Bourgeois Hinduism, or the Faith of the Modern Vedantists

Bourgeois Hinduism, or the Faith of the Modern Vedantists

Rare Discourses from Early Colonial Bengal

BRIAN A. HATCHER

OXFORD
UNIVERSITY PRESS

OXFORD
UNIVERSITY PRESS

Oxford University Press is a department of the University of Oxford.
It furthers the University's objective of excellence in research,
scholarship, and education by publishing worldwide.

Oxford New York
Auckland Cape Town Dar es Salaam Hong Kong Karachi
Kuala Lumpur Madrid Melbourne Mexico City Nairobi
New Delhi Shanghai Taipei Toronto

With offices in
Argentina Austria Brazil Chile Czech Republic France Greece
Guatemala Hungary Italy Japan Poland Portugal Singapore
South Korea Switzerland Thailand Turkey Ukraine Vietnam

Published in the United States of America by
Oxford University Press
198 Madison Avenue, New York, NY 10016

First issued as an Oxford University Press paperback, 2014.

Library of Congress Cataloging-in-Publication Data
Hatcher, Brian A. (Brian Allison)
Bourgeois Hinduism, or the faith of the modern Vedantists :
rare discourses from early colonial Bengal / Brian A. Hatcher.
p. cm.
Includes English translation from Bengali of the Sabhyadiger vaktrta.
Includes bibliographical references and index.
ISBN 978-0-19-532608-6 (hardcover); 978-0-19-937499-1 (paperback)
1. Tattvabodhinī Sabhā—History. 2. Hindu renewal—India—Bengal—History—19th century.
3. Vedanta—History—19th century. 4. Tattvabodhinī Sabhā. Sabhyadiger vaktṛtā.
I. Tattvabodhinī Sabhā. Sabhyadiger vaktṛtā. English. II. Title. III. Title: Bourgeois Hinduism.
IV. Title: Faith of the modern Vedantists.
BL1284.23.H38 2007
294.5′56—dc22 2007010414

For Gerrit
who turned sixteen
in Kolkata

Preface

You just never know where your research will lead. Years ago, while hunting down sources on the Bengali reformer Īśvaracandra Vidyāsāgara, I stumbled on a rare Bengali text in the Oriental collection of the old British Library on Great Russell Street. This short text, *Sabhyadiger vaktṛtā,* was to play an important role in my work on Vidyāsāgara, about which I shall have more to say a bit later. After completing that work, I filed away my copy of *Sabhyadiger vaktṛtā* and moved on to other projects. A decade went by before I decided to give the text a second look. This was around 2003, and *Sabhyadiger vaktṛtā* has claimed a good part of my energy and attention since then. I am pleased at last to present it to English readers in translation, along with several chapters addressing its historical context and significance. This remarkable text has prompted me to raise what I hope are new and fruitful perspectives on such issues as the legacy of Rammohan Roy, the early colonial development of neo-Vedānta, and the roots of contemporary middle-class Hinduism.

As my interpretation of *Sabhyadiger vaktṛtā* gained momentum, a number of colleagues and institutions invited me to share portions of my work with them. I want to thank especially Tithi Bhattacharya of Purdue University, Paul Courtright and Laurie Patton of Emory University, and Valerie Ritter of the University of Chicago. Some of the arguments I advance here were also run up the flagpole at professional conferences and colloquia, including the 2005 Conference on the Study of Religion in India at Albion College, the 2005

Conference on South Asia in Madison, the Nineteenth European Conference on Modern South Asian Studies in Leiden in 2006, and the 2005–6 Illinois Wesleyan University (IWU) Religion Department Colloquium. Without a doubt, my interpretation of *Sabhyadiger vaktṛtā* and the early Tattvabodhinī Sabhā has benefited from the feedback I have received on all these occasions, but I would like to give special thanks to those panel organizers and participants to whom I am especially indebted, including Selva Raj, Michael Dodson, Kumkum Chatterjee, and Gwilym Beckerlegge.

This book had an earlier incarnation that was commented on by two anonymous readers; their thoughtful and sometimes quite detailed comments were of enormous help as I reworked the material toward its present shape. The manuscript for the present book was then reviewed by another two anonymous readers, and I thank them for the care and sensitivity with which they undertook their task. At this point Dermot Killingley kindly read through the entire manuscript. With his knowledge of the historical context and his ear for argument and style, he was able to suggest numerous improvements. I cannot thank him enough. Needless to say any errors or inaccuracies are mine alone.

Because portions of this work rely on research I first conducted in connection with my doctoral studies, I would like to acknowledge again the support I received from a Fulbright-Hays Doctoral Dissertation Research Abroad fellowship in 1989–90. For this I thank both the U.S. Department of Education and the U.S. Educational Foundation in India. I am grateful as well to Illinois Wesleyan University for two Artistic and Scholarly Development grants in 1999 and 2002. These grants, and the opportunity to serve as director of the 2004 IWU London Program, made it possible for me to spend invaluable time consulting Bengali materials and missionary archives in the United Kingdom. My arguments regarding authorship of the discourses of *Sabhyadiger vaktṛtā* were largely formulated thanks to the time I was able to spend using the Bengali collections of the British Library in 2004.

Apart from the British Library, where Hedley Sutton and Leena Mitford were of particular help, I am indebted to a host of institutions, archives, and libraries that provided me with access to their collections. In the United Kingdom, I thank the Indian Institute Library in the Bodleian Library at Oxford University (with special thanks to Gillian Evison and Colin Harris for their help with my queries), the archives of the London Missionary Society at the School of Oriental and African Studies (to which institution I am indebted for the hospitality it has shown me on several occasions), and the archives of the Church Missionary Society at the University of Birmingham (which I utilized in 1989). In Calcutta (now Kolkata), I thank the Library of the Ramakrisha Mission Institute of Culture, the Baṅgīya Sāhitya Pariṣad, the National

Library, and the Asiatic Society of Bengal. And in the United States, I thank the libraries of the University of Illinois, the University of Chicago, and Harvard University. I hope I will be forgiven if I have failed to mention other institutions or individuals who have assisted me in this work.

My colleagues and students at IWU are always a source of support and encouragement. None have been better boosters than Carole Myscofski and April DeConick (now at Rice University). In addition, I am grateful to Regina Linsalata for her help with any number of tasks, but especially for transcribing the messy manuscript of my translation. Patrick Halloran was kind enough to read some of the manuscript in the early going and made several helpful suggestions regarding the translation.

I am delighted that Adam Farcus agreed to create three illustrations for the book. I thank him for his time and effort; I'm sure readers will enjoy his contemporary rendering of some icons of modern Bengali culture. Alison Hatcher introduced me to Adam, and that is just one small measure of her involvement in my work. She's been everywhere with me—from Debendranath's home in Kolkata to Rammohan's grave in Arno's Vale—and has enlivened every step of every journey. I thank her for all her love and support. The book itself I dedicate to our son Gerrit, who visited India in 2007 and liked Kolkata best of all.

Some of the material in this book draws on my earlier work. I thank Oxford University Press for permission to reprint portions of chapter 9 of *Idioms of Improvement: Vidyāsāgar and Cultural Encounter in Bengal* (Delhi: Oxford University Press, 1996), as well as some material from chapter 5 of *Eclecticism and Modern Hindu Discourse* (New York: Oxford University Press, 1999). I also thank the University of Chicago Press for permission to reprint portions of my essay "Remembering Rammohan: An Essay on the (Re-)emergence of Modern Hinduism" (*History of Religions* 46/1 [2006]: 50–80). My essay, "Bourgeois Vedānta: The Colonial Roots of Middle-class Hinduism" (*Journal of the American Academy of Religion* 75/2 [2007]: 298–323) appeared too late to be included in the bibliography, but I thank Oxford University Press for permission to reprint portions of that essay here.

Finally, I would like to thank Beth Cunningham, Provost and Dean of Faculty at IWU, who generously provided funds to support costs associated with the production of *Bourgeois Hinduism*. I remain immensely grateful to Cynthia Read at Oxford University Press for her interest in the original manuscript, as well as to Daniel Gonzalez and Linda Donnelly for providing timely and patient assistance throughout the entire process of editing.

Contents

Note on Transliteration and Primary Sources

In transliterating Sanskrit and Bengali terms, I have chosen to use forms that will be most easily recognizable to the widest range of readers. This means that I have attempted to follow Sanskrit orthography rather than Bengali pronunciation. Thus I have chosen to write *viṣaya* rather than *bishoy*, and *yoga* rather than *jog*. Major exceptions to this rule involve names and phrases that have become familiar, such as Brāhmo (instead of Brāhma), Rammohan (instead of Rāmamohana), and Upanishad (instead of Upaniṣad). In cases where proper nouns may be known in alternate spellings, I have tried to indicate these at the first usage. Unless otherwise noted, all translations are my own.

A word about the primary sources I have used. The principal source and focal point of the present volume is the Bengali book *Sabhyadiger vaktṛtā*, published by the Tattvabodhinī Sabhā in Calcutta in 1841. As far as I know, there exists only one copy of this work, preserved in the former Oriental and India Office collection of the British Library [call number: 14123.d.4.(9)]. The challenge of analyzing this rare text forms the burden of chapters 6 and 7, while a complete annotated translation of the work itself is provided in chapter 8. To make sense of the context out of which *Sabhyadiger vaktṛtā* arises, other primary sources have been invaluable, none more so than the early numbers of the *Tattvabodhinī Patrikā*, which began publishing in 1843. Perhaps this is the appropriate place to thank Rachel Van Meter Baumer for generously passing on to me her personal microfilm copies of the *Patrikā* back in the 1980s and thus opening my eyes to this wonderful periodical.

Several of the discourses from *Sabhyadiger vaktṛtā* were later published in the pages of the *Tattvabodhinī Patrikā*. There are partial runs of this journal (that was published throughout the nineteenth century) in several libraries around the world. However, there is a handsome bound edition of the journal (through 1878) in the Indian Institute Library at Oxford University that appears to include penciling by Debendranath Tagore, founder of the Tattvabodhinī Sabhā (see chapter 7). Other more or less complete sets of the *Patrikā* are in the British Library and the library of the Ramakrishna Mission Institute of Culture in Kolkata (as Calcutta was officially renamed in 2001).

Those interested in details about the Tattvabodhinī Sabhā's membership and organization would do well to consult various annual reports published by the Sabhā, though sadly none are extant for the association's earliest years. Several of these reports are preserved in the collection of the Asiatic Society of Bengal in Kolkata; they are listed in the bibliography under Tattvabodhinī Sabhā. I remain indebted to the late Dilip Kumar Biswas for alerting me to the existence of these publications.

Because one of the arguments of *Bourgeois Hinduism* is that *Sabhyadiger vaktṛtā* includes the earliest extant published work of men such as Debendranath Tagore, Īśvaracandra Vidyāsāgara, and Akṣayakumāra Datta, it is my sincere hope that scholars and editors interested in these figures will see fit to include these discourses in any future editions of their respective collected works.

Bourgeois Hinduism, or the Faith of the Modern Vedantists

Introduction

On the evening of September 29, 1839, a small group of earnest young men met in a small room on the premises of the Tagore mansion in north Calcutta. The leader of the group was Debendranath Tagore, eldest son of the influential entrepreneur Dwarkanath Tagore. It was Dwarkanath who had raised the Tagore family of Jorasanko to a place of social and economic preeminence in the first decades of the nineteenth century. The Tagores could be called the cream of civilized, or *bhadralok*, society. They ranked among the "sentinels of culture" who were the movers and shakers in native business, industry, and arts and letters.[1] However, Dwarkanath's son, Debendranath, hadn't convened this particular meeting to discuss wealth and power. Rather, the twenty-two year old was in search of religious truth, what in Sanskrit or Bengali could be called *tattva*, a term connoting fundamental principles or ultimate truth. The recent death of his grandmother, from whom he had imbibed a good deal of informal religiosity, had been a severe jolt to his spiritual moorings, leaving him to seek with ever greater intensity for something that would be both lasting and true. The September 29 meeting was the first institutional expression of his search.

Debendranath was initially inclined to name his new group the Tattvarañjinī Sabhā, the Society of Those Who Delight in Truth. However, this idea was eventually vetoed by the group in favor of the closely related title Tattvabodhinī Sabhā, or Truth-Propagating Society. Insofar as the inauguration of this society, or Sabhā, came at a time when colonial Calcutta was becoming directly acquainted with forms of Christian proselytizing, the adoption of the rubric of propagation might suggest a desire not merely to enjoy religious truth but to share it with others. How much this desire to propagate truth was a primary motive for the group's creation will be a subject to consider in due course. For now, it is enough to note that the Tattvabodhinī Sabhā would go on to become a major conduit through which new ideas of religion, society, ethics, science, and education would begin circulating among the educated elite in Calcutta and the remainder of Bengali-speaking eastern India. Throughout the nineteenth century, the Sabhā's journal, the *Tattvabodhinī Patrikā*, would rank among the most widely read and influential of periodicals associated with what has come to be known as the Bengal Renaissance.[2]

The chief goal of the Sabhā was to educate the Bengali reading public regarding the religion its members liked to call Vedānta, a religion they believed to be enshrined in India's ancient Upanishads. The Upanishads are texts that date from the first millennium of the pre-Christian era (ca. 800–200 BCE) and are widely understood to form the end or culmination of the sacred canon known as the Vedas. As *veda-anta*, the "end of the Vedas," they are understood to be the quintessence of revealed knowledge. In classical Hinduism, the Upanishads provide the spiritual foundation for several schools of Vedānta philosophy. The most well known of these is the school of Advaita Vedānta, which teaches that reality is non-dual (*a-dvaita*) and all appearance of plurality is illusory, grounded in ignorance of ultimate truth. In the modern era, Vedānta has come to be widely associated by both Hindus and non-Hindus with the essential core of Hinduism. It is not unusual to find modern Hinduism construed as a species of "neo-Vedānta" (see King 1999: 69). But just how did Vedānta acquire its central status within modern constructions of Hinduism?[3] Who were its earliest proponents? What factors of the colonial social and religious milieu fostered its growth and transformation? Put simply, how did Vedānta become neo-Vedānta? Such questions are at the heart of this volume.

The genealogy of modern Vedānta rightly begins with Rammohan Roy, a Bengali brahmin, who after 1815 initiated the project of making Vedānta modern through an ambitious program of translation, publication, and public debate. Rammohan was among the first to creatively engage both the Upanishads and the classical tradition of Advaita Vedānta associated with Śaṅkarācārya (ca. eighth century CE) from a perspective of Enlightenment rationality. As a Deist, a student of comparative religion *avant la lettre*, and a practitioner of a rationalist textual hermeneutic, Rammohan effectively initiated the task of re-tooling Vedānta to fit the spiritual needs of his generation. Rammohan's efforts during the 1820s to articulate a rational and modern form of Vedantic theism culminated in the creation of the Brāhmo Samāj in 1828, an organization and later a broad movement that would have immense influence across India.

After Rammohan's departure from India in 1830 (followed by his untimely death in England in 1833), the Brāhmo Samāj experienced a serious decline in membership and vitality. Little was done to advance his project until the founding of the Tattvabodhinī Sabhā by Debendranath in 1839. The formation of the Tattvabodhinī Sabhā, and the steps it took toward the further interpretation of Vedānta for the modern world, thus mark a second crucial moment in the emergence of modernist Hinduism. However, this particular moment has not received the kind of careful scrutiny it deserves—certainly nothing like the attention that has been lavished on Rammohan Roy. Part of the problem has been the relative paucity of sources, especially primary sources that might allow us to understand the earliest motivation and values of the Tattvabodhinī Sabhā. But just as important, it might be said that a fascination with origins has led scholars to focus so intently on the work of Rammohan Roy—the so-called Father of Modern India—that they have overlooked the work done by his immediate intellectual and spiritual heirs.

My goal is to address this unfortunate imbalance by bringing to light a small but remarkable text that provides a valuable window onto the earliest thought of members of the Tattvabodhinī Sabhā. *Sabhyadiger vaktṛtā*, the text that is translated here for the first time in its entirety, has lain unnoticed for over a century among Bengali publications preserved in the British Library.[4] The text was originally published in Calcutta in 1841. Its title means simply "Discourses by Members," and it records twenty-one discourses delivered before the Tattvabodhinī Sabhā during the first year of its existence, 1839–40. These discourses (*vaktṛtā*) offer us a precious glimpse at the articulation of modern Vedānta in the decade after Rammohan Roy's death, when the task of reinterpreting Vedānta for the modern era was only just getting under way.[5] This translation of *Sabhyadiger vaktṛtā* offers English-language readers direct evidence of the way the reconstruction of Vedānta was carried forward in colonial Bengal in the immediate wake of Rammohan's work. Far from simply magnifying the significance of Rammohan's work, I offer here an interpretation of *Sabhyadiger vaktṛtā* that highlights the independent and influential role of the Tattvabodhinī Sabhā in the ongoing transformation of Vedānta. I argue that a balanced understanding of Rammohan's achievements and reputation as a Vedantic reformer depends on our paying due attention to the initiatives of Debendranath Tagore and the Tattvabodhinī Sabhā.

I first began research on the Tattvabodhinī Sabhā around 1989 as part of a project to reconstruct the religious worldview of the Sanskrit pandit, reformer, and educator Īśvaracandra Vidyāsāgara. Knowing from a variety of corroborating sources that Vidyāsāgara had been an active member of the early Tattvabodhinī Sabhā, I became interested in exploring how far back that connection could be demonstrated. Sources were scarce, but an examination of early numbers of the *Tattvabodhinī Patrikā* revealed that he had played an important part in that publication, even serving for a time on its editorial board (or "Paper Committee," as it was known). But the *Patrikā* only began to publish in 1843. Was there any evidence that Vidyāsāgara had been involved with the Sabhā before this? I had a hunch he had been, but I could find no sources to back it up. It seemed an intractable problem—until I happened upon *Sabhyadiger vaktṛtā*.

I came across the text while searching through J. H. Blumhardt's printed catalogue of Bengali printed books in the old Oriental collection of the British Library. *Sabhyadiger vaktṛtā* had been bound by librarians into a volume of miscellaneous religious tracts from the 1830s and 1840s. A quick perusal of the title page and contents was enough to suggest the incredible value of the text. Hitherto, there had been no known record of what members were saying at the earliest meetings of the Tattvabodhinī Sabhā. Now I found there was. It was an exciting realization. However, my excitement was quickly tempered when I saw that *Sabhyadiger vaktṛtā* posed at least one formidable problem: it provided no unambiguous information as to who had actually delivered each of its twenty-one short discourses. Instead, it employed a system of initials that were placed at the end of each discourse. These initials were apparently intended to identify the speakers. Only after lengthy study was I able to arrive at what I think are reasonable conjectures regarding the identity of these speakers. From the very outset, my attention was focused on two discourses that I believe should be attributed to none other than Īśvaracandra Vidyāsāgara. These two short compositions help push the date for his membership in the Sabhā back as early as 1839–40.

For all that Vidyāsāgara is renowned (or notorious) for his skepticism—or, if you prefer, his agnostic reluctance to discuss matters of religion—these two discourses provide compelling evidence that Vidyāsāgara's world was in fact shaped in significant ways by a coherent religious worldview. In my earlier work, I drew directly from the discourses of *Sabhyadiger vaktṛtā* to flesh out the content and internal logic of this worldview, which may be conveniently summarized as a species of rational theism and moral striving. It is this worldview that provides the basic framework for understanding Vidyāsāgara's varied life as an educator, social reformer, and philanthropist.[6] These discourses also demonstrate in concrete terms Vidyāsāgara's involvement in an association that was to play a unique part in the history of early modern Vedānta. When read alongside the other discourses in *Sabhyadiger vaktṛtā*, Vidyāsāgara's discourses reveal to us a moment when Vedānta was articulated simultaneously in the idioms of modernist theism and Upanishadic Vedānta. No Vedantin in any ordinary understanding of that category, Vidyāsāgara was nonetheless clearly invested in and empowered by the Tattvabodhinī Sabhā's attempt to reinterpret Vedānta for the modern world.

Sabhyadiger vaktṛtā allows us to enter into this crucial moment in the early colonial history of Vedānta. For this reason alone, it deserves to be made available to others. If nothing else, here is a text that provides a window into the thought of the earliest members of Tattvabodhinī Sabhā, including Debendranath himself. This text is clearly too important to ignore. This is precisely why I found myself compelled to take it up again, to translate it, and to attempt to put it in some kind of context. This volume is the fruit of that effort. *Bourgeois Hinduism, or the Faith of the Modern Vedantists* presents for the first time not just a complete, annotated translation of *Sabhyadiger vaktṛtā* but also several chapters dedicated to placing this remarkable text in its historical context.

While it is tempting to say this is a book about the Tattvabodhinī Sabhā, it is both less and more than that. Because it attempts to bring into sharp focus the thoughts and activities of Tattvabodhinī members during the Sabhā's inaugural year, 1839–40, it cannot claim to be a comprehensive history of the Sabhā. But insofar as it attempts to view the Sabhā's origin—and its "original" text, *Sabhyadiger vaktṛtā*—in relation both to the earlier work of Rammohan Roy and to the subsequent development of modern, Vedantic Hinduism, this book can claim to offer far more than simply a study of the Tattvabodhinī Sabhā. Put simply, it offers insights into the complex dynamics of Vedantic reform and bourgeois Hinduism in early colonial India. If it should prompt others to explore the broader history and enduring legacy of the Tattvabodhinī Sabhā, I would be delighted.

Bourgeois Hinduism and the Faith of the Modern Vedantists

I chose the title of this book to focus attention on two broad conceptual categories: "bourgeois Hinduism" and the "faith of the modern Vedantists." These call for some preliminary explication. It should be noted straight away that neither bourgeois Hinduism nor modern Vedantist is a descriptor used by the earliest members of the Sabhā. Certainly, this sort of language figures nowhere in the text of *Sabhyadiger vaktṛtā*. Rather, these are two labels I have devised in the interests of framing an interpretation of the social context and theological program of the Sabhā. The former phrase is my own coinage; the latter is intended to echo a category employed by Christian observers when responding to the work of the Sabhā in the early 1840s.

Vedānta was a contested category in early colonial Bengal. As I show in chapter 5, the phrase "modern Vedantists" was originally deployed in the writings of Christian missionaries and native converts in Calcutta who sought to refute the theology of the Sabhā. While the phrase may strike readers today as a relatively benign description of the Sabhā, at the time the force of the adjective "modern" was to call into question the authenticity of the Vedānta propagated by Debendranath and his associates. While to Rammohan, the Brāhmos, and the early Tattvabodhinī Sabhā the category of Vedānta connoted a rational and scriptural monotheism, to Christian commentators it stood for such things as world-negation, pantheism, and immorality. Christian scrutiny of the Sabhā, in fact, eventually compelled its members to take a more assertive approach to the defense and propagation of Vedānta.

Because the discourses of *Sabhyadiger vaktṛtā* were composed before the Bengal Christian community had begun to take note of—and thence to stigmatize—the program of the Tattvabodhinī Sabhā, they allow us a rare chance to get inside the faith of these so-called modern Vedantists more or less on its own terms. As such, we should be careful not to retroject issues and concerns drawn from subsequent polemical skirmishes between the Sabhā and the local Christian community. Having said this, I should add that if I choose to employ the category of "modern Vedantists," it is certainly not to validate the spirit or the substance of later Christian critique; quite the contrary. If anything, I would like to pursue the possibility of both using the phrase to capture what is distinctive about the program of the Sabhā and encoding within that phrase a reminder of how the kind of thinking enshrined in *Sabhyadiger vaktṛtā* would in time come to represent a challenge to Christian observers.[7] In so doing, I hope to suggest how important it is that we keep in mind both these dimensions when discussing the subsequent history of Vedānta in modern India.

I have adopted the phrase "bourgeois Hinduism" to suggest something of the context and the content of this rational Vedantic faith. In particular, I use this phrase to foreground the way in which the earliest Tattvabodhinī articulation of Vedānta worked in tandem with the identity and interests of a particular social group in early colonial Bengal—namely, the so-called *bhadralok*, men like the Tagores. In chapter 4, I suggest that there was what Max Weber might have called an "elective affinity" between the worldly values of the educated, elite members of the Tattvabodhinī Sabhā and the kind of updated Vedantic theism that was first articulated by Rammohan. One goal of this volume, then, is to explore how the discourses of *Sabhyadiger vaktṛtā* work to inculcate a bourgeois religion of godly worship grounded in the diligent pursuit of worldly success. This bourgeois Hinduism merits our attention insofar as it marks an important—if admittedly early—forerunner of contemporary forms of middle-class Hinduism.

The proposition that aspects of contemporary Hinduism lend themselves to analysis in terms of middle-class religion is one that has gained fairly wide currency of late (see, for instance, Hawley 2001, Lutgendorf 1997, and Waghorne 2005). Whether in temple-building, ritual practices, contemporary guru and self-realization movements, or popular iconography, scholars have begun to turn their attention to what might be called, borrowing from Sanjay Joshi, the "middle class-ness" of recent Hinduism (2001: 8). Writing of Sathya Sai Baba as many as twenty years ago, Lawrence Babb wrote that "one would have to be asleep" not to have noticed his enormous appeal among the middle classes (1986: 167).

This middle class-ness of contemporary Hinduism correlates with an upwardly mobile socioeconomic class that has expanded rapidly in post-1990 India and in the global diaspora, as well as with broader themes of middle-class identity, such as syncretic religious practices, wide use of the vernaculars, the movement of religion from the private into the public sphere, increased urbanization, and the attempt to find univocal (often dubbed "eternal" or *sanātana*) expressions of what it means to be Hindu. One aspect of the public-sphere religious activities of contemporary middle-class Hindus that is particularly striking is the attempt to find meaningful linkages between spiritual concerns and material aspirations. As Philip Lutgendorf has memorably remarked, the monkey-faced god Hanuman is popular today among the middle classes because he can deliver both the gods and the goods (1997: 325).[8]

But what can we say about the historical roots of today's middle-class Hinduism? Can we establish a genealogy, or at least articulate some thematic connections, that would link contemporary Hinduism to developments in the colonial period? Joanne Waghorne's recent book, *The Diaspora of the Gods* (2005), is an excellent example of just such an effort. Waghorne attempts to ground our understanding of contemporary expressions of Hindu religiosity in an appreciation of the colonial and postcolonial experience of an emergent Hindu middle class.[9] By focusing on such issues as temple construction in colonial and post-independence South India (especially in Madras, or present-day Chennai), Waghorne calls attention to the dynamics of religion in the context of a colonial seaport metropolis that found itself drawn into an emerging global system. I suggest that in *Sabhyadiger vaktṛtā* we gain a similar vantage point from which to consider the question of how modern middle-class Hinduism may have first come to expression in the discourse and activities of prominent representatives of Calcutta's urban *bhadralok*. This study does not mirror or match Waghorne's in its historical scope or interpretive fieldwork, but it does attempt to follow her lead by asking to what degree the discourses of *Sabhyadiger vakṭṛtā* might be used to demonstrate how the Tattvabodhinī theology of hard work and moral restraint both encoded and legitimated a colonial bourgeois worldview.

The delineation of just such a bourgeois worldview, in fact, was a central concern of my earlier work on Īśvaracandra Vidyāsāgara. As I mentioned, the discourses he delivered before the Sabhā provide a particularly concrete example of his religious worldview, which we might characterize as one of moral restraint, rational knowledge, and obedience to the laws of God as revealed in the order of the natural and social world. While my earlier work on Vidyāsāgara began to delineate the distinctly bourgeois character of his worldview, a complete translation of *Sabhyadiger vakṭṛtā* allows us to explore both in more detail and with more nuance just how a species of *bhadralok* Vedantic theism emerged in a context of colonial bourgeois aspiration. This in turn allows us to consider how the faith of these modern Vedantists laid the initial groundwork for subsequent forms of middle-class Hinduism.

In chapter 4, I show that the authors of these discourses represented the cultured movers and shakers in colonial Calcutta. Some, like Debendranath, came from wealthy families deeply invested in commerce and trade. Many of them sought avenues for advancement in public life during a decade that was experiencing something like an "industrious revolution" (borrowing a delightful concept from de Vries 1994).[10] The 1830s in Calcutta seemed to present the *bhadralok* with opportunities for prosperity and increased political participation alike. Trade flourished, and official positions were beginning to open up for Bengalis. Voluntary associations began to spring up as if overnight, representing the urge to promote collective endeavors in publishing, education, agriculture, philanthropy, and political representation. *Sabhyadiger vakṭṛtā* allows us to consider the moral and theological resources utilized by the Sabhā's members as they increasingly took on public-sphere activities and commitments. On the one hand, these discourses appear to confidently express the religious and the worldly ambitions of the Sabhā's members; on the other hand, if we read them against the grain, we may also notice in these discourses a record of the anxious quest by members to legitimate their new social status in a rapidly changing colonial environment.

What makes *Sabhyadiger vakṭṛtā* so remarkable?

Beyond its significance as an early expression of bourgeois Hinduism, there are at least three things that make the text of *Sabhyadiger vakṭṛtā* rather remarkable. My purpose here is not to exhaust these topics but to look ahead to the following chapters, which take them up in greater detail. Alternatively, by addressing these topics here in brief, those readers who wish to proceed directly to the translation will have a better sense of what they might look for in the text. Needless to say, there is much more that could be said, and others will no doubt find far different ways to comment on the text. Nothing would better reward the effort of translating *Sabhyadiger vaktṛtā*.

The first and most obvious thing that makes *Sabhyadiger vaktṛtā* so remarkable is that it provides us with an opportunity to examine the spiritual motivations and interpretive methods of the highly influential Tattvabodhinī Sabhā. Along the way, we are able to form a far better sense of the relationship between Tattvabodhinī theology and the theology of Rammohan—arguably two of the most important original components in the modern construction of Vedantic Hinduism. This is no small matter, since the relationship between the movement inaugurated by Rammohan, known as the Brāhmo Samāj, and the society formed by Debendranath is still understood in only the most general terms. For instance, it is easy to view the Tattvabodhinī Sabhā as largely Brāhmo in its orientation. However, *Sabhyadiger vaktṛtā* provides concrete evidence that the Sabhā has independent origins: far from being a mere spin-off of Rammohan's work, it grew directly out of the spiritual yearnings of Debendranath Tagore.

To be sure, the Sabhā later came to see itself as carrying on the work of Rammohan. But *Sabhyadiger vaktṛtā* reminds us that while initially running parallel to Rammohan's work, the work of the Sabhā had an independent origin and found its own unique expression.[11] To anticipate somewhat, we might just note here the remarkable fact that Rammohan, who had done so much to focus attention on Vedānta as the grounds for a non-idolatrous Hindu monotheism, is nowhere mentioned in *Sabhayadiger vaktṛtā*. This isn't to say his theological presence isn't felt. It surely is. Yet these discourses do not trumpet Rammohan's name, nor do they merely parrot his ideas. These discourses reveal the degree to which this new group was searching for independent ways to articulate what amounts to a parallel theological vision.

Fully as much as Rammohan, therefore, the Tattvabodhinī Sabhā stands at the beginning of the modern articulation of Vedānta. The translation in this volume allows readers to reflect on the unique articulation of the Tattvabodhinī worldview. But if we are to appreciate this worldview on its own terms, we must bear in mind that the discourses translated here precede by at least a half century what is generally seen as the full flowering of so-called neo-Vedānta. We should not read into *Sabhyadiger vaktṛtā* all the concerns of neo-Vedānta as expressed in the writings of figures like Śri Aurobindo, Swami Vivekananda, and Sarvepalli Radhakrishnan.[12] *Sabhaydiger vaktṛtā* may preserve some early, probing steps toward what would become neo-Vedānta, but readers will quickly realize that these discourses read differently than do the teachings of latter-day Vedantins. These discourses strike a different spiritual chord, and they promote a slightly different moral code. If later Vedantic mystics such as Śri Ramakrishna and Ramana Maharshi famously elevated the quest for liberative wisdom over the anxious pursuit of moral rectitude, the authors of these discourses share the conviction that "we will never obtain Ultimate Reality merely by wisdom; we must first forsake evil" (quoting from Discourse Seventeen, as translated in chapter 8). To be sure, the concerted effort to construe Vedānta in terms of moral restraint makes these discourses important harbingers of such concepts as Swami Vivekananda's "Practical Vedanta." However, it is important that we allow the Sabhā's early articulation of Vedānta to stand on its own, to reveal the particular set of interpretive choices made by one particular group regarding the relevance of Vedānta within a life of bourgeois aspiration. Once the uniqueness of this Vedantic standpoint is recognized, others might then wish to begin tracing further patterns of filiation, congruence, or divergence.[13]

I don't wish to give the impression that *Sabhyadiger vaktṛtā* is somehow an essential or pivotal text for the emergence of modern Hinduism. This would be going too far; the text has long been forgotten, by Hindus and others. Nevertheless, it does hold special rewards for readers, and one of the goals of this volume is to suggest the sorts of things we might learn from it. That said, I do wish to be sensitive to the complexity of the history we're discussing. Because the story of modern Hinduism has been—and continues to be—bound closely to arguments about the truth of religion, the relative merits of "Western" and "Eastern" culture, the identity of the Indian nation, and the status of particular communities within the South Asian social world, it is imperative that we seek to problematize as far as possible all overly simplistic narratives. This includes narrratives of improvement, modernization, and progress (all bywords of Bengal's so-called nineteenth-century "renaissance"), as well as narratives that essentialize such phenomena as religion, Vedānta, Hinduism, nation, and community.

This is, in fact, the second topic worth exploring with respect to the discourses of *Sabhyadiger vaktṛtā*. This text can potentially help us highlight those areas of anxiety and conflict, processes of negotiation, acts of resistance, or gestures of accommodation that shaped and complicated the task of articulating Hinduism in the colonial context. While narratives of colonial improvement make much of the heroic advances achieved by Bengal's reformers, the "chronicle of emergent Hinduism," as Brian Pennington has recently suggested, is in fact often a tale of anxiety.[14] And while *Sabyadiger vaktṛtā* appears to be anything but an *anxious* text, if we read it against the grain, we can, in fact, discern within it—as well as within the concerns and program of the Tattvabodhinī Sabhā—several registers of discontent and multiple layers of uneasiness.[15]

Take, for example, the problem of religious proof. One of the fascinating things about *Sabyadiger vaktṛtā* is that its discourses speak with multiple voices when it comes to articulating the grounds for making religious truth claims. While the question of religious proof is never systematically or exhaustively discussed in the text, it does exert a pull on the discourses. The problematic is addressed two, or even three, different ways. On the one hand, we are offered the testimony of scripture—principally those texts drawn from the revealed literature of the Vedas (known as *śruti*), notably the Upanishads. On the other hand, several authors rely on proofs grounded in rational argumentation (what we might loosely call *tarka*). Then again, some of the authors seek to marry both standards of proof. They pursue an informal merger of scriptural religion and the religion of reason that is in many ways reminiscent of Rammohan Roy's hermeneutic.[16] Equally reminiscent of Rammohan—but completely out of keeping with later nineteenth-century formulations of Vedantic Hinduism—is the fact that these discourses do not foreground the concept of "experience" (*anubhava*). This should strike any student of Vivekananda or Radhakrishnan as extremely curious, since for the latter authors, experience is viewed as the touchstone of all valid religious knowledge.

Some time back, the late Wilhelm Halbfass pointed out that Rammohan himself does not pay much attention to experience in this respect (Halbfass 1988: 395). In particular, Rammohan never looks to the Upanishads as documents of a particular kind of human religious experience; nor does he use them to validate experiences he himself claims to have had.[17] According to Halbfass, it was Debendranath Tagore, founder of the Tattvabodhinī Sabhā, who first began the shift toward construing personal experience as the ultimate criterion of religious truth. In support of this claim, Halbfass cites sources in which Debendranath promotes the concept of *ātma-pratyaya*, or "intuitive knowledge," as the authoritative guide to truth (Halbfass 1988: 396).[18]

Readers of *Sabhyadiger vaktṛtā* have good reason to revisit Halbfass's conclusions, since these early discourses do not advance experience as the ultimate ground of knowledge. What is more, if my analysis of this text is correct (see chapters 6 and 7), Debendranath himself appears to have composed at least five of its twenty-one discourses. Yet, again, none of these five discourses makes an appeal to experience. What, then, are we to make of Halbfass's claim? Upon close examination of Halbfass's sources, it becomes clear that they date from a period fully fifteen years later than the discourses recorded in *Sabhyadiger vaktṛtā*. It is very likely that Halbfass simply had no knowledge of this text (which is entirely understandable, given its obscurity). Halbfass formed his conclusions based on what evidence he had, which came from Debendranath's later writings. However, from the discourses of *Sabhyadiger vaktṛtā*, we can now see that there was a time when Debendranath did not accord "intuitive knowledge" any special significance. Rather, like the other authors represented in the text, he seems to have been content with calling on the "merciful" texts of scripture and arguing from the evidences of nature.[19]

It is beyond the scope of this introduction to follow out the series of developments that eventually led Debendranath to abandon his original confidence in *śruti* as authoritative knowledge. Some of the later history of the Sabhā has been discussed by others, and some will be treated in the chapters that follow.[20] But for now, the silence of *Sabhyadiger vaktṛtā* on the question of experience reminds us that this text dates from a time in the Sabhā's earliest history, well before Debendranath was led to question the doctrine of Vedic infallibility. To be sure, whatever certainty the members felt in 1839–40 regarding the rational and scriptural authority of Vedānta would not last long. It is reasonable to speculate that doubts about revelation were already beginning to trouble members at this time. We shall see, for instance, that alongside Debendranath, one of the earliest guiding lights of the Sabhā was the arch-rationalist Akṣayakumāra Datta, who is known to have had little time for such vagaries as prayer. Were he and Debendranath already beginning to lock horns over the problem of reconciling reason and revelation at this early point in the Sabhā's history?

Akṣayakumāra's extreme rationalist position, informed as it was by his training in the colonial educational matrix, reminds us that anxieties over the grounds of religious proof did not simply represent a carrying over of particular intramural debates within Hinduism. The discourses of *Sabhyadiger vaktṛtā* are clearly tinged in varying ways with the colors of Enlightenment thought, as mediated to its members through the English-language curriculum and schoolbooks of colonial Calcutta. Readers may well find that the invocation of evidential theology in this text is highly reminiscent of European Deist responses to the problem of such themes as miracle and revelation in the Christian tradition. As it was for Rammohan, the adoption of a rationalist interpretation of the Hindu tradition was one strategy employed by members of the Sabhā to jettison such purported Hindu errors as polytheism and image worship. Precisely how contemporary Christian missionaries viewed the work of the Sabhā in this respect is a matter discussed in a later chapter. But for now, we may simply note that the Sabhā's agenda was not without its critics, Hindu and Christian.

There may be no better indicator of how anxiously such matters were discussed in early colonial Calcutta than the system of initials employed in the text. Why are the authors not identified by name? On the one hand, it is possible that *Sabhyadiger vakṭṛtā* was intended strictly for use among members and that therefore initials might have been seen as a sufficient mnemonic aid to help members identify speakers. On the other hand, if the text was intended for wider circulation (and its status as a printed book seems to attest to this intention), there could well have been some reluctance on the part of members to be publicly and explicitly associated with a species of reform that was by no means universally endorsed. In view of the heated atmosphere of religious polemic in early colonial Bengal—especially after the contentious debate over the abolition of *satī*/suttee—one could understand if its authors had no desire to suffer the kind of vilification to which Rammohan Roy had been subjected.[21]

This makes it all the more exciting if we can connect these discourses with particular individuals. Our understanding of the dynamics of debate and reform stands to gain appreciable complexity if we can identify the range of authors represented in *Sabhyadiger vakṭṛtā*. While the text as a whole allows us to ponder the worldview of the early Tattvabodhinī Sabhā in some detail, the various authors of these discourses are more than mere persona embodying abstract issues; they are distinct individuals, with particular voices and unique concerns. By identifying these voices and concerns, we open a window into the diverse intellectual and social makeup of the Sabhā.

This, then, brings us to the third remarkable aspect of the text—not just its curious system of initials, but the promise of identifying in it a range of authors. As I argue, we can go some way toward providing convincing proof of authorship—perhaps not for every discourse and not with equal certainty in every case, but, nonetheless, we can make some important advances in this regard. And when we do this, we find that *Sabhyadiger vakṭṛtā* contains some very rare examples of writing by major figures in the intellectual and social history of colonial Bengal. In fact, these essays are often not just *rare*; in several cases, they amount to the *earliest* extant published thoughts of prominent members. And as the case of Debendranath's silence on the authority of experience illustrates so well, our ability to identify earlier specimens of writing from such individuals can repay us in the form of some startling discoveries.

Although attributing particular discourses to particular authors is not without its problems, if the arguments I present in later chapters are deemed valid, then in *Sabhyadiger vakṭṛtā* we have the earliest extant writings by such men as Debendranath Tagore and Īśvaracandra Vidyāsāgara.[22] Aside from Rammohan, it is hard to imagine men whose impact was felt more profoundly across the world of the early colonial *bhadralok*. And here we have samples of their thinking from when they were still just young men on the cusp of their public careers. When the first discourses of *Sabhyadiger vakṭṛtā* were delivered in December 1839, Vidyāsāgara was only nineteen and still a student at

Sanskrit College. Debendranath would have been three years older but still, by his own account, wrestling to find a way to balance between service to God and the pursuit of mammon. Besides Debendranath and Vidyāsāgara, there are discourses here by the great rationalist Akṣayakumāra Datta (again certainly his earliest extant), as well as by Rāmacandra Vidyāvāgīśa, Rammohan's colleague and right-hand man in the Brāhmo Samāj.

The case of Rāmacandra alone is worth noting here as an example of the treasures to be found in *Sabhyadiger vaktṛtā*. While it is true that there are independent published versions of Rāmacandra's Brāhmo sermons that date from as early as 1828, what is striking about *Sabhyadiger vaktṛtā* is that it allows us to listen to Rāmacandra speaking outside the context of the Brāhmo worship service.[23] His voice and his ideas will be familiar to those who know his Brāhmo sermons (though these are hardly known to English-language readers), but here we encounter him in his role as a proponent of Debendranath's Tattvabodhinī agenda. *Sabhyadiger vaktṛtā* thus confirms my earlier contention that Rāmacandra was an important bridge between the rather disparate intellectual worlds of men like Rammohan, Debendranath, and Vidyāsāgara (Hatcher 1996: 206–12).

Among the other exciting, if admittedly brief, specimens of writing by prominent figures is a short contribution by the renowned poet and journalist Īśvaracandra Gupta. While historians have known of Gupta's early association with the Tattvabodhinī Sabhā, *Sabhyadiger vaktṛtā* provides the first example of Gupta's writing to emerge from this association. The selection is little more than a prayer or benediction, but for that very reason it speaks directly of Gupta's heartfelt engagement with the work of the Sabhā. To anyone interested in the intellectual history of the period, even such a short prayer must seem a minor treasure.

Overall, then, this hitherto little-known text offers us a glimpse into a decisive and fruitful—if not entirely confident—moment when the leading *bhadralok* voices of new learning and religious change in colonial Calcutta collaborated to promote a modern theistic agenda under the rubric of Vedānta. As a record of this moment, a window into this period, and a document testifying to the individual viewpoints of a range of early members, *Sabhyadiger vaktṛtā* is indeed a remarkable text.

Plan of the book

In the chapters that follow, I attempt to provide background information on, and a basic orientation to, the text of *Sabhyadiger vaktṛtā* and the group that created it. As chapter 1 suggests, the best place to begin is with the life and message of Rammohan Roy. In simple terms, his endeavors in the area of religious reform are the appropriate backdrop against which to consider the significance of Tattvabodhinī theology. Viewed in a bit more detail, the Tattvabodhinī Sabhā stands in a curious relationship to Rammohan; they follow him, but in some respects they also helped to create the now legendary image of Rammohan who lives on as the father of modern Indian religious reform. Understanding this dynamic is essential for appreciating what is distinctive about the Sabhā's work.

In chapter 2, I take up the origins of the Tattvabodhinī Sabhā. Here I draw on Debendranath's account of his spiritual awakening and the events that led to the founding of the Sabhā. Chapter 3 is dedicated to identifying what sorts of individuals joined the Sabhā and why. This provides an occasion to highlight the surprisingly diverse social and intellectual background of the Sabhā's *bhadralok* members; this chapter also briefly sketches developments after the publication of *Sabhyadiger vaktṛtā*. The goal of chapter 4 is to provide an interpretive overview of the theological and social concerns that emerge from the discourses of *Sabhyadiger vaktṛtā*. Once again, the interpretation I offer of Tattvabodhinī thought as the expression and legitimation of bourgeois interests is not meant to be either definitive or exhaustive. It is principally meant to promote reflection on one fruitful way to understand the moral and spiritual values of the Sabhā as they intersect with the worldly concerns of its *bhadralok* members. While we have no evidence of a direct Christian response to the discourses of *Sabhyadiger vaktṛtā*, there is much evidence that the creation of the Tattvabodhinī Sabhā and its subsequent endeavors were to become a cause for a great deal of concern among Christians (missionaries and converts) in Calcutta. The goal of chapter 5 is to consider in broad terms Christian suspicion of these so-called modern Vedantists. This is the context out of which the rubric of neo-Vedānta first emerged. Consideration of Christian attitudes toward the Sabhā thus highlights a central theme, not only in the further development of Tattvabodhinī thought but also in the subsequent emergence of modern Hinduism.

In chapters 6 and 7, I turn to the text of *Sabhyadiger vaktṛtā* itself, paying particular attention to the challenges it poses for the reader—most notably, the burden of deciphering its system of initials. Central to these chapters is the task of outlining the methods I have employed to go about determining the authorship of its several discourses. This is also the place to advance in detail my arguments for particular authorship. As I have said, if my arguments are accepted, then we should be able to discern the distinctive voices of several principal players in the Sabhā. In addition, if these attributions are considered valid, one might hope that scholars interested in documenting the life and works of such figures would take note and add these discourses to the list of works—and the collected writings—that we already associate with such men.[24]

These seven chapters are then followed by a complete translation of the twenty-one discourses of *Sabhyadiger vaktṛtā* in chapter 8. Readers who are less interested in the more arcane matters of authorship may wish to proceed directly to the text, either after this introduction or after reading the first five chapters. I have chosen to annotate the translation to clarify interpretive decisions and to provide textual citations not given in the text itself. In the textual notes, I have also attempted to indicate wherever possible those cases in which the original discourses may have been reprinted (for instance, in the later journal, *Tattvabodhinī Patrikā*). A series of appendixes follow chapter 8, providing readers with a variety of tools that may prove useful for closer study of the text—notably, a glossary and a list of Sanskrit works cited in *Sabhyadiger vaktṛtā*. I hope that these tools, when combined with the presentation of central issues in chapters 1 through 7, will allow readers to appreciate the overall significance of this remarkable text.

I

Vedānta According to Rammohan Roy

To understand the genesis of the Tattvabodhinī Sabhā, we must begin by considering the life and work of Rammohan Roy (1772–1833; Fig. 1.1).[1] This may not seem immediately obvious. For one thing, Rammohan took no direct part in creation of the Sabhā in 1839. In fact, he had died six years earlier in Bristol, England. For another thing, as conceived by Debendranath Tagore—the man we could rightly call the prime mover behind the creation of the Sabhā—the Sabhā was initially intended neither as an explicit testament to Rammohan's vision nor as a vehicle for the propagation of Rammohan's teachings. As discussed in chapter 2, the origins of the Tattvabodhinī Sabhā lie squarely in the personal religious experiences of Debendranath.

If we nevertheless begin with Rammohan, it is for two reasons. First, Rammohan looms large over Debendranath's early spiritual and moral development. Debendranath's father, Dwarkanath Tagore (1794–1846), had been an important supporter of Rammohan's reformist movement, the Brāhmo Samāj. As a child, Debendranath was exposed both to Rammohan and to Rammohan's ideas. We know that before attending Hindu College, Debendranath had been enrolled in a school founded by Rammohan. It is therefore not unreasonable to think that young Debendranath's aversion to image worship and his quest for a rational and ethical Hinduism owed something to the example of Rammohan. Second, although the Tattvabodhinī Sabhā was not initially established with Rammohan in mind, in time its members would come to look on Rammohan as a kind of founding figure.

FIGURE 1.1. Rammohan Roy (carbon transfer and ink on paper by Adam Farcus, used by permission of the artist)

This is an intriguing development that sheds important light on the dynamics behind the revival of the reformist movement that had been established by Rammohan, the Brāhmo Samāj. I return to this development in chapter 3.

I have found it helpful to think of the members of the early Tattvabodhinī Sabhā as "Brāhmos without Rammohan." Such a description reminds us that while the Tattvabodhinī Sabhā may have broadly sought to promote the kind of theology advocated by the Brāhmo Samāj, the Sabhā was nevertheless a unique and independent outgrowth of Debendranath's own spiritual vision. Although there was a profound connection between the Sabhā and Rammohan that eventually became clear to members of the Sabhā, this was not the self-understanding of those few young men who initially gathered with Debendranath in late September 1839. As Bhavatoṣa Datta has remarked, in the beginning there was a clear difference between the Sabhā and Rammohan's movement (1968: 121).

As I point out in the introduction, this is one of the things that makes *Sabhyadiger vaktṛtā* so interesting. This text dates from the earliest inception of the Sabhā, a short-lived but vital period of transition. The discourses of *Sabhyadiger vaktṛtā* translated here are clearly indebted to Rammohan in a loose sense, insofar as they generally build on the ideals of his Brāhmo Samāj. The vision of these discourses is broadly Brāhmo in that it is grounded in a rationalist Vedantic monotheism of this-worldly worship. Yet neither Rammohan nor the Brāhmo Samāj is anywhere mentioned in *Sabhyadiger vaktṛtā*. Indeed, it is precisely because these discourses remind us vividly of the Brāhmo movement that we are so surprised by the absence of Rammohan from them.

Another way to approach this problem is to say that the discourses recorded in *Sabhyadiger vaktṛtā* are, in a sense, decidedly post-Rammohan. At the same time, we might say they are also pre-Rammohan. What I mean to suggest is that, as of 1839, Rammohan existed in the Sabhā's past—as the man who put theistic Vedānta on the reform agenda in Bengal. But for all that, Rammohan had yet to figure in the Sabhā's self-understanding; he lay in the Sabhā's future, as the man who would in time be revered as a sort of founder ex post facto. The rediscovery of Rammohan did not come until 1842, when Debendranath resolved that the Tattvabodhinī Sabhā should begin managing the affairs of the Brāhmo Samāj. A year later, when the Sabhā launched its own periodical, the *Tattvabodhinī Patrikā*, the editors listed among its principal goals the propagation of Rammohan's Vedantic theism. This truly marks the point after which Debendranath and the Tattvabodhinī Sabhā not only began to actively think of themselves in terms of Rammohan's work but also began to revive and extend the visibility of the Brāhmo movement. By self-consciously taking upon itself the mantle of Rammohan, the Tattvabodhinī Sabhā in time became instrumental in securing his enduring legacy as a religious reformer. We might even say that Rammohan's fame as the "father" of modern Hindu reform depended on the subsequent initiatives of the Sabhā.[2] But in 1839 all this was yet to come.

For now, we need to bear in mind that the discourses of *Sabhyadiger vaktṛtā* predate the Sabhā's active promotion of Rammohan even if they nonetheless stand in an important relation to his work. Whether we choose to view them as pre- or post-Rammohan, there can be no doubt that an appreciation of these discourses depends on some understanding of the life and work of Rammohan. In what follows, I provide a brief overview of salient themes from Rammohan's work. By highlighting these themes, readers of the translated discourses in chapter 8 not only will be able to appreciate the general Brāhmo "feel" of *Sabhyadiger vaktṛtā* but also will be able to recognize just what the Tattvabodhinī Sabhā contributed to the emerging discourse of Vedānta in early colonial Bengal.

On Rammohan

Among Rammohan's crowning achievements one would have to include the following: promoting a version of monotheism he hoped would restore the rational and moral basis of Hinduism; translating the ancient Upanishads into Bengali and English; publicly debating the truths of Hinduism and Christianity with a variety of interlocutors, both Hindu and Christian; actively supporting the spread of English education in India; and campaigning to suppress the practice of widow immolation, known to the British as "suttee." In the present context, Rammohan's most relevant accomplishment was the founding of a society in 1828, the Brāhmo Samāj, to foster his vision of Hindu monotheism.

Though born a brahmin, Rammohan's spiritual development took him down a number of intellectual avenues that are not routinely associated with Hindu learning; his progress down these various avenues gave a distinctive color and tone to his theological writings. He is said to have studied early in life in both Patna and Benares, centers for Arabic and Sanskrit learning, respectively. His first published essay was a lengthy rationalistic appeal for monotheism, written in Persian, *Tuḥfat al-Muwaḥḥidīn* [A Present to the Believers in One God].[3] Much of his most mature work focused on mastering and translating Sanskrit texts on Vedānta from the Upanishads to the Brahmasūtras. In addition to his immersion in Indo-Persian and Vedantic learning, Rammohan also studied Tantra and had worked in close contact with an English official for a dozen years in the outlying districts of Bengal. By the time Rammohan finally settled in Calcutta in 1815, he had amassed the kind of experience that would equip him to stand forth as both a polymath scholar and a skilled polemicist.

In Calcutta he created one storm after another, attacking both Christian trinitarian doctrine and what he took to be the idolatry of Hindu religious life. Whether drawing on Muslim theology or Enlightenment ideals of reason, Rammohan was a quintessential rationalist. In his *Tuḥfat al-Muwaḥḥidīn*, Rammohan offered a rationalist critique of religion in which he observed that while rituals and creeds may vary, all people possess an "innate faculty" that allows them to infer the existence of a God who creates and governs the universe. He elaborates on this faculty:

> There is always such an innate faculty existing in the nature of mankind that in case any person of sound mind, before or after assuming the doctrines of any religion, makes an impartial and just enquiry into the nature of the principles of religious doctrines, of different nations, there is a strong hope that he will be able to distinguish the truth from untruth and true propositions from fallacious ones, and also he, becoming free from the useless restraints of religion, which sometimes become sources of prejudices of one against another and causes of physical and mental troubles, will turn to the One Being who is the fountain of the harmonious organization of the universe, and will pay attention to the good of society. (Roy 1906: 947)

Put simply, for Rammohan, belief in one God and a sense of duty toward one's fellow human beings were the essential criteria for judging the truth of any religion.

Rammohan applied his rationalist critique to the Christian tradition, finding fault with the miracles that abound in the New Testament, as well as with the mysteries of Trinitarian theology that seem to confound reason. For Rammohan, the essence of Christianity was nothing more than a "simple code of religion and morality" epitomized by two commandments from the book of Matthew: "Thou shalt love the Lord thy God with all thy heart, and with all thy soul, and with all thy mind," and "Thou shalt love thy neighbor as thyself."[4] As he elsewhere put it, "love to God is manifested in beneficence towards our fellow creatures."[5]

While in many respects he was a rationalist, Rammohan was also a scripturalist. He felt that the same simple code of religion and morality confirmed by reason could be found at the heart of the Hindu tradition as well. For Rammohan, this code was enshrined in the last layer of Vedic revelation, the Upanishads, the so-called end of the Veda (Vedānta). In the Upanishads, Rammohan claimed to find the core of authentic Hinduism. These texts were for Rammohan the valid means for knowing (*pramāṇa*) the Supreme Lord. Such knowledge Rammohan and his followers referred to as *brahmajñāna*.

By labeling Rammohan a scripturalist, I mean to suggest that it mattered to him that the spiritual worship he advocated had a sanction in revealed scriptures. Sometimes this side of Rammohan is overlooked, which is understandable if one looks principally at his English-language writings, in which the Deistic and rationalist approach is foregrounded. However, in his Bengali writings, Rammohan makes clear and consistent appeals to the authority of scripture. We can understand this in at least three ways.

First, by tracing the source of his worldview to the ancient Upanishads (which for him marked the sacred fountainhead of Hindu wisdom), Rammohan sought to provide a recognized hermeneutic rationale for rejecting idolatry and polytheism.[6] Such errors, he argued, were later corruptions of the original wisdom of the Upanishads. As he noted in the preface to his translation of the Īśā Upanishad, the Upanishads reveal to us a Lord who is one and all-pervading. While Rammohan admits that the later Purāṇas and Tantras also confirm the oneness of God, at the same time, in his view they are also rife with the myths and rituals of polytheism. If Rammohan was unprepared to accept the Christian narrative of incarnation and the theology of the Trinity, he was equally unprepared to tolerate the doctrines of divine descents (*avatāra*) as found in the mythology of Vishnu or the rituals of image worship (*pūjā*) so promiment in the religious life of Bengali Hindus, whether they be devotees of Krishna, Rama, Durga, or Kali.

This suggests a second way we might think of Rammohan's appeal to scripture. From what I have said so far, it is obvious that Rammohan was engaged in a critique of contemporary Hindu thought and practice fully as much as he sought to challenge the claims of trinitarian Christianity. As a result, on the Hindu front he could well expect to be accused of disbelief. Within Hinduism one can hold a variety of positions, but to reject the authority of the Vedas is by many accounts to go beyond the pale. Such a person is dubbed a *nāstika*, one who says the things described in the Vedas don't exist (*na asti*). Rammohan's recourse to the Upanishads as the litmus test for religious truth shielded him from any such charges. No *nāstika*, he might even claim he was a better Hindu than those who indulged in image worship.

Third, and finally, Rammohan's steadfast equation of truth with Vedānta, understood as the teachings of the Upanishads, allowed him to reject other formulations of Vedānta philosophy that had developed during the post-Vedic and classical periods.[7] While Rammohan had studied, edited, and translated certain of these later Vedānta texts—notably the Brahmasūtras of Bādarāyaṇa with the eighth-century commentary of Śaṅkara—he also questioned and rejected central aspects of classical Vedānta.[8] Prominent in Śaṅkara's conception of Vedānta is the stipulation that only the brahmin renouncer is entitled to undertake the kind of training that leads to ultimate knowledge. Such a view was doubly suspect in Rammohan's mind. To begin with, it validated a conception of caste hierarchy at odds with his own democratic sensibilities and conviction that the religious life was open to all. Furthermore, by grounding the pursuit of saving knowledge, or *brahmajñāna*, in the praxis of the renouncer, Śaṅkara made it impossible for the ordinary householder to strive for salvation. Rammohan therefore sought to distance himself from the renunciatory logic and exclusivism of classical Vedānta by appealing to the more ancient and revealed authority of the Upanishads. As it turned out, this strategy simultaneously shielded his position from potential attack by Christian missionaries, who tended to look with suspicion at the philosophy of Vedānta precisely because of what they took to be its world-negating posture.

In sum, Rammohan's position was that if one disentangled the primordial truths of Vedānta from the fanciful myths, idolatrous rites, and renunciatory logic of classical Hinduism, one could return to a simple and sensible belief in one ultimate Being, who is "the animating and regulating principle of the whole collective body of the universe" and who is the "origin of all individual souls." Far from renunciation, temple-worship, images, myths, and rituals, all that was required for true worship was knowledge of the Supreme Lord and "benevolence towards each other."[9]

This twofold concept of worship was to form the theological and moral bedrock upon which Rammohan founded the Brāhmo Samāj. On the one hand, worshipers were encouraged to know "the only true God" (see Killingley 1982). For Rammohan worship depends on *brahmajñāna*, knowledge of the relationship between the individual self and ultimate reality. Following a logic deeply embedded in the Hindu tradition, acquisition of such saving knowledge comes only through a combination of study, meditation, and diligent restraint of the senses (the last of which the classical sources refer to as *indriya-nigraha*). On the other hand, worship must have its social and moral manifestation. Rammohan insisted that what we do in this world should be done in a spirit of dedication to God (Biśvās 1989: 368–69).

Putting these two dimensions of Rammohan's teachings together allows us to appreciate why he was just as opposed to renunciatory forms of Hindu worship (which lead humans to forsake their duties to others in society) as he was to idolatry and polytheism (which detract from the unity and transcendence of the Supreme Lord). His ideal was therefore not the ascetic renouncer, or *saṃnyāsin*, who flees the world, but the *brahmaniṣṭha gṛhastha*—the "godly householder" who worships the Supreme Lord while carrying out his worldly affairs (Hatcher 1996a: 201–6).

In 1815, Rammohan created a small association known as the Ātmīya Sabhā, the Society of Friends. This was apparently little more than an informal gathering—Sophia Dobson Collet calls it "not quite public"—for conversation and debate (1988: 76). At this point, there was no provision for formal worship within the group, which was largely devoted to reciting scripture and chanting hymns composed by Rammohan and others. Regarding worship and theology,

Rammohan was rather famously drawn for a time toward Unitarianism, because there he found no talk of incarnation and the trinity. According to one contemporary account, however, two of Rammohan's closest associates, Candrasekhar Deb and Tarachand Chakravarti, suggested to him that it would be a good idea to establish their own place of worship that would be analogous to what Christians had in their churches.[10]

Their suggestion led Rammohan to found the Brāhmo Samāj, or the Society of Worshipers of the Absolute, which was formally established in north Calcutta on Wednesday, August 20, 1828 (Collet 1988: 224).[11] At the inaugural meeting, a discourse on the spiritual worship of God was delivered by Rammohan's close associate, the Sanskrit pandit Rāmacandra Vidyāvāgīśa (1786–1845). In subsequent years, after Rammohan's death, this same Rāmacandra had a pivotal role not just in preserving the faith and worship of the Brāhmo Samāj but also in mediating Rammohan's ideas to a new generation of Bengali Hindus, most notably Debendranath Tagore.

Two years after the founding of the Brāhmo Samāj, Rammohan left for England. He carried with him the honorary title of Raja, which had been bestowed upon him by Akbar II, the Mughal emperor in Delhi. While in England, Rammohan had been asked to seek assistance for the emperor on a mission that was, as one scholar has noted, "a strange one for a liberal with republican sympathies": the emperor wished him to sue for an increase in the pension he was receiving from the East India Company (Killingley 1993: 11). But in England, Rammohan also sought kindred spirits chiefly among the Unitarians. He had been in regular contact with Unitarians both in England and America for several years. In fact, his message was received with great enthusiasm by the Unitarians, who saw in him not just a fellow believer in the unity of the godhead, but a commited rationalist. In England, Rammohan would have had an opportunity to deepen these Unitarian contacts while completing his mission for the emperor. As it turned out, his visit and his life's work were cut short by his untimely death in 1833, when he was staying with friends in Bristol.[12]

After Rammohan's death

In the wake of Rammohan's departure and eventual death, the energy and activities of the Brāhmo Samāj were severely weakened. Attendance dwindled at the weekly meetings. To many, it must have seemed as if Rammohan's vision and his movement would both soon fade from memory. This might have been the end of the Brāhmo movement were it not for the dedicated work of Rammohan's closest associates. None was more instrumental in keeping the Brāhmo Samāj alive than Rāmacandra Vidyāvāgīśa, the member who had delivered the first discourse before the Samāj in 1828. As first preceptor, or *ācārya*, of the Samāj, Rāmacandra presided over weekly meetings in the months and years after Rammohan's death. As one later Brāhmo commented, "Only the faithful Ram Chandra Vidyabagish remained steadfast; and for seven years he regularly and punctually conducted the weekly service, as directed by Rajah Ram Mohun Roy, often alone like the solitary watcher by the dim-burning pyre at the burning-ghat" (Sarkar 1931: 5).

Like Rammohan, Rāmacandra was a brahmin by birth. Unlike Rammohan, he went on to train as a Sanskrit pandit. In 1827 he was hired to fill a vacancy teaching Hindu legal texts at the Calcutta Government Sanskrit College, a position he would hold for ten years, until being dismissed under curious circumstances.[13] His world was drawn close to Rammohan's in many ways, not the least because Rammohan had studied Tantra under Rāmacandra's older brother, who had renounced worldly life and become an Avadhūta ascetic known as Hariharānanda Tīrthasvāmī. It may even be that Rammohan and Rāmacandra met one another through Hariharānanda.

Rammohan was so impressed by Rāmacandra's mastery of Sanskrit that he sent him to study Vedānta with one of his own pandits. Rāmacandra is reported to have mastered Vedānta in a very short time.[14] It is clear from all accounts that Rāmacandra and Rammohan formed a powerful intellectual friendship. Sources indicate Rammohan gave Rāmacandra funds with which to open a traditional Sanskrit school for teaching Vedānta, while Rāmacandra's mastery of Sanskrit literature was a valuable asset to Rammohan. Precisely because their friendship transcended what might well have seemed otherwise impassable intellectual barriers—Rammohan a modern, rationalist reformer and Rāmacandra a custodian of brahmanical tradition—it serves to suggest how careful we must be in making generalizations about ideological orientations in colonial Calcutta.

This is not to say that Calcutta society wasn't at the time fractured by competing ideologies, both religious and social. In fact, it is to these fractures that we must attend if we are to appreciate why the Brāhmo Samāj went into decline after Rammohan's death. According to Benoy Ghosh, the Brāhmos generally faced intellectual challenges on three fronts: (1) from English-educated Hindu youth, (2) from Christian missionaries, and (3) from advocates of existing forms of Hindu orthodoxy (Ghoṣa 1963 24–25). We should examine each of these groups in a bit more detail in order to appreciate both the forces that impinged on the early Brāhmo Samāj and the intellectual matrix within which any restatement of Rammohan's goals would need to be situated.

For all that it was based on a rational investigation of religious truth, Rammohan's movement was itself open to critique from even more strident rationalists. The most prominent group of rationalists at this time were the English-educated youth associated with such colonial institutions as Hindu College. Students of the college, inoculated with the enlightened skepticism of their Eurasian instructor, Henry Louis Vivian Derozio (d. 1831), had little patience for religion. A loose-knit cadre of atheists, rationalists, and skeptics known as Young Bengal, these students quickly became notorious in Calcutta society for flaunting all religious orthodoxies.[15] Their motto was, in the words of Ramgopal Ghosh, "He who will not reason is a bigot; he who cannot is a fool, and he who does not is a slave" (cited in Sarkar 1958: 19). To the members of Young Bengal, even an indigenous religious movement such as the Brāhmo Samāj might have appeared to be just another form of religious sectarianism. No doubt their antipathy to sectarian dogma owed much to their schooling in a curriculum grounded in Enlightenment mistrust of religion, exemplified by the role of Christianity in Europe.

And Christians were an active presence in Calcutta. The anti-religious feelings of Young Bengal were thus fueled not only by colonial critiques of Hinduism as an erroneous and degraded religious system but also by their disgust with the persistent proselytizing of the Christian missionaries. In the previous decade Rammohan had taken on the Protestant missionaries—the Baptists in particular—luring them into public debates over religious truth. For their part, the missionaries realized that movements like the Brāhmo Samāj provided a way for Hindus to be theists without converting to Christianity. In response, the Christian missionaries took it upon themselves to combat not just stereotypical notions of Hindu superstition and idolatry but also the Vedānta-based reforms of the Brāhmos. I discuss in chapter 5 how such concerns shaped Christian perceptions of the Tattvabodhinī Sabhā in the 1840s.

In addition to the English-educated youth and the Christian community in Calcutta, Brāhmo reform faced resistance from less progressive Bengali Hindus, notably those who formed the Dharma Sabhā in 1830 in opposition to Rammohan's campaign against suttee. Such Hindus took affront at the Brāhmos' critique of idolatry and their explicit rejection of the myths and ceremonies associated with Puranic Hinduism. In the immense corpus of the Sanskrit Purāṇas (narrative texts from the middle of the first through the middle of the second millennium CE), and in the broader range of local and oral religious discourse that flowed from them, the vast majority of Hindus found the legends, myths, and maxims that framed their religious and moral universe. Bolstered by the ritual and legal traditions associated with orthodox Hindu practice, popular Puranic Hinduism offered a world grounded in the transcendent laws of *dharma*, articulated socially in rules of caste and family law, and punctuated by the regular performance of domestic and temple rituals. These rituals were largely centered on devotion to the deities widely worshiped in Bengal—namely, Krishna, Rama, Shiva, Durga, and Kali. But it was this entire mythic and ritualistic framework that Rammohan had threatened to undermine; his call was for a nonidolatrous, egalitarian mode of worship, centered not on the personal deities of the Purāṇas but on the transcendent absolute of the Upanishads.

We can say, then, that after Rammohan's death, there were many who would have been happy to see the Brāhmo Samāj fade into obscurity. It is important to bear in mind that the advent of the printing press in the last quarter of the eighteenth century had fostered the rapid explosion of publishing and print journalism in Calcutta. And the printed word provided contending groups with the means to advance and defend their ideological positions. Theology was debated in the pages of both Bengali and English periodicals.[16] In this atmosphere of vigorous public debate, the loss of a dynamic and integrating figure like Rammohan cost the Brāhmos dearly. Declining attendance at the Samāj is not hard to understand. Even if one were sympathetic to the goals of the Samāj, it was no doubt far safer to stay out of public view. As one scholar has noted, many members of the Samāj at this time "simply accepted its principles intellectually and did not follow them in their daily lives and activities" (Sen 1979: 12). As the same scholar perceptively notes, what was lacking were the vital institutional means to counter the charges leveled at the Brāhmo Samāj by its various opponents. Something was required that would go beyond what Rammohan had been able to initiate—something that could parry the jabs of Young Bengal, silence the missionaries, and reassure Bengali Hindus that the ideals presented by Rammohan were neither dangerous nor deracinating.

The afterlife of Rammohan's Vedānta

Somewhat ironically, the means to save the Brāhmo Samāj were found neither through aggressively recruiting new members nor through more active advocacy of the Samāj in print, but by the creation of yet another association. This new association would take up Rammohan's cause, but it would do so under the terms of a new synthesis (see Sen 1979: 13).[17] And though the fortunes of the Brāhmo Samāj and this new association would be closely bound from the outset, there would initially be no formal relationship between the two; that would only come with time.

This new association was the Tattvabodhinī Sabhā, or Truth-Propagating Society. The creation of the Tattvabodhinī Sabhā was to become a defining moment in Brāhmo history, a singular moment that would have enormous consequences for the shape of modern Bengali culture. In the simplest of terms, it is a story about the meeting of two men, Rāmacandra and Debendranath—the latter anxiously seeking God, the former faithfully tending to the legacy of Rammohan. Their encounter not only marked an upswing in the fortunes of the Brāhmo Samāj, it also sparked a range of new developments in the areas of Bengali literature, social reform, and scientific learning. *Sabhyadiger vaktṛtā* captures the promise and the complexity of this encounter.

Those familiar with Rammohan's work will find themselves on familiar terrain when reading *Sabhyadiger vaktṛtā*. The affinity between Rammohan's theological message and the Tattvabodhinī spiritual vision is readily apparent. Sometimes the authors represented in *Sabhyadiger vaktṛtā* invoke a concept of Vedānta that seems to build directly on Rammohan's Upanishadic theology. The idioms of *ātman* (the Self), *brahman* (Ultimate Reality), *jñāna* (knowledge), and *mokṣa* (liberation) are all employed to speak of the quest for salvation. And, in keeping with Rammohan's ideals, these discourses remind us that the possibility for salvation does not depend on an act of world renunciation (*saṃnyāsa*). Rather, as Rammohan had taught, right worship of God is grounded in an ethic of worldly responsibility. In *Sabhyadiger vaktṛtā*, as in Rammohan's works, it is not the renouncer but the householder (*gṛhastha*) who stands at the heart of religious life.[18]

At other times, the authors of these discourses abandon Upanishadic language in favor of the idioms of modernist theology and rational theism. The concepts of a creator God, divine purpose, the reasonableness of creation, and the sanctity of God's laws are regularly deployed in *Sabhyadiger vaktṛtā*. When this is the case, readers will notice the authors of the discourses resorting to what amounts to a species of evidential theology. From this perspective, God is not the impersonal *brahman* of Vedānta but a wise and purposeful creator. By creating the world, God has brought into existence a marvelous realm of order, proportion, and lawfulness. The Tattvabodhinī authors encourage their audience to recognize that their duty is to know God as revealed in his created order and to strive to conform to his purpose by following his laws. This is not a message entirely alien to Rammohan's thinking, but it is one that receives a distinctive treatment in *Sabhyadiger vaktṛtā*.

Thus while the Tattvabodhinī authors use Vedantic language to speak of the oneness of Self and Ultimate, they simultaneously make claims we might otherwise associate with classical theism. Reading across these discourses, from author to author, one notices that Vedantic axioms such as "Who knows

Brahman, he alone becomes Brahman" (Discourse One) are juxtaposed with theistic proclamations such as "The Lord creates nothing without a purpose" (Discourse Three). To find these two theological idioms nestling side by side in a single text suggests both the diverse intellectual membership of the group and the degree of openness that characterized the group's theology at this particular moment. Taken in its entirety, *Sabhyadiger vaktṛtā* provides striking evidence of a new conception of theistic Vedānta.

In chapter 4, I show that, no matter the idiom chosen, the authors of the Tattvabodhinī discourses tend to approach their theology less in terms of metaphysics than in terms of morality, the morality of human community. For these authors, the focus of religious life is neither philosophical argument nor meditative absorption; rather, it is moral exertion: making a diligent and careful effort to control one's passions so as to live according to the laws of God's creation. Though he is never mentioned by name in the text, one clearly recognizes the debt owed by this group to Rammohan. Here we find re-articulated his vision of a theistic and rational form of Hinduism grounded in the sources of Vedānta. However, as shown in the next chapter, the relationship between the Tattvabodhinī Sabhā and Rammohan is not as simple as that between original and replica. There was a second source for the Sabhā's vision, and this source was Debendranath Tagore.

2

Debendranath Tagore and the Tattvabodhinī Sabhā

The origin of the Tattvabodhinī Sabhā is intimately bound to the spiritual awakening of Debendranath Tagore (Devendranātha Ṭhākura, 1817–1905; fig. 2.1), who later came to be revered in the Brāhmo movement as the Maharṣi, or "great seer." It is time now to recount the story of Debendranath's spiritual development and to explore how it triggered the formation of the Tattvabodhinī Sabhā. As we approach this topic, it is worth bearing in mind that my account of the origins of the Sabhā depends heavily on Debendranath's autobiography. As such, it is easy to draw the conclusion that the Tattvabodhinī Sabhā was created by Debendranath alone. However, while Debendranath was obviously the primary catalyzing influence in the creation of the Sabhā, other individuals had crucial roles from the very beginning. Chief among these was Rāmacandra Vidyāvāgīśa. In chapter 1 we learned in particular of Rāmacandra's efforts to maintain the Brāhmo Samāj after Rammohan's death. It is important to keep Rāmacandra in mind as we proceed. For not only was he to play an important part in the drama of Debendranath's spiritual awakening, but Rāmacandra reminds us of the ongoing and immensely fruitful interplay between the Brāhmo movement and the independent spiritual quest of Debendranath.[1]

FIGURE 2.1. Debendranath Tagore (carbon transfer and ink on paper by Adam Farcus, used by permission of the artist)

The early religious experiences of Debendranath Tagore

Debendranath was the eldest son of Dwarkanath Tagore, the worldly patriarch of the Tagore family of Jorasanko in north Calcutta. The family history of the Tagores is intimately bound to the Brāhmo movement and the so-called renaissance of Bengali culture more generally during the nineteenth and twentieth centuries. Without doubt, the family's brightest light was Debendranath's son, the Nobel laureate Rabindranath Tagore. But as David Kopf long ago pointed out, for all the adoration paid to Rabindranath, it is all too rare to find adequate attention paid to the debt he owed to his father, Debendranath, and his grandfather, Dwarkanath (Kopf 1979: 287).

Dwarkanath has been hailed by many as "India's first modern-style entrepreneur" (Kopf 1979: 162). He was a businessman who developed extensive contacts with European traders and Englishmen in Calcutta and who displayed an astounding range of commercial interests.[2] At the same time, he was a great friend and patron of Rammohan. Dwarkanath had been a trustee of the original Brāhmo Samāj and was among a handful of stalwarts who went on attending meetings of the Brāhmo Samāj after Rammohan's death. In fact, it was Dwarkanath who paid the bills to keep the Samāj afloat during those lean years (Śāstrī 1983: 171). But for all his interest in and support of Rammohan's spiritual mission, Dwarkanath's heart was wed to business. It was his hope that his son Debendranath would follow him by taking over management of the family's business concerns. Dwarkanath was none too pleased when Debendranath began to show more interest in spiritual questions than in business dealings (Kling 1976: 185).

While an English-language biography of Debendranath is long overdue, what concerns us here are the events of Debendranath's early life that were to trigger a profound religious experience. This experience issued into Debendranath's search for a nonidolatrous mode of divine worship, which in turn led to the creation of the Tattvabodhinī Sabhā. We are fortunate that Debendranath left us a moving and detailed account of his spiritual journey in his autobiography, written late in his life and known in Bengali as *Ātmajīvanī* (Tagore 1909, 1980). What follows draws heavily but not uncritically on the first five chapters of *Ātmajīvanī*, in which Debendranath provides an account of his youth and the genesis of the Tattvabodhinī Sabhā.[3]

The figure who looms largest over the earliest pages of Debendranath's autobiography is not his father but his father's mother, his Didimā. Debendranath recalls her with great affection, noting in particular the shape and quality of her religious faith. Didimā was what one might call a devout Hindu, who followed patterns of worship and practice typical for a high-caste Bengali woman of her day. She was a Vaiṣṇava who bathed daily in the Gaṅgā (which in Calcutta is known as the Hooghly River) and who worshiped God at home in the form of the aniconic *śālagrāma* stone. She was known to travel occasionally to the holy site of Puri on the seacoast of Orissa just south of Bengal to worship at the great temple of the Vaiṣṇava deity, Lord Jagannātha. During much of his childhood and adolescence, Debendranath came in close and daily contact with his Didimā and, as his autobiography makes clear, he was devoted to her. He speaks fondly, for instance, of the joys of accompanying her on her morning trip to bathe in the Gaṅgā.

When Debendranath was eighteen, his father left on a journey to Allahabad in north India. While he was away, Debendranath's Didimā fell ill. It soon became evident that her condition was critical. Sensing the end, her family decided to move her to the banks of the Gaṅgā as the first step in her preparation for death. This would have been quite customary for Hindus of her station. Though Didimā protested vigorously that such a decision would not have been made had her son Dwarkanath been at home, her pleas were not heeded. She was moved to the riverside, where the family attended her in what they felt sure would be her quick decease. But Debendranath's Didimā was apparently a stubborn soul. Angered at being shifted to the riverbank in this fashion, she vowed not to make things any easier by dying. And so she lingered on for several days, living in a temporary shelter on the riverbank, with a view of all the activity around the adjacent burning ghats.

For much of this time, her grandson Debendranath stayed right beside her. No doubt he was deeply distraught at the prospect of losing his grandmother, but he was also moved by the depth of his grandmother's devotion and her calm confidence in the face of death. It was in just these circumstances, as she lay dying in her riverside shelter, that Debendranath was to have a profoundly moving spiritual experience. His story rightly ranks among the paradigmatic accounts of transformative religious awakening.

Debendranath recounts for us in some detail the night before his Didimā died. It was a full moon night, and Debendranath was sitting on the riverbank not far from his grandmother. He could see the moon rising amid the smoke and flames of the nearby funeral pyres. At this moment, he suddenly felt all worldly concerns melt away; he recollects that he felt all desires for worldly power (*aiśvarya*) leaving him. Instead, he was flooded with a profound feeling of joy, or more precisely, religious bliss (*ānanda*). Later on, as he pondered this moment, he realized that up until this point he had lived a life of ease, finding pleasure wherever and however he might. Lost in worldly concerns, he had hitherto paid no particular attention to the quest for ultimate truth (*tattvajñāna*).

Up to this point, he had shown no real interest in pondering religious duty (*dharma*) or in knowing God.

Now he fell to thinking. Where could this unprecedented feeling of bliss have come from? He realized there was no way to attain such a state by reasoning or logic. Scholars of religious studies will recognize in his account a classic example of the sort of sui generis religious experience identified by the likes of Friedrich Schleiermacher in the modern West around this very same time. This experience, as Debendranath and Schleiermacher would agree, was something irreducible, something that could only be understood in its own terms. Unable to account for an earthly cause of his bliss, Debendranath concluded it could only be a gift from God. As he put it, this blissful experience was in fact certain proof of God's existence.[4] It was with just such thoughts running through his head that he returned home that evening, although he failed to sleep that night.

The next morning, his grandmother died. Debendranath was fortunate to be by her side. He recalls in particular the way she chanted the name of Krishna and the way she held her hands over her breast, one finger pointing upward. To the young and spiritually sensitive Debendranath, this was a kind of signal from his grandmother. As he put it, she who had shown him how to love God in this life was now showing him the way to heaven.

Not long after this, Debendranath fell into a deep and extended meditation on the religious life. While he despaired at being able to re-create or recover the experience of bliss he had had on the banks of the Gaṅgā, he nevertheless began to feel increasingly detached from all worldly concerns about wealth and status. He speaks in his autobiography of a growing sense of dispassion, or *vairāgya*, the classic attitude of detachment thought by many renunciatory traditions of Hinduism to be an essential prerequisite for growing closer to the divine. He recalls feeling drawn to a new life, yet he also remained uncertain what such a life would entail. His narrative is reminiscent of the biography of Siddhārtha, in particular of the young and sheltered prince who was suddenly brought face to face with the grim reality of old age, suffering, and death. Like Siddhārtha, Debendranath responded to this pyschic shock not with despair but with a feeling of hope that it might point him toward a higher realization. At one point, we find Debendranath alone on the grounds of the Botanical Gardens downriver from Calcutta. Here he found a bench on which he could sit in solitude and meditate. There, in the afternoon, with the sun streaming through the trees, he tells us he spontaneously sang his first religious song.

He was now nineteen or twenty. His decision to take up the study of Sanskrit is one indication of his growing desire to engage more directly with the great spiritual texts of the Hindu tradition. While he had studied some Sanskrit as a boy, he now requested the family's pandit, Śyāmacaraṇa, to point him to the best texts for learning about God. Śyāmacaraṇa recommended the Mahābhārata. Reading the Mahābhārata, Debendranath claimed to find early clues to ultimate truth, which he refers to as *tattvajñāna.*[5] At the same time, he also went in search of *tattvajñāna* in English-language books, reading what he could of European philosophy. While he doesn't tell us the names of the authors he read at this time, he does make it clear that he was disappointed to find that the philosophers he studied displayed a clear penchant for materialist explanations. He rejected all such explanations. They could be of no help in understanding the deepest sources of spiritual bliss that he had experienced. This decision aside, if we can judge from his autobiography, it was around this time that he began to develop an interest in evidential, theology. This attempt to reason back from the wonders of creation to the creator may well have been an intellectual tool he had picked up from his reading of contemporary European thinkers.

Debendranath's narrative gives us the impression that he eventually concluded that God must be utterly beyond the realm of sense and forms. He reasoned that God can have no body, no feelings, no earthly attributes. This being so, how could he endorse his own family's traditions of image worship, whether they involved devotion to Krishna the flute player, Kali the sword-wielding goddess, or Vishnu as embodied in the *śālagrāma* stone so dear to his late Didimā? He simply could not. His spiritual understanding had arrived at a point where he could no longer countenance what he took to be the irrational superstition and sensual idolatry of Hinduism.

As he tells it—and here we do well to remember that hindsight is always twenty-twenty—this is when he remembered the work of Rammohan Roy. Rammohan had been close friends with his father, Dwarkanath. After Rammohan's death, his books on religion had been stored in Dwarkanath's library at Jorasanko. What is more, Dwarkanath had arranged for the young Debendranath to attend a school Rammohan had helped Rāmacandra start in north Calcutta.[6] Debendranath had fond memories of playing in Rammohan's garden as a boy, picking lichees, and being pushed on the garden swing by none other than the great reformer himself (for example, Tagore 1909: 13 and Chakravarty 1935: 172–77). In particular, he recalled that Rammohan "did not take part in any image-worship or idolatry" (Tagore 1909: 14). Remembering the principles that had guided Rammohan's life, Debendranath vowed to follow them in his own life. He joined his brothers in a secret promise to no longer bow before the family idols during such ceremonies as Durga Puja.

These, then, are some of the major developments highlighted by Debendranath as his narrative approaches the period that witnessed the founding of the Tattvabodhinī Sabhā. In light of what we have already discussed regarding the question of the precise relationship between Rammohan's teachings and the founding of the Sabhā—and not losing sight of the fact that in his autobiography Debendranath looks back at this period from much later in his life—there is surely cause to continue asking just how explicitly Rammohan figured in Debendranath's thinking at this time. If judged merely from the evidence of the text of *Sabhyadiger vaktṛtā*, in which there is no reference to either Rammohan Roy or the Brāhmo movement, it is reasonable to surmise that in his autobiography Debendranath may have projected Rammohan back into this period, giving him a more central role as inspiration for the new society.

Why might he do this? If the discourses preserved in *Sabhyadiger vaktṛtā* contain no explicit mention of Rammohan or the Brāhmo movement, why would Debendranath introduce Rammohan so squarely into his later narrative of this period in his life? The answer to these questions is quite simple. In the years immediately following the creation of the Tattvabodhinī Sabhā, Debendranath came to see ways in which the work of the Sabhā and the Brāhmo Samāj could be mutually supportive. I discuss some of these developments later, but for now it is enough to highlight one important event. In 1843, four years after the founding of the Sabhā, Debendranath decided to undergo formal initiation into the Brāhmo Samāj. This did not bring his involvement in the Tattvabodhinī Sabhā to a close; if anything, in his eyes, it marked the fulfillment of his spiritual quest. From that time forward, his energies were applied to fostering the growth of both the Tattvabodhinī Sabhā and the Brāhmo Samāj. As he turned more explicitly to the task of articulating the meaning, scriptural sources, and founding principles of the Brāhmo movement, it naturally became necessary to invoke the life and work of Rammohan. Likewise, it became essential to link Rammohan directly to the history of the Tattvabodhinī Sabhā. These decisions constituted the steps that would lead to Rammohan to attain the status of "founder," not just of the Brāhmo Samāj but also, in a secondary sense, of the Tattvabodhinī Sabhā.[7]

Debendranath's great awakening

Before I can address these developments, however, I need to reconstruct the actual events that led to the creation of the Tattvabodhinī Sabhā in 1839. Despite Debendranath's later narrative reconstruction, it will become clear that Rammohan was in fact not the primary or even the decisive factor in the Sabhā's creation. Rather, the impetus for establishing the Sabhā came from Debendranath and should be understood as the outgrowth of a second profound spiritual experience that befell him. This second great awakening effectively sealed his commitment to a life of rational and nonidolatrous monotheistic worship. Even accounting for the subtle background influence of Brāhmo ideals, it remains clear that the experience and its aftermath were rooted squarely in Debendranath's personal story.

The story of his awakening is well known to scholars of this period, but it deserves retelling for both its dramatic and its thematic content. By this point, Debendranath had turned his back on image worship. But having recognized what he rejected, he remained uncertain where to turn for guidance. Then he tells us that "one day all of a sudden I saw a page from some Sanskrit book flutter past me" (Tagore 1909: 14). Out of curiosity, he picked it up, but he was unable to make out what it said. He brought it to the family pandit, Śyāmacaraṇa, and asked him to have a look at it for him.

According to his autobiography, it was at this very moment that Debendranath's worldly duties intruded. He told Śyāmacaraṇa that he would have to leave to go to work at his father's bank, where he was employed as an assistant cashier. With the world of mammon summoning him he left, but not before giving Śyāmacaraṇa explicit instructions to "decipher the meaning of the verses so that you can explain it all to me on my return from office" (Tagore 1909: 14).

It should have been a long day at the office, but Debendranath was too agitated to stay. He pled his case and received permission to return home early. Racing back to Jorasanko, he sought out Śyāmacaraṇa. Sadly, Śyāmacaraṇa informed him that he had been stumped by the passage. Debendranath was surprised by this. Shouldn't a pandit know all sorts of Sanskrit literature? Still, he was too excited to dwell on such concerns. Instead, he asked Śyāmacaraṇa who might be able to help him. Śyāmacaraṇa's reply is quite telling. He said, "That's all Brāhmo Sabhā stuff" (Tagore 1980: 14).[8] And then Śyāmacaraṇa added that "Ramchandra Vidyavagish of the Sabhā could probably explain it" (Tagore 1909: 15). Debendranath didn't let a beat pass; he asked that Rāmacandra be sent for immediately.

As Rāmacandra had been a close colleague of Rammohan's and was then serving as the "preceptor" of the Brāhmo Samāj, he would have known the Tagore family well. He was soon summoned to the Jorasanko house. When Rāmacandra was shown the page, he instantly informed Debendranath that the passage in question was taken from the Īśā Upanishad. Then he read the Sanskrit passage out loud for Debendranath:

> Īśāvāsyam idaṃ sarvaṃ yatkiñca jagatyāṃ jagat
> tena tyaktena bhuñjīthā mā gṛdhaḥ kasysvit dhanam

As Rāmacandra began to explain the meaning of the text, Debendranath remarked, "nectar from paradise streamed down upon me" (Tagore 1909: 15). Debendranath had found what he had so desperately been searching for—proof of a transcendent deity beyond names and forms, as revealed in Hindu scripture. As he tells it, he had been granted a foretaste of *brahmajñāna*—knowledge of *brahman*, or Ultimate Reality. He had found the Supreme Lord. And he had done so with the help of the one man who had endeavored to keep the Brāhmo vision alive since Rammohan's death, Rāmacandra.[9]

What, though, was the meaning of this verse that so changed Debendranath's life? As it turns out, the Īśā is among those Upanishads that had been translated by Rammohan into English. It is perhaps fitting to consider the way Rammohan chose to translate this passage:

> All the material extension in this world, whatsoever it may be, should be considered as clothed with the existence of the Supreme regulating spirit: by thus abstracting your mind from worldly thoughts, preserve thyself from self-sufficiency, and entertain not a covetous regard for property belonging to any individual. (Roy 1906: 75)

One cannot help but be struck by the coincidence between the message and the context of its revelation. First, Debendranath finds the enigmatic torn page. Then, his clerical work at the bank calls him away. Only later, after fleeing the world of mammon to return home, was the ambrosia granted. Debendranath's account thus underscores the text's emphasis on the tension between knowing God and coveting wealth. And heeding the Upanishad's injunction, Debendranath resolves that his life will no longer follow the material and sensualist path of his father. As Tithi Bhattacharya has pointed out, if Dwarkanath was known widely as the "Prince," Debendranath would henceforth go down in history as the "Maharṣi," the great sage (Bhattacharya 2005: 79). However, it is best not to draw the contrast between the Prince and the Sage too sharply, since the very tension between worldly desire and spiritual aspiration that is at play in the passage from Īśā Upanishad, serves to characterize the bourgeois faith of the Tattvabodhinī Sabhā, as demonstrated in chapter 4.

The incident with the Upanishad is a clear turning point, a conversion. Henceforth, Debendranath would begin working to translate the content of his great awakening into a message and an organization. Clearly, Rammohan is standing in the wings. It was Rammohan, after all, who had told his readers (in the preface to his Bengali translation of this same Upanishad) that the Upanishads teach us of a Supreme Lord (*parameśvara*) who is omnipresent, beyond our senses, and unknowable by our intellect, but who is the source of final liberation (for example, Robertson 1995: 117n16). This is the very God Debendranath would dedicate his life to serving. Whereas hitherto life had seemed meaningless, Debendranath could now see a divine presence behind creation. And he could also now see a kind of purpose for himself. He knew what his role must be from this time onward. He would need to understand for himself—and then help others to understand—the profound truths delivered to him in this Upanishad. This would be the goal of the Tattvabodinī Sabhā.

Founding of the Tattvabodhinī Sabhā

Debendranath's first task was to learn more about *brahmajñāna*. Toward this end, he read through several Upanishads (Īśā, Kena, Kaṭha, Muṇḍaka, Māṇḍukya) with Rāmacandra; later, he studied the remaining major Upanishads under the tutelage of other pandits in his circle. He made a habit of memorizing the texts and repeating them on subsequent days to his teachers. His goal was to internalize the texts in the hope of becoming "illumined by the light of truth" (Tagore 1909: 16). As his sense of illumination grew, a second major task announced itself.

He writes that he "felt a strong desire to spread the true religion" (Tagore 1909: 16).[10] This desire would lead to the creation of a small group that shared his vision of theism, the Tattvabodhinī Sabhā. The context and timing behind the creation of the Sabhā bears noting. Most important, we notice that Debendranath made his decision to form a theistic association at the very height of Bengal's most exuberant season of image worship, the autumn festival of the goddess Durga (a celebration of great pomp and display known as Durga Puja). While the rest of the Jorasanko household reveled in worship of the goddess, Debendranath gathered with some friends and relatives in a small room by a tank on the grounds of the family mansion. The year was 1761 of the Śaka era. It was the fourteenth day of the dark fortnight during the Bengali month of Āśvina (corresponding to September 29, 1839). Everyone present had bathed first, and Debendranath tells us the room was "filled with an atmosphere of purity" (Tagore 1909: 17).

The novice now became the guru, as Debendranath launched into a sermon on the meaning of a verse from the Kaṭha Upanishad, yet another text upon which Rammohan had lavished attention.[11] He emphasized how important it was not to become so attached to this world that one denied the existence of the life to come (*paraloka*). For Debendranath, this was to be but the first of many discourses (*vaktṛtā*) and sermons (*vyākhyāna*) he would deliver over the course of his life, a life that would become increasingly defined by the mission of propagating the truths of Upanishadic theism.

At this point, Debendranath was not thinking of himself as a Brāhmo. In fact, at his suggestion, the group agreed to call themselves the Tattvarañjinī Sabhā. Their goal would be promoting knowledge of God, or *brahmajñāna*. The group also resolved to meet on the first Sunday of every month. Then they adjourned. It was a promising beginning, but it wasn't really a proper inauguration; that would come at the next meeting.

The next meeting took place on October 6, 1839, in a spacious room on the ground floor of Dwarkanath's house in Jorasanko (fig. 2.2).[12] Rāmacandra was invited to attend. The invitation presumably came from Debendranath, for it was Debendranath who appointed Rāmacandra to the position of *ācārya*, or preceptor, of the new association. Interestingly, one of the earliest English-language records of the meeting, written by the Reverend Joseph Mullens, appears to see in Rāmacandra the true motive force behind the group: "On the sixth of October (Aswin 21st, 1761), the Pandit Ram Chandra with his scholars and friends, ten in number, met in the house of Babu Dwarkanath Thakur, established the present Tattwabodhini Sabhā, and determined, by actively advocating their views, to endeavor to gain converts to their faith" (Mullens 1852: 5).

It is striking that Debendranath is not even mentioned. Striking, too, is the rather ominous tone Mullens lends to the events when he speaks of the group's goal of seeking converts to their new "faith." Mullens apparently sensed something dangerous about this group, which (as discussed in chapter 5) was a theme

FIGURE 2.2. Tagore residence at Jorasanko (carbon transfer and ink on paper by Adam Farcus, used by permission of the artist)

that would characterize missionary views of the society almost from the outset. But why is there no mention of Debendranath?

I can think of at least three reasons. The first is that Mullens wrote his account at a later date, working only from secondhand sources or testimony. It wouldn't be surprising if he simply didn't have all the facts. A second reason could be that, unlike Debendranath, Rāmacandra was by this time well known in Calcutta as the preceptor of the Brāhmo Samāj. To any missionary with an ear to the ground, Rāmacandra's link to this new group would no doubt have raised an eyebrow. What were those Brāhmos up to now? A third reason may be that it was Rāmacandra, after all, who took the lead at this meeting. A prominent leader within the Brāhmo community, the group may well have looked to him for guidance.

We cannot reconstruct what went on at this first meeting beyond what Debendranath tells us. From his narrative, we learn that Rāmacandra put forward an important proposal to rename the association the Tattvabodhinī Sabhā, or Truth-Propagating Society. Debendranath betrays no disappointment at having had his initial idea for a name revised, but then we should recall that he owed his spiritual awakening and subsequent tutelage to Rāmacandra. As for why Rāmacandra changed the name, it seems likely he preferred the powerful idiom of *bodha*, or "awakening," over Debendranath's choice of the less metaphysically charged, and perhaps too sensual, idiom of *rañjana* ("gratification"). Additionally, to refer to the society as *tattvabodhinī* is to convey two meanings. On the one hand, it suggests a group individuals dedicated to the realization of truth; on the other, it suggests that this group also wished to make the truth known to others. It is this latter, crucial sense that is missing from Debendranath's original choice of *tattvarañjinī*. Whatever the reasoning, it would be Rāmacandra's name that would stick. And henceforth, this—the de facto second meeting of Debendranath's group—would be remembered as the de jure inauguration of the Tattvabodhinī Sabhā. The date of 21 Āśvina 1761 Śaka would be for some time an important anniversary date for the Tattvabodhinī group.[13]

It was at the meetings of this group, during its inaugural year, 1839–40, that the discourses translated in this volume were read aloud to members. According to Debendranath, a pattern for the meetings was very quickly established. Rāmacandra would begin by reading out a Sanskrit couplet, which in translation runs:

> O spiritual guide of the universe, thou art without form, yet that I have conceived thine image in the act of meditation, that I have ignored thine inexpressibility by words of praise, that I have nullified thy

omnipresence by making pilgrimages, and in other ways, for these transgressions committed through confusion of spirit, O Almighty God, I implore thy forgiveness. (Tagore 1909: 18–19)[14]

After this, anyone present at the meeting had the right to offer a discourse (*vaktṛtā*) on spiritual matters.[15] The only stipulation was that in order to be recognized to speak at a given meeting, one had to present a handwritten copy of one's remarks to the secretary of the group in advance of the meeting. Debendranath notes that this led to humorous attempts on the part of members to sneak copies of their discourses into the secretary's bed so that he would find them first thing in the morning (Tagore 1909: 19).

Understanding *Sabhyadiger vaktṛtā* in its moment

Such, then, were the terms under which the discourses translated here were delivered. It remains but to ask three simple questions: Who were the speakers responsible for these discourses? What concerns did they raise in their discourses? And how were the ideas of the Sabhā received by others, especially by contemporary Christian observers who had been so concerned in the past with the reformist work of Rammohan? These are the questions that broadly frame chapters 3, 4, and 5.

Before taking up these questions, it is worth reminding ourselves of the curious position occupied by *Sabhyadiger vaktṛtā* vis à vis the earlier activities of Rammohan and the subsequent history of the Brāhmo movement, which concerns us in chapter 3. One way to suggest the right vantage point to adopt when reading these discourses comes from considering the formally established purpose of the new society, which Debendranath summarized as follows in his autobiography: "Its object was the diffusion of the deep truth of all our *shastras* and the knowledge of *Brahma* as inculcated in the *Vedanta*. It was the *Upanishads* that we considered to be the *Vedanta*,—we did not place much reliance on the teachings of the *Vedanta* philosophy" (Tagore 1909: 18; emphasis in original).[16] Tellingly, Rammohan is not explicitly invoked. Rather, the mission of the Sabhā is presented as the propagation of Vedantic truth. And yet we know that this was precisely the reform strategy that Rammohan had so effectively inaugurated. We are reminded, thus, of the ambivalent relationship between the Sabhā and Rammohan at this point.

Clearly echoing Rammohan, Debendranath grounds his theological vision on the root teachings of the Upanishads. For Debendranath, as for Rammohan, it mattered that the spiritual worship of the Sabhā had its ultimate sanction in revealed scripture. For all that the Sabhā endorsed the rational pursuit of God, its members nevertheless did so on the basis of assurances granted in what were to them, as to all Hindus of the time, sacred writings. This would subsequently become a point of contention within the larger Brāhmo community. In the decades to come, the problem of reconciling reason and revelation would have to be more squarely faced. And the verdict would eventually be that the concept of revelation was untenable. However, that moment had not yet arrived. Rather, if we are to properly understand the discourses translated here, we must bear in mind that the original Tattvabodhinī group generally took for granted the revealed status of the Vedas. And for the moment, this position worked to shield the group from attack by other, more orthodox, Hindus.

Debendranath's statement of the Sabhā's purpose also emphasizes the group's rejection of the classical philosophy of Vedānta (here to be understood to refer to the system of Advaita Vedānta). This posture is again reminiscent of Rammohan's approach to Vedānta.[17] Rammohan had relied on, edited, and translated certain philosophical texts important for classical Vedānta philosophy (notably the Brahmasūtras of Bādarāyaṇa with the commentary of Śaṅkara).[18] But, he had also avoided endorsing central aspects of classical Vedānta, notably its endorsement of the caste hierarchy and its mandate that the renouncer's life was a prerequisite for gaining ultimate knowledge. Debendranath and the Sabhā carried forward these concerns.

Overall, then, the Sabhā's emphasis on the scriptural authority of the Vedas worked to shield the group from attacks by other Hindus. At the same time, by putting some distance between Debendranath's concept of saving knowledge, or *brahmajñāna*, and the renunciant exclusivism of Śaṅkara, the Sabhā may have hoped to discourage criticism from Christian missionaries, who were known to look with suspicion upon the philosophy of Vedānta.

It didn't necessarily work out this way. While the Sabhā was received with somewhat more favor by so-called conservative Hindus (who may well have appreciated the Sabhā's initial attempt to distance itself from Rammohan), it did not escape the critical scrutiny of the missionaries. It wasn't long before Christian missionaries began to attack the Sabhā's theology for its purported pantheism and immorality. But, again, it must be noted that the discourses translated in this volume predate these debates. To be sure, "like all moments in an intellectual development," these discourses "contain a promise for the future." But they also reveal "an irreducible and *singular* present" (Althusser 2005: 156; emphasis in original). We should not, therefore, project the terms of subsequent controversies onto the twenty-one short discourses found in

Sabhyadiger vaktṛtā. Instead, we must endeavor to read these discourses on their own and in their singular moment. If we do this, we may hope to better understand the earliest concerns of the Sabhā—concerns that were neither a mere repetition of Rammohan's Brāhmo faith nor an entirely independent theological vision.

3

New Members and a New Founder

According to the account left for us by Debendranath Tagore in his autobiography, the first meeting of the Tattvabodhinī Sabhā brought together a core group of just ten members. By the following year, the number of members had increased dramatically to 105,[1] and within three years, the ranks had grown to 138.[2] While these are impressive numbers, it must surely have been the case that during its earliest months the Sabhā grew somewhat slowly. No doubt news of the association initially traveled by word of mouth among friends, schoolmates, business associates, and family members. We can imagine there were those who attended an occasional meeting but for one reason or another never became regular, dues-paying members. Reports from later years of the Sabhā suggest that there were always those who claimed membership but did not keep current with their dues. This is hardly surprising. It is much the pattern we would expect for any voluntary association in an age before TV, telephones, the Internet, and sophisticated pledge drives.

Besides the question of basic membership, one wonders how many members in the earliest period were what might be called active and vocal participants in the Sabhā's meetings. Judging from the discourses translated here, there may have been only a small number of members who took an active part in meetings during the first year. While *Sabhyadiger vaktṛtā* includes a total of twenty-one discourses, only eleven distinct authors are represented. This being the earliest extant publication of the group, and for all we know its first formal publication, we have to wonder whether these eleven either represented the most outspoken members of the Sabhā or were perhaps the sole membership of the group in its earliest months. If the authors of these discourses sound as if they are preaching to the choir, if we find in *Sabhyadiger vaktṛtā* precious little evidence of proselytizing zeal, it might well be evidence that during its first months at least, the Sabhā remained a small and rather insular group. This is all the more reason, of course, to marvel at its growth in subsequent years.

In this chapter, I foreground issues of membership and identity. Just what do we know about the earliest members of the group? What did they share, and, just as important, what did the Sabhā offer that might have attracted individuals from disparate social, educational, and professional backgrounds? How did Debendranath and his colleagues go about attracting new members? To raise these sorts of question is to raise in turn questions about the group's identity and its sense of origin, mission, and purpose. As we attend to these questions, it will become apparent that the group's self-understanding changed significantly over the first few years.

No doubt, the most significant development is one to which I have already had occasion to refer in preceding chapters—namely, the Sabhā's evolving understanding of its relationship to the figure of Rammohan Roy. In this chapter I consider in a bit more detail just how, in the years after publication of *Sabhyadiger vaktṛtā*, the Sabhā came to integrate Rammohan into their own sense of communal identity. As I argue, it was by "remembering" Rammohan as their "founder" that the Sabhā was able to ensure a lasting identity for itself as a religious organization, one we would today characterize as Brāhmo in theology and social vision. This is so despite the fact that, in their earliest self-understanding, the members of the Sabhā are best described as "Brāhmos without Rammohan." We have seen very clearly that the driving force behind the Sabhā was Debendranath, and judging from the record of *Sabhyadiger vaktṛtā* Rammohan seems to have been all but ignored initially. As I have written elsewhere, there is something very interesting in the Sabhā's retroactive elevation of Rammohan to the status of founder. These developments should interest anyone curious about the nature and role of religious "founders," not to mention Rammohan Roy's contribution to the emergence of modern Hinduism (Hatcher 2006).

Who were the earliest members of the Sabhā?

We are sadly lacking in concrete or comprehensive records for the earliest phase of the Sabhā's history. We remain largely indebted to Debendranath's autobiography, to scattered historical overviews published by the Sabhā in later years, and to random accounts from missionaries like Joseph Mullens. By collating the evidence from such sources, we can at least develop a sketch of the early membership of the Sabhā. That sketch reveals a rather complex situation.

Perhaps most striking is the fact that among the earliest active members, we find a rather diverse range of personalities and backgrounds. In its earliest years, the Sabhā not only attracted prominent (or soon to be prominent) Bengali intellectuals; it also attracted individuals with widely differing views of religion, spirituality, corporate worship, public culture, education, and politics. To understand this we need to remember that by the end of the 1830s, the makeup of elite Calcuttan society was complex, and *bhadralok* commitments to public-sphere activities were manifold. Two-dimensional depictions of standoffs between "liberals" like Rammohan and "conservatives" like the Dharma Sabhā (who opposed his movement against *satī*) do little justice to the multiple and often overlapping attitudes, allegiances, and agendas among Calcutta's active *bhadralok*. A member of the ostensibly reactionary Dharma Sabhā might at the same time be a member of a European-style scientific or agricultural society.

Commitments to religious "orthodoxy" need not have prevented such an individual from endorsing norms of Enlightenment science; he might even become a corresponding member of a European or American learned society. I have in mind, of course, the case of Radhakant Deb. Conversely, a graduate of Hindu College, the so-called bastion of progressive education, might feel an earnest desire to carry forward the norms and customs of traditional brahmanical culture. This would describe the case of Bhudeb Mukhopadhyay rather well.[3] Add to this the push and pull of economics and politics—the tensions generated when individuals with vested interest in commerce or landholding become aware of the plight of landless peasants or the depradations of greedy European planters—and one struggles to find the kinds of pigeonholes that might allow for a neat categorization of Bengali Hindu society at the time.

I return to the interplay between the social status of the Sabhā's members and the particular theology they endorsed in chapter 4, where I consider the members as representatives of Calcutta's emergent bourgeoisie. For now, in preparation for that discussion, it will be enough to fill in the sketch of membership I promised above. The goal here is simply to highlight the diversity of the group. The discourses of *Sabhyadiger vaktṛtā* take on far greater interest if one can imagine them delivered not to a room full of clones, but to a rather more motley collection of Calcuttan society. Let us not forget, after all, that the earliest meetings of the Sabhā were shaped by the somewhat unlikely collaboration between the English-educated scion of one of Calcutta's great entrepreneurial families and a brahmin pandit with a penchant for reform.

Benoy Ghosh long ago called attention to the curious roster of names associated with the early Tattvabodhinī Sabhā. Building on Ghosh's analysis, we can note that among its members (if not from the very outset in every case) the Sabhā boasted:

> the socially and religiously moderate poet, Īśvaracandra Gupta
> the staunch rationalist and materialist, Akṣayakumāra Datta (Akshay Kumar Dutt)
> the Sanskrit pandit and social reformer, Īśvaracandra Vidyāsāgara
> the witty Derozian businessman, Ramgopal Ghosh
> the reclusive antiquarian, Rajendralal Mitra
> Rammohan's son, the barrister, Ramāprasāda Rāya (Ghoṣa 1963: 15)[4]

Readers familiar with the history of nineteenth-century Bengal will recognize in this roster some of the most vocal and industrious men active in educated society before the middle of the century. Even this simple list serves to reveal a range of strikingly divergent family backgrounds, ranging from rural brahmin (Īśvaracandra) to urban progressive (Ramāprasāda), as well as a gamut of attitudinal dispositions that runs from cautious scholarship (Rajendralal) to savvy business acumen (Ramgopal).

What the list doesn't reveal are the manifold fronts upon which such men were (or would become) active—notably, journalism, law, business and trade, Indological scholarship, and education (Sanskrit-, Bengali-, and English-language).[5] Furthermore, the very fact that the Sabhā grew out of the interaction between Debendranath and Rāmacandra should caution us against assuming that members of the Sabhā tended to be cut from the same cloth. Clearly, there was complexity at the very start. We know that apart from Debendranath and Rāmacandra, both Īśvaracandra Gupta and Akṣayakumāra Datta (whom Gupta had encouraged to attend) were among the earliest important members. My research indicates that Vidyāsāgara was himself present early on, which is itself rather remarkable, considering that we are talking about a nearly destitute young brahmin who had come to Calcutta from the countryside to study Sanskrit at the Government Sanskrit College (for details, see Hatcher 1996a).

How this remarkable group of individuals interacted within the association is unfortunately lost to us; we have nothing like the proceedings of meetings, which might have allowed us to listen in to the various exchanges, motions, resolutions, or quarrels that must have punctuated the group's meetings. We are left to imagine meetings charged with enormous intellectual vigor, sincere spiritual feeling, and perhaps even serious disagreement from time to time. After all, here were religiously inspired Brāhmos rubbing shoulders not simply with English-educated members of Young Bengal (those skeptical students of Derozio discussed in chapter 1), but also with highly learned men like Vidyāsāgar and Rajendralal Mitra, men who seemed by most accounts to take little interest in religion one way or another (Biśvās 1958: 36). An attentive reading of *Sabhyadiger vaktṛtā* will serve to suggest some of the disparate sources members drew on in order to make sense of their respective commitments to the group, as well as their own spiritual aspirations. These sources include obvious scriptural texts like the Upanishads, along with passages from various mythic, legal, or even tantric texts. In addition, there are passages of storytelling and rational argumentation that further remind us of the individuality of the authors of these discourses. Again, we wish we had more information, but we're grateful nonetheless to be able to witness at least this much of the group's early internal dynamics.

Reading *Sabhyadiger vaktṛtā* with this disparate membership in mind, we quite naturally ask what it was that these men shared. What common values or aspirations drew such a curious range of individuals to this forum at this time? One answer, which I explore in more detail in chapter 4, is that these men shared a set of values regarding the proper way to harmonize the spiritual life with a desire to succeed and prosper in their urban colonial environment. The 1830s were a time of optimism and aspiration for Bengali Hindu elites, who were moving into a wide variety of successful private and public roles. The Tattvabodhinī Sabhā provided one context where an up-and-coming group of young men could share both their commitment to a moral and spiritual life and their conviction that religion provided the best prop for success in the world. These were all, in effect, "godly householders," men who sought to live a religious *and* a worldly life. This desire fueled the Tattvabodinī message of confident bourgeois spirituality. This seems to have been one essential conviction shared by all the members, no matter their personal or professional backgrounds.

We should bear in mind, also, that the Tattvabodhinī Sabhā was established during a time when the youth of Bengal were being tempted, through Western education and an increasing Christian missionary presence, to dismiss the traditional sources of Indian religion and culture. It would have been relatively easy for any educated young man to conclude that his intellectual and religious options were limited either to denying the validity of religion altogether on the basis of an Enlightenment critique or to choosing conversion to Christianity as the highest form of religious truth (Ghoṣa 1963: 13). The founding of the Tattvabodhinī Sabhā offered such young men a third option: it offered a way to be rational and religious.[6] To Christians, the Tattvabodhinī Sabhā may have seemed an illegitimate sort of intellectual compromise, but to members of the Sabhā it amounted to a safe place to articulate an authentic and indigenous form of religious commitment (on this theme, see Hatcher

1999: esp. ch. 5). What's more, membership in the Tattvabodhinī Sabhā carried the additional advantage of making a direct appeal to Vedic traditions, which not only forestalled a measure of orthodox Hindu critique but also worked to promote a deepened respect for India's past (Ghoṣa 1963: 14). The offer of a non-deracinating, indigenous, and intellectually honest forum for worship and reflection must have surely been an additional factor working to unite the society's disparate membership.

Reaching out to new members

While the membership and events of the momentous first year are all but lost to us—except as we may infer from the discourses translated here—we are fortunate that in his autobiography Debendranath did leave an account of a celebratory meeting he arranged for the third anniversary of the Sabhā's inauguration. This account provides further insight into membership and activities during this early period.

Debendranath notes that, during the first two years, membership in the Sabhā was less than what he had hoped for. He feared the Sabhā suffered from a lack of visibility in the colonial metropolis. Something needed to be done to attract greater attention. In an enterprising move, Debendranath came up with what we might today call a "direct marketing" strategy:

> In those days advertising was not of much use in spreading news. So what I did was to send a note of invitation in the name of every employee in all the offices and firms throughout Calcutta. Each one came to office and saw on his desk a letter addressed to himself,—on opening which he found an invitation from the *Tattvabodhinī Sabhā*. They had never even heard the name of the *Sabhā*. (Tagore 1909: 19)

Not only does Debendranath's account confirm our suspicions regarding the challenges of getting word of the Sabhā out to potential members, his decision to target office workers helps us situate the Sabhā's membership against the backdrop of commercial and clerical Calcutta.

Having sent out their invitations, members worked hard to prepare for the event. "How to decorate well the rooms of the *Sabhā*, what lessons to read and what sermons to give, what part each one should take—these furnished the objects of our preparations. Before it was dusk we had the lamps lighted, the *Sabhā* decorated, and all arrangements complete" (Tagore 1909: 19). The excitement is palpable. One senses even from these few words how eager the members were to strike the right chord for the meeting. But would anyone come?

Debendranath's anxieties on this score were soon assuaged, as people began to show up around nightfall. He describes the scene as visitors filtered in after work, looking around cautiously, rather uncertain as to what they might be in for. At eight o'clock sharp, bells and conch shells sounded the commencement of the meeting.

According to Debendranath's description, there was a small platform, or *vedī*, at the front of the room upon which Rāmacandra was seated. On either side were arrayed twenty southern brahmins, most likely Telegu-speaking. The brahmins began to chant the Vedas. This continued until about ten, when Debendranath stood up and delivered a discourse (*vaktṛtā*) whose content clearly reflected his own spiritual journey. He noted how the spread of English education was working to enlighten the Bengali people, who no longer felt inclined to worship physical images of their deities ("stocks and stones" in the English translation; 1909: 20). However, he also lamented that while educated people were giving up image worship, they remained ignorant of the spiritual alternative offered by Vedānta—that form of worship in which God is revered as "formless, the very essence of intelligence, omnipresent, beyond all thought or speech (1909: 20).[7]

Of equal interest is the fact that after Debendranath spoke, others delivered their own discourses. Thankfully, Debendranath tells us who spoke: Śyāmācaraṇa Bhaṭṭācārya, Candranātha Rāy, Umeścandra Rāy, Prasannacandra Ghosh, Akṣayakumāra Datta, and Ramāprasāda Rāy. This took the meeting up until midnight, when Rāmacandra read a sermon (*vyākhyāna*) of his own. By the time this was over, and a set of hymns had been sung, it was two o'clock in the morning. Everyone was exhausted, but the celebration had been a huge success. Those who had never before heard of the Sabhā had turned out for the event and had thereby learned of its inspiration and its goals. Surely some newcomers must have requested membership. No doubt this went a long way toward allaying Debendranath's fears regarding the group's future.

Two years later, in a report published by the Sabhā, it becomes clear how successful Debendranath's group was becoming. Most interesting, it was taking a crucial role in reviving the flagging fortunes of Brāhmo worship:

> The exertions of the Tuttuvoadhinee [*sic*] Society . . . have imparted renewed energies to the cause. They have led a large number of the educated and respectable members of society, to appreciate the knowledge of God. The meetings of the Braumhu Sumauj [*sic*] are now attended by overflowing congregations, and religious discussions are extensively maintained in Native society.[8]

As the Sabhā's report reveals, the "renewed energies" generated by the Sabhā yielded a dividend in the concomitant revitalization of Brāhmo worship. Contrary to the pattern of moribund worship meetings throughout the 1830s, the success of the Tattvabodhinī Sabhā meant that attendance at Brāhmo meetings also began to improve. Here lies one of the ironies of the Sabhā's success. The Sabhā would eventually become so successful in rekindling Brāhmo fervor that the Tattvabodhinī group would itself be rendered redundant. And just as the Sabhā's inception was due in large part to the spiritual and organizational inspiration of Debendranath, so, too, was its eventual redundancy. For it was Debendranath who brought the Brāhmo movement back from the edge of oblivion and, in turn, restored Rammohan to a place of primacy in the minds of Vedantic reformers.

Once again, we are led to ponder the curious relationship among Debendranath, the Brāhmo Samāj, and Rammohan Roy. While Rammohan deserves credit for establishing the Brāhmo Samāj, it was Debendranath who reinvigorated Rammohan's movement, drawing skillfully on the spiritual impetus provided by the Tattvabodhinī group. Thanks to Debendranath, by the early 1840s, the Brāhmo Samāj was poised to undergo a new phase of definition—liturgical, theological, and social. In the process, the Tattvabodhinī Sabhā came to a new understanding of itself. Put simply, it discovered its debt to Rammohan. The end result of this twin set of developments was to seal the status of Rammohan as the great founding father of reform in modern India. It is worth exploring this in a bit more detail, if only to further highlight the ramifications of the worldview and organization represented in *Sabhyadiger vaktṛtā*.

Remembering Rammohan

The decisive moment that triggered the merger of the Tattvabodhinī Sabhā and the Brāhmo Samāj came one year after publication of *Sabhyadiger vaktṛtā*. In 1842, Debendranath happened to pay a visit to one of the Brāhmo Samāj's weekly meetings. Whether he had been attending on and off before this, we don't know for certain. What we do know is that he was utterly taken aback to find a gentleman preaching from the Brāhmo dais on the topic of Lord Rama, one of the incarnations, or *avatāras*, of Vishnu. Knowing what he did of Rammohan's vision, and sharing the same ideals himself, Debendranath was deeply troubled by this unapologetic reference to Puranic Hinduism in the middle of a Brāhmo ceremony. He responded immediately by resolving that henceforth the Tattvabodhinī Sabhā would take over managing the affairs of the Brāhmo Samāj. In so doing, he effectively committed the Sabhā to the mission of reviving the Samāj and restoring it to its rightful purpose.[9] Simultaneously, he decreed that the spiritual interests and activities of the Tattvabodhinī Sabhā would henceforth be overseen by the Brāhmo Samāj. Here, in effect, we have the first public admission of the Tattvabodhinī religious identity. Henceforth, Tattvabodhinī members became Brāhmos.

One index of this transformation can be found by examining the changes that were made to the liturgical calendar after 1842. Up to this point, the Tattvabodhinī Sabhā had met weekly on Sundays; the discourses collected in *Sabhyadiger vaktṛtā* would have been delivered at these meetings. Annually, the founding of the Sabhā was celebrated on 6 October in memory of the meeting at which the group decided on its name and confirmed its mission (21 Āśvina in 1761 of the Śaka era, to be exact).[10] By contrast, the Brāhmo Samāj was by this time meeting weekly on Wednesdays and monthly on Sundays. The anniversary of the Samāj was celebrated not on the date of its first meeting in August of 1828 but on the date of the formal inauguration of the Samāj, namely 23 January 1830 (11 Māgha 1752 Śaka).[11] Now, under Debendranath's new arrangement, the Tattvabodhinī Sabhā abandoned its own Sunday meetings in order to meet during the Brāhmo's regular worship time. Henceforth, all anniversary meetings would be held on the date of the formal institution of the Brāhmo Samāj (11 Māgha).[12] In time, this date would assume an aura of great sanctity, thanks in large part to the work of the Tattvabodhinī group.[13]

This process of redefinition was marked by two further developments during the following year, 1843. First, the Tattvabodhinī Sabhā launched a new Bengali periodical, the *Tattvabodhinī Patrikā*. Like the original Sabhā, it was dedicated to the goal of propagating Vedānta. However, the *Patrikā* went a step further; it announced its commitment to republishing the writings of Rammohan Roy, which it noted had fallen into near obscurity since his death.[14] In a second major development, four months after publication of the *Patrikā*, Debendranath joined twenty-one other members of the Tattvabodhinī Sabhā in taking formal initiation (*dīkṣā*) into the Brāhmo Samāj. The old Brāhmo stalwart Rāmacandra presided over the ceremony as *ācārya*. As Debendranath later wrote: "This was an unprecedented event in the annals of the Brāhma-Samaj. Formerly there had existed the Brāhma-Samaj only, now the Brāhma Dharma came into existence."[15] As his comment indicates, by this point Debendranath had come to see the Brāhmo path as *dharma*—a moral code, a religion, a way of life. And as the explicit commitment to republishing the works of Rammohan suggests, Debendranath clearly traced this *dharma* back to the pioneering work of Rammohan.

As David Kopf (1979: 163) once remarked, "it may well be argued that the Brahmo Samaj as we have known it since began with the covenant ceremony in 1843 and not earlier."[16] Kopf was astute in noting the significance of Debendranath's initiation for marking "the beginnings of a distinctly new sense of Brahmo community." However, he focused so closely on the leadership and initiative of Debendranath that he failed to notice the broader significance of the Sabhā's attempt to reconnect with Rammohan.[17] In the present context, we are able to appreciate how Debendranath's decisions served to resolve a lingering ambiguity regarding the Sabhā's relationship to the Brāhmo movement.

It is as if the followers of Debendranath had originally been moved by a spiritual vision but could not conceptualize themselves as standing in a specific religious tradition. Living as they did at the end of the 1830s, a turbulent decade during which contests over religion, culture, and politics had virtually driven Rammohan and the Brāhmo Samāj underground, the members of the Tattvabodhinī Sabhā suffered what we might call a kind of a "memory crisis."[18] The discourses of 1839–40 reveal them to be proponents of a generalized Brāhmo theology, but the absence of Rammohan from those discourses suggests the degree to which that theology had floated free of any unifying organizational memory. In order to fully understand themselves as a community, the Tattvabodhinī group needed to remember Rammohan; they needed to reincorporate him within their story.[19]

This required critical choices such as those taken by Debendranath when he merged the interests of the two groups. The significance of these choices was then ratified in the new rites of commemoration established by Debendranath, which gave pride of place to the Brāhmo anniversary date. Through these decisions, the Tattvabodhinī group began to think of themselves explicitly as Brāhmos. Once they began to see themselves as committed to carrying on the work of Rammohan and the Brāhmo Samāj, the integrity and plausibility of their organization *qua* religious movement was secured. From this point on, members could affirm, as they did in an English-language proclamation of 1844, "We follow the teachings of Rammohan Roy."[20]

While it may strike some as odd to say so, it would be these very developments that would work to transform Rammohan Roy into the true "founder" of the Brāhmo Samāj.[21] To appreciate the force of this observation, we have to bear in mind that the status of founder depends less on mere historical originality than on the creative force of a community's memory. The act of remembering Rammohan, of incorporating him into the Sabhā's story, was thus of great consequence. It not only bestowed a kind of paternity on Rammohan but also resolved the Sabhā's own memory crisis. In so doing, it worked to ensure the Sabhā's identity as an explicitly Brāhmo religious movement. A report for the year 1843–44, composed in English and published in the *Tattvabodhinī Patrikā*, shows this process at work, as the Sabhā rewrote the story of their establishment to include explicit mention of their newly remembered founder:

> The TUTTUVOADHINEE SUBHA [*sic*] was established . . . by a select party of friends, who believed in god as "the One Unknown True Being, the Creator, Preserver and Destroyer of the Universe." . . . The avowed object of the members was to sustain the labours of the late Rajah Rammohun Roy.

The conclusion of the report makes it clear that Rammohan's departure and death had dealt a serious setback to the Brāhmo movement. But it also stresses that the revitalization of the Brāhmo movement was itself directly dependent on the work of the Tattvabodhinī Sabhā:

> The members are fully aware of the extent to which the cause of religion was carried during the time of the celebrated Rammohun Roy. But it is no less a fact that, in his lamentable demise, it received a shock from which it was feared it could hardly have recovered. The exertions of the Tuttuvoadhinee [*sic*] Society, however, have imparted renewed energies to the cause. They have led a large number of the educated and respectable members of society, to appreciate the knowledge of God. The meetings of the Braumhu Sumauj [*sic*] are now attended by overflowing congregations, and religious discussions are extensively maintained in Native society.[22]

Further evidence of the elevation of Rammohan to the status of founder in the eyes of the Tattvabodhinī group is given in a passage from an annual report of the Sabhā for 1846, which describes Rammohan as having descended (*avatīrṇa*, semantically akin to the concept of *avatāra*) into Bengal to establish the Brāhmo Samāj.[23]

This is the background against which we should also read an English-language passage written by Debendranath in 1846, in which he outlines the moral and theological tenets of his new *dharma*. While Rammohan is not explicitly invoked, the concept of the "godly householder" (*brahmaniṣṭha gṛhastha*)—to which we have seen Rammohan gave pride of place—is clearly emphasized:

> As spiritual worshippers of our All-Benevolent Legislator and followers of the Vedant—of Ooponeshud, . . . [we] are *Bhrummunistha Grihustha* [*sic*], or monotheistic householders. . . . The object of our humble exertions is not merely a negative reformation in the religious institutions of our countrymen, but a *positive one too*,—not

> merely the overthrow of the present systems, but the substitution in their place of more rational and proper ones.[24]

This passage makes it apparent that a recollection of Rammohan's Brāhmo ideals had provided the Tattvabodhinī Sabhā with the means to ratify their own identity as a movement. The rearticulation of the group's self-understanding was made clear at a meeting held on 28 May 1847. Hitherto the Tattvabodhinī Sabhā had defined its goal as the propagation of the "true religion as taught by Vedānta" (*vedānta pratipādya satyadharma*). At the May 1847 meeting, it was resolved to formally replace this language with the explicit rubric of *brāhmadharma*; the Sabhā would now propagate the Brāhmo religion of Rammohan.[25]

Years later, in 1864, Debendranath gave a Bengali address in which he looked back over the previous twenty-five years of the Brāhmo Samāj. In that address, Debendranath clearly identified Rammohan as the founding father of the movement, referring to him as "the country's first friend" (*deśer prathama bandhu*).[26] Debendranath crafted a virtual creation myth that depicts Rammohan appearing in the midst of darkness and lethargy to plant the seeds of monotheistic worship. In this evocation of Rammohan as pioneer, father, and founding guru, Debendranath offered the Brāhmo Samāj a representation of itself as an ongoing lineage of belief traced to a founder whose memory could now serve to unite them as a religious association. And, as Debendranath remarked toward the close of his address, it was not as if he and Rammohan had different visions; their goals were one and the same (Tagore 1957: 35).

What is most striking about this address is that while it seems to take us back to the time of Rammohan's founding of the Brāhmo Samāj in 1828, if read carefully, one realizes that the scope of this twenty-five-year retrospective really only takes us back to 1839, the year the Tattvabodhinī Sabhā was founded. We are thus led to see in rather dramatic terms the very time lag that existed between Rammohan's creative action in 1828 and the birth of the organization that was to revive his vision in 1839. If Debendranath eventually credited Rammohan with creating the religion, or *dharma*, that he had committed himself to promoting, he nonetheless still cherished some sense of his own creative role.

Of course, the self-understanding of the Sabhā continued to evolve after this (for a brief chronology of the Sabhā, see table 3.1). In the decades to come, it was more than once forced to review and revise its store of memories. The coming years would bring a series of important developments, such as increasingly heated debates with Christian missionaries; a major internal debate within the Samāj over the viability of appeals to Vedānta as revelation; and Debendranath's eventual creation of an official Brāhmo scripture, *Brāhmo*

TABLE 3.1. Brief chronology of the Tattvabodhinī Sabhā

Year	Significant event(s)
1839	First meeting of Tattvarañjinī Sabhā (29 September)
	Name changed to Tattvabodhinī Sabhā (6 October)
	First discourse of *Sabhyadiger Vaktṛtā* delivered (1 December)
1840	Tattvabodhinī School (*pāṭhaśālā*) established in Bansberia
	Last discourse of *Sabhyadiger Vaktṛtā* delivered (17 May)
1841	*Sabhyadiger Vaktṛtā* published (1763 Śaka)
1842	Tattvabodhinī Sabhā begins to manage affairs of the Brāhmo Samāj
1843	*Tattvabodhinī Patrikā* first published (1 Bhādra 1765 Śaka)
	Debendranath initiated into Brāhmo Dharma (7 Pouṣa 1765 Śaka)
1845	Debendranath sends four students to Varanasi to study the Vedas
1850	Debendranath publishes *Brāhmo Dharmaḥ*
1851	Brāhmo Samāj officially abandons belief in Vedic infallibility
1859	Tattvabodhinī Sabhā dissolved into Brāhmo Samāj

Dharmaḥ, culled from a variety of Indian religious texts like the Upanishads, the Laws of Manu, the Mahābhārata, and the Mahānirvāṇa Tantra (Tagore 1975). While the debate over scriptural infallibility commenced in earnest around 1845 with the dispatch of four students to Varanasi to seek guidance on the matter, it would not finally be laid to rest until 1851, when a formal rejection of Vedic infallibility was issued (Damen 1988: 36). From that point on, the Brāhmos would locate the source of religion in the "pure, unsophisticated heart" (Tagore 1909: 161). One is tempted to suggest that it was this later decision to trust intuition over revelation that initiated the momentous shift toward experience in modern Vedantic Hinduism. But, as pointed out in the introduction, we must remember that this development occurred well after publication of *Sabhyadiger vaktṛtā*.

Later history of the Sabhā

The shift toward a concept of religious intuition also opened the door to the rhetoric of divine inspiration. It was through this door that Keshub Chunder Sen (Keśavacandra Sena, 1838–84) later walked, eventually luring away a portion of the Brāhmo community with his enthusiastic preaching. After midcentury we notice increasing examples of dissension and schism, as the Samāj went on to struggle, not just with the correct way to interpret the teachings of the heart but also with the correct way to balance the spiritual life with increasing demands for social reform. Space permitting, one could go on to explore the negotiation of such dilemmas within the Brāhmo community, though thankfully others have done so already (for example, Śāstrī 1911, Kopf 1979, and Damen 1988). What bears noting here is simply the fact that at critical junctures it would become imperative to accommodate new developments within the movement to new memories of the community's origins. What's more, in time, it would be necessary to invoke the creative agency of other founding figures in order to integrate and commemorate the evolving sense of group continuity and identity. In time, Debendranath himself would become another such founder alongside Rammohan, as would Keshub later still.[27]

Keshub's views on Rammohan from the mid-1860s are particularly interesting. While he recognized Rammohan as the "great man" who brought his fellow citizens together to worship the One God, Keshub did not credit him with founding a religious movement. Keshub stressed that Rammohan had merely created a place and a reason for people to worship.[28] Keshub's remarks are an excellent reminder of the degree to which the Brāhmo story remained under construction, subject over the years to new and sometimes competing claims of creative agency.

At this point, Keshub was clearly less interested in historical observation than in the ongoing validation of the movement, its memories, and its leaders. Chief among his concerns during the 1860s was the question of leadership. Who would be granted creative agency within the movement? Even as he broke to form the Brāhmo Samāj of India in 1866, Keshub could praise the role of his former patron and spiritual mentor, Debendranath, situating the latter's creation of the Tattvabodhinī Sabhā in relation to Rammohan's earlier accomplishments:

> When the patriotic, virtuous, great-souled Raja Ram Mohun Roy established a public place for the holy worship of God in Bengal, the true welfare of the country began. . . . But that great man being within a short time removed from this world, the light of Divine worship kindled by him came very nearly to be extinct.[29]

Then, refering to Debendranath, Keshub went on to say,

> God raised you, and placed in your hands the charge of the spiritual advancement of the country. . . . Thus have you generally served the Brahma community after the ideals of your own heart, but you have specially benefited a few among us whom you have treated as affectionately as your children. These have felt the deep nobleness of your character, and elevated by your precept, example, and holy companionship, reverence you as their father.[30]

Keshub's break with Debendranath in 1866 and his subsequent move in 1879 to form the New Dispensation (*nava vidhāna*) are striking illustrations of the ongoing and very fluid process that was the construction of Brāhmo religious identity throughout the nineteenth century. But his views on the respective roles of Rammohan and Debendranath also remind us of the degree to which the creative contributions of these two reformers were intertwined. Who really created the Brāhmo movement? Was it Rammohan, or was it the Tattvabodhinī Sabhā under Debendranath? Obviously, there would have been no Brāhmo Samāj—and most likely no Tattvabodhinī Sabhā—without Rammohan. One might well argue that Debendranath would not have undergone his spiritual awakening had there been no Rammohan. After all, that awakening had been precipitated by a reading of Rammohan's beloved Īśā Upanishad and was mediated by Rammohan's colleague, Rāmacandra. But would Rammohan have become "Rammohan Roy, founder of the Brāhmo Samāj," without Debendranath's retrospective attempt to provide a compelling origin story for the Tattvabodhinī Sabhā?[31]

In a final bit of irony, the decision by Debendranath and his colleagues to embrace Rammohan and the Brāhmo path also marked the beginning of the end of the Tattvabodhinī Sabhā. While the Sabhā continued to meet independently until 1859, it was eventually dissolved, its identity and its mission having become synonymous with the Brāhmo movement.[32] To be sure, before ceasing to exist, the Sabhā had garnered widespread attention and achieved enormous influence through its path-breaking journal, the *Tattvabodhinī Patrikā*. Through this journal alone, the Sabhā was to have an enormous influence on the development of religious, literary, cultural, and political life in nineteenth-century Bengal. In fact, the journal long outlived the Sabhā, continuing to publish throughout the nineteenth century and into the first decades of the twentieth century. Among its editorial staff, it counted the likes of such luminaries as Akṣayakumāra Datta, Īśvaracandra Vidyāsāgara, Rajendralal Mitra, and even (at a much later date) the great poet, Rabindranath Tagore, Debendranath's son.[33]

Much of our information regarding the Brāhmo movement during this period emerges from the pages of the *Tattvabodhinī Patrikā*. Several of the discourses originally published in *Sabhyadiger vaktṛtā* were subsequently republished in the *Patrikā*, which occasionally included them alongside reprints of Rammohan's writings; reports on the Sabhā's activities; essays on aspects of contemporary social and political life; and regular reports on membership, dues, and news of other Sabhā publications.[34] For any student of nineteenth-century Bengal, the *Patrikā* is a largely unexplored gold mine. It awaits a thorough study. However, to take up here the history of the *Tattvabodhinī*

Patrikā would be to move well beyond the specific moment that produced the discourses found in *Sabhyadiger vaktṛtā*. We might bear in mind that the discourses of *Sabhyadiger vaktṛtā* originate from a time well before the Sabhā began to enter aggressively into the realm of public debate. It should also be clear that *Sabhyadiger vaktṛtā* comes to us from a time before the Sabhā had embraced Rammohan as their founder, alerting us once again to the importance of the text as documenting a singular moment in the independent spiritual vision of Debendranath and his associates.

4

Bourgeois Vedānta for the *Bhadralok*

The formation of the Tattvabodhinī Sabhā marks an important moment in the development of what we might broadly call modern (or perhaps modernist) Hinduism. However, while the theological innovations of Rammohan and the Brāhmo Samāj have long been recognized as a major source of modern Hinduism, very little careful study has been devoted to the hermeneutics, theology, and moral concerns of a group like the Tattvabodhinī Sabhā.[1] Nor do we possess many thorough attempts by scholars to understand Tattvabodhinī theology in relation to its concrete socioeconomic milieu. And yet there is much we could learn by asking how this particular species of modernist Hindu discourse correlates with the social location and agency of its early proponents. This is precisely the question raised in this chapter. Using the discourses of *Sabhyadiger vaktṛtā* as the guiding text, I explore to what degree Tattvabodhinī theology can be said to have mirrored and, in a sense, advanced the economic, social, and political concerns of its members.

As indicated in the introduction, it is my contention that reflection on the theology and social placement of the Tattvabodhinī group provides us with an opportunity to ponder the emergence of Hinduism as a "middle-class religion" in the colonial and postcolonial period. Essays by Philip Lutgendorf (1997) and John Stratton Hawley (2001), as well as Joanne Waghorne's book, *The Diaspora of the Gods* (2005), attest to increased scholarly interest in exploring how contemporary expressions of Hindu religiosity may reflect or promote the particular values and interests of the Hindu middle class.[2] Waghorne's approach is particularly fruitful because she provides a broad historical canvas on which to situate the rise of middle-class Hinduism. Her work recognizes that we need to explore contemporary Hinduism in light of developments taking place in early colonial India and in the emerging "new world system" (with a nod to Immanuel Wallerstein) of the colonial and postcolonial periods. Waghorne's focus is Chennai, or Madras, India's earliest colonial seaport metropolis. Looking north to Bengal and Calcutta (present-day Kolkata), one might just as well inquire how the development of modern middle-class Hinduism was shaped by religious and social change in this early colonial metropolis.

If we think of the modern middle class as broadly reflecting attitudes and styles of life associated with the kinds of social mobility promoted by capitalism, urbanization, and an increasingly bureaucratic societal system (for example, Weber 1958 and Wilson 1983), there is good reason to explore the degree to which such socioeconomic changes in colonial Calcutta may have influenced those individuals who gravitated to the Tattvabodhinī Sabhā. After all, even a cursory glance at the Sabhā's programs reveals a clear emphasis on such middle-class markers as a priority for the domestic sphere, the use of vernacular forms of communication, eclectic patterns of religious thought, the importance of English-language education, growing involvement in the urban public sphere, increased involvement in patterns of commerce and consumption, a respect for impersonal law over custom, and the quest for upward mobility (Waghorne 2005: 233–34). To what degrees does *Sabhyadiger vaktṛtā* allow us to chart the effect of such factors on Tattvabodhinī theology?

The colonial *bhadralok*

In chapter 3, I note the complex makeup of the Sabhā, remarking on how diverse members were, in terms of backgrounds, personalities, and ideological orientations. In that context, I stressed this diversity in order to undercut any facile assumptions about the intellectual and social makeup of the group. In its diversity, the Sabhā mirrored, rather than departed from, the patterns of social, religious, and educational life prevailing in early-nineteenth-century Calcutta. Without in any way forgetting the diversity of the Sabhā's membership, it will now be necessary to introduce a category that will allow us to simultaneously make some basic generalizations about the Tattvabodhinī membership. The goal in this regard is to search for an answer to one of the questions raised in chapter 3: What values or interests (beyond those of theology per se) did this divergent group of individuals share that caused them to gravitate toward an association like the Tattvabodhinī Sabhā? To begin to answer this question, it will help to think of Debendranath and the other members of the early Sabhā as representatives of a category of people known in Bengali as the *bhadralok*—the "civilized" or "respectable" people.

The importance of the *bhadralok* as a category for understanding modern Bengali society has long been emphasized, receiving important attention in the 1960s and 1970s by the likes of J. H. Bloomfield (1968) and S. N. Mukherjee (1977). It was Bloomfield who portrayed the *bhadralok* as a local "dominant elite" who were "distinguished by many aspects of their behavior—their deportment, their speech, their dress, their style in housing, their eating habits, their occupations, and their associations—quite as much as fundamentally by their cultural values and their sense of social propriety" (Bloomfield 1968: 5–6).[3] In the nearly forty years since Bloomfield's study of the role of this dominant elite in Bengali cultural and political life, the category of the *bhadralok* has played an on-again, off-again role in the analysis of Bengali society, receiving extensive treatment very recently by Tithi Bhattacharya in her monograph, *Sentinels of Culture* (2005), to which I turn below.

At present, there are three things about the *bhadralok* that require special comment. First, even though it is handy to invoke the concept of *bhadralok* as a unitary category, it is, in fact, loose and expansive; it can include wealthy entrepreneurs and impoverished school teachers, powerful landholders and struggling pandits, government servants and independent journalists. Obviously, this accords well with what we have already seen regarding the earliest membership of the Tattvabodhinī Sabhā, whose ranks included English-educated skeptics, Sanskrit pandits, Bengali poets, and Calcutta businessmen, teachers, and landed gentry.

Second, as this brief roster of identities suggests, the category of *bhadralok* speaks of a peculiar nexus between ascriptive group status and bourgeois individualism.[4] That is, while many *bhadralok* were from high-caste (brahmin and kayastha) families, not all of them were. Some of the most important among the Bengali nouveaux riches during the early nineteenth century were, in fact, men of lower-caste status who had achieved wealth and reputation through their financial dealings. In a word, we should not confuse the *bhadralok* with a particular caste.

The world of the colonial *bhadralok* was one of great social mobility, as well as class and occupational diversity. And yet, for all this diversity in *bhadralok* caste status, economic background, and vocational identity, there was, in fact, something that worked to unite them—or, better put, allows us to speak of them as a collective whole. I refer to the shared educational commitments of the *bhadralok*, which formed the crucial bedrock for their particular cultural projects. The third thing we should note, then, is that this was a group of men who were both schooled in and contributed to the maintenance of the colonial educational system. In early colonial Bengal, English education was invested with a sense of great promise; it seemed to provide one grand avenue into opportunities in both public and private ventures. The *bhadralok* embodied this sense of promise, often couched in terms of grand notions of progress and improvement.

This sketch of the *bhadralok* accords well with Tithi Bhattacharya's recent analysis (2005). As she demonstrates, far from being a uniform class of social agents, the *bhadralok* was an internally complex set of social classes, ranging from the rich *bania* families (like the Tagores of Jorasanko) who had acquired immense family wealth by trading with the Europeans, through a group of comfortably well-to-do middle-class families, to the poor but respectable (*bhadra*) representatives of the urban petty bourgeoisie. Attending to the internal diversity of the *bhadralok* is essential because it allows us to make sense of both the successes and the failures of the *bhadralok*. The successes may seem obvious, insofar as groups like the Tattvabodhinī Sabhā were able to have the kinds of deep and long-standing influence over the shape of Bengali social life in the nineteenth century. The failures may seem less obvious, but bear noting, if only as a reminder of the complex legacy of reformist Hinduism.

As Bhattacharya has noted, it was the *madhyavitta*, or middle-rank *bhadralok*, who found themselves in a curious and ultimately "contradictory" class position. They were, in effect, pulled in two different directions. On the one hand, they struggled to attain the kind of prestige accorded to the wealthy *bania* and rentier families who rose to prominence in the decades after 1780; on the other hand, they often found themselves compelled to adopt service-based occupations that pulled them down the class ladder toward the petty bourgeiosie (Bhattacharya 2005: 61). The end result of this dual dynamic was to create a situation in which the middle-rank *bhadralok* were prevented from truly emerging as a hegemonic ruling class during the nineteenth century (Bhattacharya 2005: 63). As an earlier generation of Marxist historians had already emphasized, this failure meant that any hopes for a *bhadralok*-led transformation of modern Indian society were ultimately misplaced.[5]

While this failure cannot be the point of focus here, we do well to recall this theme of tension and contradiction, which is a dynamic that is also highlighted in Sanjay Joshi's recent study of the middle class in colonial Lucknow. Joshi depicts a social group much like Calcutta's *madhyavitta bhadralok*, a class that asserted its superiority over traditional elites through the invocation of progressive Enlightenment values while continuing to justify its superiority over the lower classes through appeals to traditional norms of hierarchy. Joshi demonstrates that this precarious pair of strategies both enabled and constrained the overall agenda of the middle class (2001: 24). Inherently fractured, the agency of the middle class is most apparent in its attempt to selectively enlist traditional norms and concepts in the service of constructing the modern (8–10). It is less the middle class *as class* than it is the middle class as this kind of attempt that Joshi finds to be distinctive, this "project of self-fashioning . . . which was constantly in the making" (2).

What Joshi calls a "project," Tithi Bhattacharya identifies as the distinctive *bhadralok* "ethic and sentiment" (2005: 67). Both authors employ these rubrics to allow us to see the cultural significance of the colonial middle class. While they may not have been a homogeneous socioeconomic class, they did represent a coherent set of cultural goals.[6] Call it the middle-class project or the *bhadralok* ethic and sentiment, the point is that, over the long haul, this collective mindset would work to weld a set of disparate class interests into a shared universe of values. As both authors suggest, this *bhadralok* or middle-class vision of the world was underwritten and extended by widespread commitments to colonial education and the Enlightenment project. Not merely the products of their educational milieu, the *bhadralok* went on to create the kind of educational and associational environment that gave urban, colonial India its distinctive character.[7]

This is where we should focus our attention when considering the membership and collective program of the Tattvabodhinī Sabhā. Not only did the Sabhā employ the traditional values of Vedānta to articulate a modern form of Hindu belief and practice; just as importantly, *Sabhyadiger vaktṛtā* demonstrates that the earliest members of the Sabhā were actively creating a framework of middle-class values centering on rationality, benevolence, hard work, and worldly success. Later, these core values became the very "model of middle class-ness" in colonial India (Joshi 2001: 8). What's more, as Bhattacharya has shown, the *bhadralok* sentiment eventually had a major role in the development of nationalist mobilization in the early twentieth century. One notable moment came with the anti-partition, or Swadeshi, agitation of 1905, with its slogan of *Bande Mataram*, or "Hail to the Mother(land)." On this occasion, as Bhattacharya points out, Swadeshi politics brought together a wide range of zamindars, intellectual reformers, salaried clerks, landholders, and railway workers who collectively made up the broad spectrum of *bhadralok* identity. What united them all, despite their obvious class and occupational differences, was a "project"—a set of sentimental attachments to such emerging notions as religion and the nation.

While Joshi's study explores the emergence of middle class-ness in late-nineteenth- and early-twentieth-century India, *Sabhyadiger vaktṛtā* allows us to see in clear terms how the middle-class project was already beginning to be defined as early as 1839. These discourses may not provide a detailed profile of their bourgeois authors, but they do bring to the fore key features of an emergent *bhadralok* ethic and sentiment. And if it is true that the members of the Tattvabodhinī Sabhā may not have represented the avant garde of a new and revolutionary social class (much to the Marxists' despair), they were by no means devoid of critical agency. To the contrary, the colonial middle class played a major part in codifying the norms of industry, domestic life, moral responsibility, religion, and worldly success that eventually became essential to modern Hindu identity. Precisely because these norms were articulated through the hallowed idioms of Vedānta and were bolstered by the scriptural authorities of ancient Hinduism, they clearly helped usher into existence modes of Hindu identity that were to have immense influence on the colonial and postcolonial history of India. As Joshi suggests, the "publicized religiosity" of contemporary India—whether it be Nehruvian secularism or militant Hindutva—continues to draw on conceptualizations of religion that are the byproducts of a longstanding and ongoing middle-class project.

If we are to successfully flesh out the early expression of *bhadralok* ethic and sentiment in *Sabhyadiger vaktṛtā*, we need to integrate what we have learned about the membership of the Sabhā with an appreciation for the world in which these members lived, worked, and prayed. If we can supplement the discourses with further information on the background, education, and public sphere activities of the Sabhā's earliest members, we should be able to appreciate in more nuanced terms how the *bhadralok* ethic—allied with Tattvabodhinī theology—produced a major harbinger of contemporary middle-class Hinduism.

Calcutta in the 1830s

An appreciation of the socioeconomic profile of the Tattvabodhinī Sabhā requires us to consider the decade of the 1830s in Calcutta. This was a promising decade for the *bhadralok*. It seemed to present them with opportunities for economic prosperity and increased political participation alike. Trade flourished, and official positions were beginning to open up for educated, urban Bengalis. Voluntary associations began to spring up as if overnight, representing the urge of the *bhadralok* to promote collective endeavors in publishing, education, agriculture, and political representation.

When thinking about the history of this period, it might actually prove helpful to mark the beginning of the 1830s as the year 1829, which was the year

Governor General Lord William Bentinck passed legislation banning the practice of widow immolation or "suttee"—a reformist cause that had famously been championed by Rammohan Roy. In passing Regulation XVII, Bentinck made explicit reference to the possible agitation this would cause in the "public mind." He was all too aware of the heated debates the issue had aroused among local religious factions (Muir 1969: 294). His awareness may stand as a measure of the rapidly increasing visibility and influence of the *bhadralok* in colonial life.[8]

Public debate was a prominent part of religious, political, and social life throughout the 1830s. The constraining circumstances of colonial rule notwithstanding, the decade did witness a dramatic increase in the expression of Bengali public opinion on issues closely connected to the future of the region. Notably, in 1830 the Dharma Sabhā (or Society of Religion) was established to express public opposition to Bentinck's ban on suttee.[9] In a similar fashion, prominent intellectuals, landholders, and entrepreneurs entered into open debates over the pros and cons of European colonization. To take just one example, they quarreled over the ramifications of future European settlement. How would the residence of Europeans in Bengal affect such matters as the value of land or laborers's wages? At the same time, English-educated students of Hindu College—the notorious Young Bengal faction to which I have already referred—began to openly criticize what they took to be the superstitions of traditional Hinduism. Their teacher and guiding light at college (itself a creation of indigenous effort) was Henry Louis Vivian Derozio. Because of his role in encouraging the iconoclasm of Young Bengal, Derozio was dismissed from the college in 1831, largely as a result of pressure from the Dharma Sabhā. As noted, some members of the Tattvabodhinī Sabhā were drawn from the same Young Bengal faction. Though mostly nonreligious themselves, they would have opposed the Dharma Sabhā's attempt to challenge the progressive values promoted by Rammohan.

In 1833, the East India Company charter was renewed. The new charter carried assurances of more administrative posts for Bengalis. The following year saw the creation of the Bengal Chamber of Commerce, which featured some natives as members (Sanyal 1980: 222). Remarking on such developments, one important Bengali paper reported confidently around this time that "public opinion, enlightened by the lights of growing knowledge, is almost everywhere gaining strength" (Moitra 1979: 57). That strength may be measured by the fact that residents of Calcutta began to agitate openly for a free press, as they did for the abolition of taxes on salt and the opium trade. The end of the decade brought the creation of two important expressions of Bengali public sentiment and civic engagement: the Landholders Association and the

Society for the Acquisition of General Knowledge. Both of these semipolitical organizations were established in 1838 and served to provide conservative and liberal Bengalis important contexts within which to voice their concerns about commerce, trade, government, education, and culture (Palit 1980: 77).

If the 1830s began in 1829, we might say the decade ended in October 1839, with the establishment of the Tattvabodhinī Sabhā. The Tattvabodhinī Sabhā was both a product of this particular historical milieu and a vital agent itself in the further development of Bengali public life. No mere reflection of its times, the Sabhā was immensely influential in the representation and contestation of everything from religion and morality to education and family customs. The creation of the Sabhā in 1839 attested to the unifying power of the *bhadralok*'s emerging sentiment. Clearly, members did not see eye to eye on all things social or political. But as *bhadralok* they shared a commitment to a set of religiously grounded moral values that they also found to be congruent with their rapidly improving social position. In this sense, the Sabhā was the epitome of the early-nineteenth-century voluntary association.

In general, such voluntary associations, all those *sabhās* and *samāj*es that began to pop up during the 1830s, were a striking testament to the public expression of *bhadralok* interest in religion, politics, and social change.[10] During this decade, the *bhadralok* became increasingly active, not merely in the creation of associations but also in the publication and dissemination of pamphlets, periodicals, and printed books. Taken together, these developments fostered an environment in which public debate on issues of religion, social custom, and government policy became common. Associations like the Dharma Sabhā, the Society for the Acquistion of General Knowledge, the Landholders Society, and the Tattvabodhinī Sabhā gave organized expression (sometimes through their own periodicals) to the desire of the *bhadralok* to unite in pursuit of their common intellectual, commercial, and political interests.

What makes all this activity interesting is how much it speaks of the shared sentiment—the mentality and values—of the *bhadralok* over and above their sometimes conflicting caste or occupational status. No matter whether we look at orthodox Hindus or modernizing reformers, these *bhadralok* tended to share a discernible set of values. Those values centered on the promotion of hard work, honesty, frugality, and dependability. Those values formed the moral framework of early Tattvabodhinī thought, and, as such, they provided an important basis for the expression of new notions of Hindu religious identity. These were the very values I highlighted in my earlier study of the Sanskrit pandit, Vidyāsāgara. He remains a good example of the complex convergence of indigenous norms of status and authority (as a brahmin and a pandit) with a bourgeois morality of diligent effort and responsible self-reliance (Hatcher 1996a).

By calling these values bourgeois, I hope in part to suggest how they relate to central aspects of modernity as understood by historians, social scientists, and philosophers. In particular, these values call to mind that mixture of Puritanism and the capitalist work ethic that sociologists have commented on since the influential work of Max Weber on the so-called Protestant Ethic (Weber 1958). Reading the discourses of *Sabhyadiger vaktṛtā*, it is difficult not to think of Weber's thesis regarding the "elective affinity" between religious belief and capitalist enterprise.[11] We might even borrow directly from Weber and say that what interests us is "the influence of those psychological sanctions which, originating in religious belief and the practice of religion, gave a direction to practical conduct and held the individual to it" (Weber 1958: 97). Of course, the setting in this case is colonial Bengal rather than post-Reformation northern Europe, so what requires further consideration are the unique terms in which such an affinity might have come to expression in early colonial Calcutta.[12] If the Tattvabodhinī Sabhā was invested in the task of reviving interest in the "true religion as taught by the Vedānta" (*vedānta pratipādya satya dharma*), then how did the Sabhā's religion (its *dharma*) converge with, reinforce, or transform the concerns of bourgeois morality as these found increased expression in a variety of colonial contexts, from education and journalism to law and government?

In *Sabhyadiger vaktṛtā* we can hear *bhadralok* members thinking out loud about the role and function of a Vedānta-based path of spiritual worship in addressing the stresses and strains that accompanied the rapid socioeconomic transformations that were taking place in Calcutta. While the overt concern of these discourses is the articulation of the meaning and duties of a Vedantic worldview, we may also come to see that the discourses reveal an attempt by members to legitimate their unique social role and sense of moral leadership in the colonial metropolis. In the remainder of this chapter, I examine these discourses to see how they manifest the Sabhā's attempt to think out loud about these concerns.

Just a note on the approach I adopt in the rest of this chapter. While the twenty-one discourses found in *Sabhyadiger vaktṛtā* were crafted by a number of individuals—including Debendranath and Vidyāsāgara—I do not focus on individual identities here. Rather, I treat the text as if it were one integral document, referring to the discourses only by their number (so readers may consult the complete text in the translation). My goal is to search for the patterned expression of shared *bhadralok* values across the discourses. This will allow me to sketch in broad terms the fundamental theological and moral concerns of the group. Later, in chapters 6 and 7, I discuss in detail the question of who the different authors were and how we can identify their work. Interested readers might then choose to study the translation on their own in an attempt to flesh out the important, if sometimes more subtle, differences among the various authors. For now, I read the text as one unified *bhadralok* testament to a bourgeois conception of Vedānta, what I shall call for present purposes a bourgeois Vedānta for the *bhadralok*.

Bourgeois Vedānta

For a text created by a group with a strong commitment to Vedānta, it may come as a surprise to find that those things most often associated with Vedānta—that is, the metaphysics of *ātman* and *brahman*; the relationship between ignorance (*avidyā*) and illusion (*māyā*); and the characteristics of an ultimate reality that is beyond name and form—do not dominate the discourses of *Sabhyadiger vaktṛtā*. In part, this is due to the attempt made by the group to distance itself from the classical Advaita Vedānta of Śaṅkarācārya (eighth c. CE), in which the aforementioned themes take precedence. Dissaffection with the Vedānta of Śaṅkara had begun already with Rammohan, who subtly distanced his Vedantic reform from any taint of brahmanical elitism, world negation, and illusionism (Killingley 1981). For his part, Debendranath tells us explicitly that he could not accept Śaṅkara's denial of a self that is other than the supreme reality. He tells readers of his autobiography that the relationship between the worshiper and God was the very "life breath" (*prāṇa*) of his theology (Tagore 1980: 83). In the following chapter, I discuss how ironic it would be that missionaries nevertheless attempted to fault the Tattvabodhinī group for its failure to recognize a distinction between the individual and God.

While renunciation and mystical union are not the focus of these discourses, another important aspect of the classical Vedantic path is given a great deal of emphasis: that is, the need to control one's passions and senses. This is obviously not an original doctrine for the Tattvabodhinī group to endorse. Rather, it reflects an ancient Indian concern, one far more widespread even than Vedānta. Hindus, Buddhists, and Jains had for centuries emphasized the need to come to grips with the interplay of the senses and the passions in shaping the spiritual life. In one way or another, all these traditions share an emphasis on desire as the motive force behind continued existence in the realm of rebirth known as *saṃsāra*. The Tattvabodhinī group was no different in this regard; for them, the teachings of Vedānta promoted mastery of the senses and passions as the key to knowledge and worship of the Supreme Lord, a creator God variously called *paramātman*, *parabrahma*, *paramārtha*, or *parameśvara* (for terminology, see appendix 3, the glossary of Bengali terms).

What makes *Sabhyadiger vaktṛtā* so interesting is that in it we have the opportunity to study the way this concern for sense-restraint (*indriya-nigraha*) emerges from the lived experience of the colonial *bhadralok*. For instance, one can easily visualize the bustling seaport world of colonial Calcutta as the backdrop to the following meditation on the transiency of sensory objects:

> So many people expend enormous effort and time amassing wealth. They travel to distant countries; they traverse the ocean; they follow the commands of proud and wealthy individuals; and they suffer rebuke when their obedience falls even the slightest bit short. Eventually, they reach their appointed hour, overcome by old age and death. Then there are those who have copious wealth and various avenues for enjoyment, but who are unable to enjoy it because of illness. (Discourse Fourteen)

This passage foregrounds the general human predicament of desire or lust (*kāma*). It is a concern as old as the Upanishads and the Buddha. However, we note that here it is construed concretely in terms of the specific craving for wealth. As the author of Discourse Eleven remarks, a person under the sway of the senses "gazes at unearned riches and imagines them to promise endless possibilities for happiness. And yet, no sooner do those riches come to him by dint of countless afflictions than he is left unsatisfied. Driven by a longing for happiness, he once again grows agitated to acquire more riches." Would we be wrong to sense in these words an implicit reference to the rapidly changing fortunes of an upwardly mobile colonial *bhadralok*?

The same author reminds us that it is this very desire for sensory objects that drives "the business of life" (Discourse Eleven). Farmers grow crops, artisans produce wares, investors acquire those goods, and merchants ship them around the world. As if looking out the window at the sailing ships moored in the Hooghly River, the author of Discourse Twenty-One points out that the residents of Calcutta have clearly benefited from all this trade and entrepreneurial activity. Thanks to the fundamental force of human desire, all these marvelous goods flow into the colonial metropolis from around the world, and men grow wealthier by the day.

But this is not all. We are reminded that it is the very desire for wealth, power, and glory that also ultimately fosters the "welfare of the country" (Discourse Eleven). For instance, because government officials desire further professional advancement, they work hard to ensure the public order. Similarly,

"Wise men, desiring greater glory, expend great energy preparing a variety of books for the welfare of the country, by means of which we all gain knowledge and fulfillment" (Discourse Eleven). If the earlier references to investment and trade put us in mind of traders and merchants like Dwarkanath, Debendranath's entrepreneurial father, this passage reminds us that these same *bhadralok* increasingly took up philanthropic activities during the 1830s. Among the many voluntary associations formed during this period were several dedicated to the creation and publication of schoolbooks to promote the interests of "native education."[13]

As the example of the philanthropist suggests, in the eyes of the colonial *bhadralok*, desire in itself is not the problem. It can yield good, in fact. Human beings only encounter real trouble when they fail to submit their desires to a proper hierarchy of values. If all we are after in life is wealth and power, we are likely to be misled by the allure of illusory and transient signs of success. Such is delusion (*moha*), a standard Vedantic category. This is one point where some of the authors in *Sabhyadiger vaktṛtā* choose to adopt familiar Vedantic terminology. They speak of our failure to know reality as it is. For Vedānta, such ignorance is the root cause of suffering and rebirth. Liberation (*mokṣa*) comes with knowledge (*jñāna*) of ultimate reality (*brahman* or *tattva*). And knowledge of ultimate reality necessarily corresponds to knowledge of the self (*ātmabodha*; see Discourse Twelve). As in the ancient Upanishads, the fundamental question for these *bhadralok* remains, Who are you? One author even goes as far as to assure us that Vedānta is a "supremely compassionate" set of "revealed texts" that let us discover our "true nature" (Discourse Three). If one studies Vedānta, one looks in a mirror and finds out who one truly is.[14]

One goal of these discourses, then, is to identify the rich spiritual resources of Vedānta for members of the Sabhā and, presumably, for Bengali Hindu society more broadly. This explains the generous sampling of Upanishadic texts cited in *Sabhyadiger vaktṛtā*. Another goal is to apply these scriptural resources not just to personal spiritual growth but to the betterment of one's world. The energetic *bhadralok* authors of these discourses were intent on both spiritual comfort and worldly happiness. We might even think of them following Rammohan's simple code of religion and morality: know God and love your neighbor. Consequently, as we have seen, Debendranath and his colleagues believe the ideal practitioner of Vedānta is the "godly householder" (*brahmaniṣṭha gṛhastha*), not the cave-dwelling yogi. If renunciation is motivated by fear (as Discourse Seventeen suggests), the life of the householder turns on love of family and society. The trick for these authors is to remain in touch with ultimate reality while engaged in one's worldly affairs. It is in this context that one author invokes the figure of Śaunaka, the archetypal godly householder of ancient myth and legend (see Discourse Fifteen). Several other discourses engage more or less directly with the question of how to pursue life in this world. Again, it all turns on the need for sense restraint.

We are reminded that, according to Vedānta, in order to worship God, we must first restrain our "fickle senses" (Discourse One). It is only through sense restraint that ultimate reality can be known and liberation attained:

> With minds purified through faith, senses restrained, the passions of lust, anger, greed, delusion &c. restrained by the practice of calmness and restraint, diligent individuals worship the Supreme Lord directly by following the injunctions of Vedānta. Thereby they attain liberation. (Discourse Two)

As a corollary, more than one author argues that since God has given human beings the power to restrain their senses, such restraint must certainly be within our grasp. However, the key to sense restraint is not radical renunciation, as it is in many classical traditions, but simply constant diligence and personal effort. The authors of *Sabhyadiger vaktṛtā* concur that it is ultimately pointless to wander off to the forest to subdue one's passions; distraction is still all too possible, even in the depths of the jungle. The better strategy is to pursue sense restraint right within the ordinary world of family, business, and government (Discourse Eighteen). Our senses and our passions don't need eradication; they just need subduing. Subdued, "they are the cause of happiness in this life and liberation in the next" (Discourse Two).

One index that *Sabhyadiger vaktṛtā* provides us with a bourgeois rescripting of the Vedantic message can be found just here, in the authors' view of the role of the passions in the religious life. The passions are not to be suppressed or devalued outright. Rather, just as Baron Mandeville had suggested in his 1705 "Fable of the Bees," these authors find it simplistic to view pride, vanity, envy, and the like as mere vices. If anything, the passions could be seen as a motive force behind "the public benefits of industry and prosperity" (quoting de Vries 1994: 259). That is, were it not for such passions as lust, anger, and greed, human society would fall apart.[15]

Mandeville's parable was immensely important for shaping social theory during the Scottish Enlightenment (for example, de Vries 1994: 259). Its popularity with thinkers like Thomas Reid and Adam Ferguson coincided with a rejection of Lockean social contract theory, as well as a repudiation of Hume's skepticism. In Reid's writings, one is able to sense the same comforting interplay of rational philosophizing with conservative social philosophy and theistic belief that characterize the discourses of *Sabhyadiger vaktṛtā*. For instance, at one point Reid writes:

> We are placed in this world by the Author of our being, surrounded with many objects that are necessary or useful to us, and with many that may hurt us. We are led, not by reason and self-love only, but by many instincts, and appetites, and natural desires to seek the former and to avoid the latter. (Quoted in Johnston 1915: 164)

The similarity between Reid's argument and the attitudes of the Tattvabodhinī authors should come as no surprise. The Scottish Enlightenment made its way to India in the curriculum of English-language schools. John Abercrombie's repackaging of the so-called Scottish Common Sense philosophy in particular was widely read. For Debendranath and the former Young Bengal faction who had been educated at Hindu College, Reid, Abercrombie, and Adam Smith were likely to have been familiar topics of study and examination. And we find clear traces of the legacy of such thinking in the discourses of *Sabhyadiger vaktṛtā*. As with the "Fable of the Bees," we are told that, without a bit of lust, we wouldn't love our wives and children. Without a bit of selfishness, we wouldn't seek friends. If humans weren't prone to anger, we wouldn't worry about shame or honor. As one author asks, "How could the duties of worldly life be carried out in such a situation?" (Discourse Thirteen).

A passage from the seventeenth discourse in the collection provides a representative example of this kind of argument:

> Were humans not to help one another, the world would instantly collapse. If fathers and mothers did not nourish and care for their children, then how would the frail bodies of the young be protected? The Supreme Lord has instilled affection in the hearts of human beings to protect these young ones. Were it not for this love, how would we know it is our duty to nourish and care for our children? Were it not for such love, the birth and death of our children would bring no more sense of gain or loss than the birth and death of a fly or an ant. Truly, how could the world carry on if we didn't make some careful effort to protect our children? To ensure the well-being of the world, the Lord has created affection so that we will devote our full attention to nourishing and caring for our children. (Discourse Seventeen)

Rather than renouncing our passions, we must learn to frame our desires appropriately. "Were you put on this earth solely for sensory pleasure?" No, you were created "to respect your father and mother, love your neighbors, work for the welfare of the government, rescue people from the torment of suffering, provide religious instruction to your son and students, and give knowledge to the ignorant" (Discourse Fifteen). The authors of these discourses concur that when we reflect on the purpose behind God's creation, we cannot help but arrive at a corresponding sense of our worldly duties.[16] Through the measured restraint of our passions, we can work to fulfill God's purpose by seeking the welfare of ourselves and others.

Overall, these discourses deliver a very conservative social and political message, one that favors the responsible maintenance of precisely those structures of family life and social order that allow for the smooth practice of worldly affairs. As one author puts it, "wiser and happier still . . . are those who pray for wealth and power solely in order to promote the welfare of the country" (Discourse Eleven). These discourses do not counsel social revolution; they do not question the legitimacy of colonial government. They offer guidance for making one's way within the world as it exists; more, they suggest the key to finding success in such a world. As an emergent bourgeoisie, the *bhadralok* members of the Sabhā found in their theological worldview not simply a spiritually ennobling path but also a powerful means for understanding and legitimating their newfound social status. If they were gaining increased access to wealth, influence, and social mobility, these were not just the irrelevant by-products of their worldly activity; they confirmed the truth of a theology of success grounded in the diligent and restrained pursuit of worldly desires.

The optimism of the group and its confidence in the promise of prosperity through landholding, trade, commerce, and benevolent government is signaled by the rhetorical question that opens the final discourse in *Sabhyadiger vaktṛtā*: "Is there a single member of this Society who doesn't know how much the world is helped by business?" (Discourse Twenty-One). Sitting in Calcutta at the end of the 1830s, surrounded by striking evidence of the transformation of the local economy, who could deny it? The Sabhā's very membership seemed to offer visible confirmation of the just confluence of their theology and their business. The author of the final discourse goes on to conjure up a legion of traders diligently involved in buying up local goods and shipping them off to other nations. The author asks us to marvel not only at how such commerce increases the welfare of local farmers and craftsmen but also at how it benefits those who "live in the one place where all these delightful goods are prepared, here on the shore of the mighty ocean."

It is difficult not to think of Max Weber's industrious Puritans when reading these discourses, especially since the authors so clearly work to subsume the pursuit of wealth beneath a higher spiritual calling.[17] We are reminded that while traders will, in fact, brave the high seas in order to win "wealth, reputation and fame," this really isn't all there is to life. There is a higher norm. The devout will remember God, who has endowed humans with the capacity to seek more than mere personal gain. Look closely, these discourses suggest, and you will always find some traders and merchants who are conscious of serving a greater good. Such men are labeled the "true votaries of the Supreme Lord" (Discourse Twenty-One). The religious life is less about renunciation and asceticism than it is about intention: "It is only through intention that men are guilty or blameless. . . . This is why it is essential that we guard our intention according to the law!" (Discourse Twenty-One).

In many ways, this *bhadralok* effort to balance worldliness and religious devotion calls to mind Hermann Hesse's unflattering portrait of the bourgeois, who "will never surrender himself either to lust or to asceticism. He will never be a martyr or agree to his own destruction. On the contrary, his ideal is not to give up but to maintain his own identity. . . . He is ready to be virtuous, but likes to be easy and comfortable in the world as well" (Hesse 1969: 59). The members of the Sabhā seek ease and comfort as well, but only as these can be made meaningful within a framework of Vedantic effort and restraint. There is no nationalist aspiration here or chafing at colonial rule; there is mostly hard work and the peace of mind that comes from conforming one's work to God's laws.

Idioms of law and duty in *Sabhyadiger vaktṛtā*

The idiom of "law" in these discourses provides a powerful tool for legitimating the social status and worldly pursuits of the *bhadralok*. This idiom is invoked in two registers. On the one hand, the idiom of law operates to remind us of the regularity and purposefulness of God's creation. Creation conforms to the Creator's laws (*niyama* or *dharma*). Were there to be any relaxation in this law, "the world would be completely destroyed" (Discourse Three).[18] On the other hand, the idiom of law is used to identify the kinds of duties human beings must observe. Thus we are told that the religiously awakened person is one who "performs all his actions in life in accordance with the Lord's laws" (Discourse Nine). Weber's discussion of the Calvinist view of duty rings remarkably well in this context: "The world exists to serve the glorification of God. . . . The elected Christian is in the world only to increase this glory . . . by fulfilling His commandments. . . . But God requires social achievement of the Christian because he wills that social life be organized according to His . . . purpose" (1958: 108).

These references to God and the purposefulness of his creation offer a clear reminder that even though the Tattvabodhinī Sabhā looked to Vedānta for its inspiration, its members often chose to express their vision of the human-divine relationship using the idioms of modern, rational theism. As they might have put it, we must do our duty and live according to our human capacities, because this is how God has ordered the world. Observation of the ordered and harmonious structure of the created order serves to convince a rational being of God's plan, of God's law:

> Following this universal law, you . . . were created to respect your father and mother, love your neighbors, work for the welfare of the government. . . . If you try to defy it out of a desire for sensual happiness, you will instantly fall into a sea of affliction. (Discourse Fifteen)

As the reference to working for the 'welfare of the government' makes clear, members of the Sabhā tended to believe that the social and political order is itself grounded in God's law. When the social and political order is honored and upheld, it provides a reassuring matrix within which to conduct human affairs. Therefore, just as people who violate God's laws suffer in this life and the next, those who violate the laws of the state end up being punished.[19]

These discourses suggest that both God's divine law and all human laws are reflected in our internal sense of duty. Weber spoke of "natural intuition" (1958: 109), but the members of the Sabhā invoke the idiom of *dharma*. By drawing creatively on the semantics of *dharma*—an ancient and multivalent concept expressive of cosmic order, divine rule, natural law, and human religious instinct—these authors demonstrate the ways in which their bourgeois ethic came to expression in vernacular categories. And, of course, by invoking the concept of *dharma*, these authors provide an important sanction for their worldview. In particular, by grounding the moral life in *dharma* as an internal sense of duty, these discourses effectively, if subtly, rule out any objection that the group's values are based in either an irrational supernatural power or an unreliable political authority.

We know the Sabhā had members whose education had inclined them to distrust not only the powers of the clergy but also the unchecked authority of despots and kings. Those members drawn from the Young Bengal faction, in particular, would have been hard pressed to endorse any theology based simply on a purported divine mandate. By invoking *dharma*, such concerns evaporate. Duty is innate; we act on our values because they make up the very "law of our hearts" (Discourse Seventeen).[20] In other words, it is in our very nature as human beings to do those things we should, such as love and care for others. Duty is naturalized. In the process, the legitimacy of the Tattvabodhinī worldview is further ensured.[21]

The idiom of *dharma* was a particularly fruitful one for the Tattvabodhinī group, precisely because it promised to offer a middle ground between theistic and humanistic morality. It spoke to the interpenetration of divine law, human legislation, and an innate human moral sense. Through the idiom of *dharma*, the members of the Sabhā arrived at a further convincing argument for legitimating their worldly activities. It was enough to suggest that engaging in profit-making business was an essential part of the omniscient Lord's creative plan (Discourse Twenty). Business is good not simply when it is done well, but when it is done according to *dharma*. To live according to *dharma* is to live with the right intention—with diligence and with concern for the well-being of others.

With the themes of diligence and care, we return to a key issue I explored in my earlier work on Vidyasagar's bourgeois morality. In looking at Vidyāsāgar's worldview, I emphasized the concept of *yatna*, a word that in this context evokes what we might call an ethic of diligent effort. To act with *yatna* is to exert onself energetically, but within a framework of care and concern. In effect, *yatna* enshrines an ethic of care, care for oneself and care for others. In these discourses, we find the same idiom invoked, especially in the last discourse, whose author closes by exhorting his listeners to live lives of diligent effort. As he puts it, whether it is in the company they keep, the counsel they give, the sick they attend to, the knowledge they bestow, or the suffering they comfort, good people "always exert themselves with care" (Discourse Twenty-One).[22]

In this idiom of "taking care"—this concern to be diligent and careful in one's restrained behavior and in one's concern for others—we find the very essence of this particular species of Bengali bourgeois ethic. This "industrious disposition," to borrow de Vries's phrase (1994: 262), promotes a life both of spiritual worship and of worldly profit-making. And it legitimates both by reference to a set of theological claims expressed in the idioms of Vedānta, duty, law, effort, and care. As these short discourses make abundantly clear, this is a confident, optimistic vision of the world. One can sense the enthusiasm of the members, not only for their newfound religious vision but also for the framework they have found for rationalizing success and happiness in this life.

It would take us too far beyond these discourses to reflect on the afterlife of this bourgeois vision. We can close this chapter simply by noting that the bourgeois hopes of the *bhadralok* for expanded opportunities in the colonial public sphere—for increased participation in the commercial, political, and administrative life of colonial Bengal—would begin to crumble not long after the founding of the Sabhā. As Sumit Sarkar has written, the 1840s witnessed "the end of large-scale Bengali entrepreneurship, with the collapse of the Union

Bank being often taken as a benchmark" (1997: 226). The same period witnessed the folding of the once promising venture begun by Debendranath's father. In 1848, the assets of the Carr, Tagore, and Co. were sold—an event that signaled the "declining role of the *bhadralok* in the business life of their province" (Kling 1976: 242). Simultaneously, groups like the Sabhā began to feel increased heat from Christian polemic, prompting significant reevaluation of their identity and their mission. This is the subject of chapter 5.

As the century progressed, the melioristic bourgeois theology of the earliest Sabhā began to seem quaint and perhaps a tad irrelevant, as subsequent generations turned to more assertive forms of Hindu identity, especially in the face of growing British racism after 1857. Looking back on these discourses now, they may therefore strike us as naïve, complacent, and self-absorbed.[23] Be that as it may, *Sabhyadiger vaktṛtā* nevertheless reveals an important, if short-lived, moment in the early decades of colonial Calcutta when merchants and entrepreneurs were looking to redefine their religious world. The theology they developed speaks to the creative convergence of ancient South Asian religious norms and modern rationalist theology within an ethos of confident bourgeois aspiration. Even though this particular association, and even the broader Brāhmo movement with which it eventually came to be affiliated, have faded into near obscurity, we do well to consider how this moment of theological reflection contributed to the emergence of what might today be called middle-class Hinduism. In the latter part of the nineteenth century, this bourgeois ethic would reappear in a variety of modernist guises, whether it be Swami Vivekananda's "Practical Vedanta" or Bankim Chatterjee's vision of a Hindu humanism. This quest to harmonize the spiritual truths of Vedānta with modes of worldly activity, even worldly success, remains a vital factor even in today's manifold expressions of postcolonial and diasporic Hinduism.

5

Missionaries and Modern Vedantists

Rammohan's most celebrated debates with the Baptist missionaries centered on such issues as the question of miracles, the doctrine of the atonement, the nature of Jesus Christ, and trinitarian theology. A skillful polemicist, Rammohan was able to put Christian doctrines on trial, requiring the missionaries to publicly respond to his interpretation of Christianity. By contrast, the creation of the Tattvabodhinī Sabhā came about with no overt reference to the Christian missionary presence in Bengal. After reviewing the circumstances leading up to Debendranath's spiritual awakening and the founding of the Sabhā, and judging from his autobiography, we can see that Christianity had no role, postive or negative, in those events. If the creation of the Sabhā chiefly bore the imprint of Debendranath's spiritual vision, then we may fairly conclude that at the outset his religious concerns did not take the shape of either overt polemic or nervous apologetic. This fact is corroborated by the evidence we find in *Sabhyadiger vaktṛtā*, whose discourses make no mention of Christianity, Christian missionary activity, Jesus Christ, the Bible, or even European civilization more generally.

These facts notwithstanding, as noted in the introduction, even if *Sabhyadiger vaktṛtā* is silent regarding Christianity, this does not mean that we cannot find evidence of interreligious tension, either within the text of *Sabhyadiger vaktṛtā* or in the concerns of the Tattvabodhinī movement more broadly. The very fact that the authors represented in *Sabhyadiger vaktṛtā* felt the need to bolster their religious worldview not simply with scriptural proofs but with appeals to rationally derived evidences of God's activity in the world may be taken to suggest at least two things: first, that they understood themselves to be living in a world in which religious epistemologies were beginning to come into more persistent conflict; second, that they sought a form of proof (alongside their cherished scriptural traditions) that had some claim to being universal. And if the various members who contributed discourses to *Sabhyadiger vaktṛtā* betray no desire to engage in either an assault on the truth of Christianity or an outright defense of their own beliefs, the time for such tactics was nevertheless not far off.

Anxiety, Hindu and Christian

It is difficult to judge precisely when Christian missionaries first became aware of the work of the Tattvabodhinī Sabhā. There are scattered references to the founding of the Sabhā in the writings of various missionaries, but these were typically written at the distance of a few years or more. One of the earliest references to the Sabhā comes, not surprisingly, from the brahmin convert, Krishna Mohan Banerjea (1813–85). Banerjea was a contemporary of Debendranath and, like him, had been schooled at Hindu College, where he became one of the leading voices of the Young Bengal faction. However, in 1832 he broke with his radical cohort and converted to Christianity, largely through the efforts of the Rev. Alexander Duff (1806–72). The following year, Duff encouraged the young convert to write a critical review of Rammohan's interpretation of the Upanishads (Banerjea 1833; see also Kopf 1979: 161). It is worth noting that Banerjea was immensely active on the Calcutta intellectual scene and continued to have regular contact with his Hindu peers. A member of such prominent organizations from the 1830s as the Society for the Acquisition of General Knowledge, he would have had easy access to intellectual developments among his elite counterparts—far more so than any of his European missionary co-religionists.

In 1840, Banerjea published *Sermons Addressed to Native Christians and Inquirers*, a Bengali work that is often referred to as *Upadeśa kathā*.[1] The book carries an English preface that provides a valuable early reference to the Sabhā:

> However defective and meager this little volume may be, it may perhaps be humbly hoped that it will contribute, in a limited extent, to the improvement of Sacred Literature in Bengalee; while the recent reprints, by a distinguished Hindu gentleman, of Vedantic tracts composed and edited by the late Raja Rammohun Roy and his friends,

> and the exertions lately made in the Tattwa bodhini Sabha to oppose a barrier to the progress of the Gospel, render this not altogether an improper season for the publication of a number of Christian Sermons. (Banerjea 1840: iii)[2]

Two things are interesting about this passage. First, Banerjea seems to indicate the existence of two factions, however loosely these are construed. One centers on a "distinguished Hindu gentleman" and the other on the Sabhā. This seems consistent with the picture we have developed thus far, in which the original Tattvabodhinī Sabhā operated independently from Rammohan's followers. Second, Banerjea suggests that the goal of the Tattvabodhinī Sabhā was to "oppose a barrier to the progress of the Gospel." This is a rather curious remark, given the absence of references to the Gospel or Christianity in *Sabhyadiger vaktṛtā*. One wonders whether Banerjea's remark was based less on specific proclamations of the Sabhā than on his own anxiety that any attempt by native intellectuals to promulgate a reformed Hindu message would work to impede the advance of Christian teachings in Bengal.[3]

As discussed, there is little in Debendranath's version of events to suggest that opposition to Christianity was a primary—or even a particularly relevant—factor in the creation of the Sabhā. Now, it is not unreasonable to suspect that in writing his autobiography Debendranath adjusted his account of events in order to emphasize the independent spiritual origins of the Sabhā. This is the position taken by M. M. Ali, who some time back argued that the origins of the Sabhā were firmly grounded in anti-Christian sentiment (1965). Ali speculates that Debendranath's later autobiographical account must have papered over this fact in favor of a more spiritualized narrative. In his widely read study of the Brāhmo Samāj, David Kopf (1979: 162–63) clearly followed Ali's interpretation, quoting the same texts in support of this position. However, the strongest evidence advanced by Ali (and later by Kopf) to prove the supposed anti-Christian origins of the Sabhā is an English-language "Report of the Tattvabodhinī Sabhā" from 1843. The relevant passage from that report reads as follows:

> The educated native mind relieved, as it were, from the burden which superstitition had so long imposed, was naturally left to receive the first impression it could lay hold on. It was to have been feared, therefore, that, as a natural result of this course of events, the great body of the people, unshakled [*sic*] from the fetters of superstition, would either imbibe the pernicious principles of atheism, or embrace the doctrines of Christianity, so successfully promulgated by its teachers—a consummation which the members could not bring themselves to look on with indifference, consistent with their regard

for the welfare of their countrymen. It was to counteract influences like these . . . that the Society was originally established.[4]

In light of the developments surveyed in chapter 3, it should be clear that this report needs to be put in its proper context. Much had changed within the Sabhā by 1843. It should be recalled that this is the very same report I cite in chapter 3 as evidence of the Sabhā's newfound allegiance to Rammohan after Debendranath's 1842 decision to join forces with the Brāhmo Samāj.[5] There is every reason to think that just as the Sabhā eventually projected its reverence for Rammohan back to its point of origin, it might also have retrojected anti-Christian sentiments as an original motivating factor when composing the 1843 report. In other words, this report does not offer an accurate picture of the way things stood in 1839.

By contrast, one of the strongest signs that the Sabhā's origins were not in fact motivated by anti-Christian sentiment must be the text of *Sabhyadiger vaktṛtā* itself. As readers of the present translation may confirm for themselves, these discourses are almost resolutely engaged in an intra-Hindu act of interpretation. Ironically, this may give some weight to David Kopf's other contention that Debendranath's decision to form an independent Sabhā rather than joining the Brāhmo Samāj was inspired by his desire to arrive at a more "culturally apologetic" message than Rammohan's "universalist Unitarian" position (Kopf 1979: 162). However, whereas Kopf thinks this was Debendranath's way to more effectively defend Hinduism from Christianity, one might equally argue that the Sabhā initially sought to distance its own reformist message from the taint of missionary polemics into which Rammohan had been so forcefully drawn. Of course, as the 1843 report suggests, in the end it proved impossible for the Sabhā to avoid such concerns.

A careful review of the sources suggests that the years 1843–45 mark an important juncture in the self-awareness of the Sabhā. Missionary activity in Bengal had increased steadily throughout the 1830s, beginning with the arrival of the outspoken Alexander Duff in 1830 and followed closely by the conversion of a prominent brahmin intellectual like Banerjea in 1832. More conversions followed, including the visible instance of two students of Duff's General Assembly's Institution in 1839.[6] In 1843, two more promising young men of rising talent were converted, Lal Behari De and Michael Madhusudan Dutt (who had already begun to distinguish himself as a poetic genius by this time). Then, in 1845, came the notorious case of the fourteen-year-old Umesh Chandra Sarkar and his young wife of eleven, who took shelter in Duff's home and then subsequently converted. This case caused immense uproar within the local Hindu community. It even wound up in the courts, while public discussion of the circumstances surrounding the conversion raised concerns among local Hindus regarding parental rights over their children (Ali 1965: 79–80).

In all, as Kopf rightly notes, the visible and startling success of Duff in converting educated Hindu youth had served to make the Bengali public anxious about the role of missionaries in education. In response, prominent Hindus began calling for independent initiatives in education to reduce the risk of losing their children to Christianity. Ali's study of the Hindu response to conversions reminds us that appeals for Hindu schools were often published in prominent Bengali periodicals like the *Saṃbād Prabhākara* and *Samācāra Candrikā*, which had begun to proliferate during the period from 1843 to 1847. While some were more successful than others, few of these new journals were as long-lived as the *Tattvabodhinī Patrikā*. Its appearance in 1843—at just this juncture in time, notice—is further evidence of a clear shift in the program, and no doubt the underlying rationale, of the Sabhā.

As discussed, the Tattvabodhinī Sabhā witnessed astounding growth during these years. That this growth coincided with increased Hindu concerns about conversion can help us appreciate how, in time, the Sabhā came to take a leading role in challenging missionary initiatives. The conversion of the two students of Duff's General Assembly's Institution in 1839 is often cited as the spark that led the Tattvabodhinī Sabhā to establish its own school during the very next year, the Tattvabodhinī Pāṭhaśālā, located in Bansberia, north of Calcutta.[7] As more and more anxious Hindus joined the Sabhā, we can well imagine how the aura of benign theological introspection that characterizes the discourses of *Sabhyadiger vaktṛtā* might have turned into a more heated atmosphere of fear, outrage, invective, and—eventually—polemic. That the Sabhā's orientation and sense of mission changed correspondingly is hardly surprising.

From the perspective of an educated Hindu convert like Banerjea, these developments would have been cause for great concern. The more local elites were drawn to organizations like the Tattvabodhinī Sabhā, the less likely they would be to open their ears or hearts to the Christian message.[8] At the same time, Debendranath's decision in 1842 to use the resources of the Tattvabodhinī Sabhā to promote Rammohan's message would have given the missionaries further grounds for serious concern. Rammohan's name was by then synonymous with the energetic and sophisticated attempt by native intellectuals to reject Christianity. We can imagine that Christian observers had watched happily throughout the 1830s as the Brāhmo movement faltered and appeared ready to fade away. We can likewise easily imagine their consternation when Debendranath suddenly pledged his new association to reviving the Brāhmo movement. What had apparently begun as a largely nonpolemical association was now more explicitly becoming aware of a grander mission to preserve a sense of Hindu truth and identity. In 1840, it may have looked to Krishna Mohan Banerjea that the Brāhmos and the Sabhā represented two independent developments, but by 1842 these two groups were clearly drawing together.

Sources indicate that by the mid-1840s several missionaries were beginning to take a closer and more critical look at the Tattvabodhinī Sabhā. Ali cites evidence from 1843 that shows members of the Calcutta Christian Tract and Book Society (notably the Revs. Morton and Ewart) expressing anxiety about the efforts of a particular society (unfortunately unnamed) to promote the teachings of Vedānta (Ali 1965: 44). We can well imagine these missionaries asking themselves, Who are these people? Why are they organizing? What is their relationship to Rammohan's Brāhmo movement? And what is going to be the best way to address their increasing appeal among educated Bengalis? These are precisely the sorts of questions that lurk behind the handful of missionary accounts we have of the Sabhā from this period.

It is in 1845, two years after the Sabhā became more publicly visible through its journal *Tattvabodhinī Patrikā*, that we begin to notice a flurry of references to the Sabhā in missionary publications. These references are rather remarkable for the consistency of the language used to refer to the Sabhā, which may suggest that the missionaries had had time to talk among themselves about the significance of this new association. Though not always lengthy, sensitive, or detailed, these accounts nevertheless allow us to form an idea of the major concerns missionaries had regarding Tattvabodhinī theology. The most important missonary voices during the mid-1840s are those of Alexander Duff and his convert, Krishna Mohan Banerjea; Joseph Mullens, a missionary representing the London Missionary Society (LMS); and James Long, an Irish-born Anglican representing the Church Missionary Society (CMS).

Doubly Suspicious Vedānta

It is largely to these early missionary depictions of the Sabhā, and, most important, to their attempts to interpret the ramifications of Tattvabodhinī theology, that we owe the now-familiar rubric of "neo-Vedānta." The phrase is today used to describe a wide range of modern Hindu philosophies grounded in one way or another in the teachings of Vedānta.[9] But few today are sufficiently aware of how the term originally emerged from missionary accounts of the early Tattvabodhinī/Brāhmo alliance. To Christian missionaries and local converts during the 1840s, dubbing the members of the Tattvabodhinī Sabhā "neo-Vedāntists" was a way of saying—none too kindly—that this was a group bent on the modern revival of Vedānta. It is not going too far to say that the category of neo-Vedānta, far from being a mere descriptive label, is in its origin a polemical one, born in a moment of high anxiety.

It is to Duff and Banerjea that we can most directly trace the origin of the rubric neo-Vedānta, since both men speak of the Tattvabodhinī group as modern Vedantists. Banerjea also ventures the related rubrics of "modern revivers of the Vedant," and "New Vedantists" (Duff 1845: 52; Banerjea 1845: 112–13). Joseph Mullens arrives at much the same way of categorizing Debendranath and his co-members. Speaking more generally of the Brāhmos, Mullens styles them "modern worshippers of Brahma" but adds that "sometimes the members have been called Vedantists" (1852: 109).[10]

While it may seem to us that the adjectives "new" and "modern" make perfect sense when applied to the Vedānta of the Tattvabodhinī Sabhā—which, after all, was a newly formed association dedicated to the propagation of Vedānta—it is important to bear in mind that such terms would have had a doubly perjorative significance for the missionaries. First, the theme of newness announced by the epithet "modern" carried with it a sense of "newfangled." To these missionaries, who saw themselves as guardians of the eternal word of God, newfangled meant "inauthentic." By construing this Vedānta as newfangled, the missionaries were able to suggest that sensible people should beware of this group. Though the Sabhā, like Rammohan, claimed to revive the ancient teachings of the Upanishads, Christian observers considered its position to be theologically unprecedented. We should bear in mind, too, that in those days newness was not valorized as avant-garde, or what we might today call "cutting edge." In this context, newness was devalued as something for which little or no authority was thought to exist.[11] What precedent there was for such theology could be found only in one place—not the Upanishads, but Rammohan, a figure whose theology and republican politics the missionaries would surely have opposed.

To appreciate the second connotation of newness in this respect, we have to think of what was conveyed by speaking of a modern Vedānta. To begin with, the rubric of Vedānta naturally highlighted the Sabhā's problematic association with Rammohan. To the missionaries, these were just Brāhmos by another name, and their commitment to Vedānta really signaled a desire to revive suspect elements of the Hindu religious system. The missionaries I have mentioned thus far tended to broadly characterize these elements as world renunciation, pantheism, and immorality. All of these purported Hindu errors were premised on a vision of the universe that the missionaries took to be a kind of theological nihilism. As if this weren't enough, the missionaries also pointed out that by grounding their worldview in Vedic scripture, the modern

Vedantists were obligated to recognize not just the lofty vision of the Upanishads (the *jñāna*, or knowledge-centered, portion of the Vedas) but also the clear emphasis on sacrifice and the worship of multiple deities enshrined in the remaining Vedic collections (the *karma*, or ritual-centered, portion).[12] When all this evidence was mustered against the modern Vedantists, the missionaries felt it only right to conclude that this newfangled Vedānta represented the worst of possible situations: an attempt to dress up ancient error in new clothes.

That the creation of an organization to promote modern Vedānta among the Bengali public was indeed a source of serious concern to the missionaries is made evident in a letter written in 1855 by the Rev. A. F. Lacroix (also of the LMS), in which he refers to the existence of "a new sect in Bengal" whose members he refers to as "Vedantists." Going on, Lacroix adds that "this new phase in the religious history of this country . . . causes some anxiety to the missionaries."[13] We should not lose sight of this anxiety, since its specter haunts all subsequent manifestations of neo-Vedānta. Later invocations of Vedānta by the likes of Vivekananda and Radhakrishnan surely gained some of their contestatory force during the nationalist period precisely because they represented an attempt to construe this formerly suspicious Hindu system as the clarion call of Hindu spirituality. No matter how mainstream neo-Vedānta may have become within contemporary Hinduism, it is worth bearing in mind its contested beginnings.

The Vedānta debates of the 1840s

Earlier I referred to Krishna Mohan Banerjea's critique of Rammohan's interpretation of Vedānta. His 1833 review of Rammohan's translation of the Muṇḍaka Upanishad announces in no uncertain terms the missionary's desire to master and then refute any modern reformulation of Vedānta. Though credited to Banerjea, the work bears the clear stamp of Banerjea's spiritual mentor, Alexander Duff, who set Banerjea to this task (Banerjea 1833). Did Duff ask this of Banerjea as a test, a way to gain proof of the convert's commitment to his new faith? If this is too harsh an interpretation, we can nonetheless say that Duff's role in the creation of the review suggests how closely the two men worked to advance a thorough critique of Vedānta.

In the 1833 work, Banerjea begins by questioning the very use of the term "Vedānta" to refer to the Upanishads. He understands this term to refer principally to the later, classical school of monism known as Advaita Vedānta. As for the meaning "end of the Veda" (that is, *veda-anta*, or Vedānta), which

Rammohan applied to the Upanishads, Banerjea says that such a usage is found only in more "modern" works; he denies that this idea of "end" is found in the Vedas themselves (Banerjea 1833: 1). However, he claims to see all too clearly why Rammohan would "wish to have it understood that the vedant is a 'principal part of the veds [i.e., Vedas].'" Being "heartily ashamed of the silliness and sensuality of the real veds" (that is, the *karma* portion, taken together with the *jñāna*), Rammohan might well have wished to simply disregard them altogether. But since the Vedas clearly form the scriptural basis of the Hindu tradition, he could not do this. Instead, Banerjea suggests, Rammohan looked to the far more recent school of Vedānta, which honored only the *jñāna* portion of the Vedas, and "set it forth as embodying the tenets of the founders of Hindooism" (3).[14]

Having rather briskly (and no doubt unfairly) dismissed the category of Vedānta as an appropriate designation for the Brāhmos' Upanishadic faith, Banerjea moves just as quickly to highlight key criticisms of Vedānta. He begins by saying that "Ram Mohun asserts that 'the books of the Vedant, with great consistency, inculcate the unity of God.'" But then Banerjea adds that what they inculcate is more truthfully "the existence of an infinite *something*; but that something is not God" (1833: 6; emphasis in the original). Carrying on, Banerjea adds that this "infinite something" is neither a creator nor a moral ruler or a benefactor of humanity. We may be in awe as to his omnipresence and immutability, but "we cannot thank, or love, or reverence him" (9–10). In an interesting twist on the origins of so-called Hindu polytheism, Banerjea suggests it was natural that the ordinary Hindu should have "formed gods for themselves of every shape and character" since the Vedantic philosophers had robbed believers of any God they could adore and revere. Echoing a common Christian complaint of the day, Banerjea adds that the God of the Vedantins does not even have a personality (10–11). The implication is that no revived Vedānta is likely to help solve this problem, since it continues to offer no God worthy of sincere devotion.

The core features of the later missionary assault on Vedānta from the 1840s are thus already present in Banerjea's 1833 essay. We do well to take note of this work, therefore, since it allows us to identify the sort of arguments that would have been circulating among educated Calcuttans during the years leading up to the creation of the Tattvabodhinī Sabhā. Even if Debendranath's autobiography and the discourses of *Sabhyadiger vaktṛtā* betray no overt concern with missionary critiques, such critiques had clearly begun. Where Rammohan had first addressed Christian concerns, Banerjea kept the debate going. It would be naïve to think that the Tattvabodhinī Sabhā's early attempts to propagate Vedānta were not informed in some sense by such exchanges.

A major watershed in the advance of the Christian critique came in 1839, when Duff published his lengthy tome, *India and India Missions*. In this work, which was published in the very year Debendranath created the Tattvabodhinī Sabhā, Duff advances a pitiless attack on Hinduism.[15] Deploying an array of violent, militaristic metaphors, Duff makes clear his goal of demolishing Hinduism. Using Western education to inaugurate a kind of "silent warfare," Duff seeks to lay down a "species of raking fire" intended to leave "the fortress of Hinduism" in "ruins" (587).[16] According to this ardent Scotch Calvinist, Hinduism was no better than Popish Catholicism. Both promote what he calls doctrines of "exclusive self-reliance." If anything, in Hinduism this doctrine is even "more absolute than that of Roman Catholicism itself" (297). For Duff, such error can only be overthrown by the Protestant trust in *sola fides*, salvation by faith alone (301).[17]

As for Hinduism's emphasis on self-reliance, Duff chalks this up to the belief in *brahman*, which he styles (in tones reminiscent of Banerjea's earlier essay) "one great universal self-existing spirit" (1939: 74). Defining final beatitude as the soul's participation in this spirit, Duff goes on to suggest that such a goal could only be achieved by cutting away all human concerns and responsibilities in order to focus on one's true self. It follows for Duff, therefore, that to become *brahman*, one must necessarily become selfish (207–8). And so two major missionary objections to Hinduism are advanced: it is a pantheistic religion that emphasizes self-reliance in the form of radical—and self-serving—renunciation of the world.

Further leitmotifs of the missionary critique emerge in turn. For Duff, attaining *brahman* is tantamount to a kind of "infinite negation." That is, salvation can really be nothing but an annihilation of the self in the infinite *brahman*. The state thus achieved can only be understood as utterly passive, emotionless, and, by extension, amoral. Never one to mince words, Duff dismisses the goal of liberation as being like "the blessedness of a decayed vegetable" (1939: 207). Thereby another charge is advanced against Hinduism, insofar as it promotes a kind of passive—Duff might even say nihilist—immorality.

An answer to Duff and his colleagues was not long in coming. While his assault was launched in 1839, we have seen that the early Sabhā was perhaps not inspired by, let alone geared up for, the smoke and thunder of religious polemics. However, we have also seen that by 1843–44, this situation had begun to change. One indication of the Sabhā's growing desire in the early 1840s to defend its position may be found in a pair of unsigned English-language works that appeared in the newly launched periodical, *Tattvabodhinī Patrikā*. The first essay, from September/October of 1844, was entitled (in

Bengali) "Ḍāpher prativāda," or "A Reply to Duff." The second appeared in February/March of 1845 and carried the English title, "Vaidantic Doctrines Vindicated."[18] The deliberate choice to write in English and not Bengali (as was the Sabhā's routine practice) is further indication of the Sabhā's resolve to become more seriously engaged in some form of interreligious communication.

The earlier essay begins by commenting on how "remarkable and characteristic" it is of missionary polemics in India that authors who begin by denouncing the errors of polytheism and idolatry do not spare their scorn even for those Hindus who have themselves abandoned such errors. Making deliberate allusion to Duff's violent language, the author notes that, rather than crediting such Hindus with making important advances, these missionaries simply "shifted the ground of their aggressive warfare, and levelled the whole artillery of their argumentative tactics against the stronghold of Unitarianism itself, as inculcated in the Vaidanta." Only after this does the author reveal that he has the "polemical hostility" of Alexander Duff in mind, notably his *India and India Missions* (quoted in Ghoṣa 1981: 89–90).

Having thus called Duff to task for his unnecessary hostility, the author goes on to cast the Sabhā in a far different light. A passage from the first tract illustrates the way this unnamed apologist for Vedānta seeks to occupy the moral high ground, while making the group's theology of moral theism clear. Referring to Duff's misreading of ultimate reality (*brahman*), the author remarks:

> But such vague and untenable assertions ought, after all, to excite no surprise in us, as emanating from one of those who, trusting to their own infallibility, profess to believe that they alone are the select and beloved children of our common Almighty Father; that they alone are blessed with a full and perfect knowledge of the true religion, that by a fearful distinction . . . millions of their fellow creatures have, since the beginning of the world, been doomed to live and die in utter mental darkness. . . . We thank the great Architect of the universe that such are not our own doctrines,—that it is, on the contrary, our chiefest source of comfort and happiness, firmly to believe, and zealously to inculcate, that all mankind are morally and spiritually equal in the eye of a beneficent, an impartial, and an eternal Deity. (Ghoṣa 1981: 91)

Space does not permit us to thoroughly review these two remarkable tracts, and we must bear in mind that they were created some years after the discourses of *Sabhyadiger vaktṛtā*. We can state, however, that they reveal the confidence and conviction of the Tattvabodhinī group that their theology of Vedānta represented not just a theologically viable form of Hinduism but, in fact, a superior (because more universalist) theism.[19]

Needless to say, the Tattvabodhinī attempt to plead its case made little impression on the missionaries. Duff and his colleagues continued to caricature the Sabhā, and the Brāhmos generally, as promoting a form of theological pantheism and a moral path of spiritual self-abandonment. Despite the Sabhā's attempt to challenge the missionaries' charge of Vedāntic "pantheism," Duff and his colleagues continued to rely on the negative connotations of this polemical category.[20] For them, Vedānta not only taught the unity of the creature and the creator, it also required its believers to seek ultimate dissolution into a formless, abstract deity called *brahman*. As the Rev. James Long wrote toward the end of the 1840s, the so-called modern Vedantists offered "a materializing pantheism" that was as "deficient in moral truth" as "the current idolatrous polytheism is senseless and debasing" (1848: 351–52). In other words, no matter how modern it might claim to be, this new Vedānta was still just Hinduism by any other name. And Hinduism to these missionaries was error, pure and simple.

It may be one small index of the success of the Tattvabodhinī essays, "Reply to Duff" and "Vaidantic Doctrines Vindicated," that Long at least felt compelled to acknowledge that the modern Vedantists were attempting in their own way to oppose such things as the worship of images and the widespread Hindu belief in multiple deities. However, far from redeeming the followers of Rammohan and Debendranath, such an admission really only highlighted for the missionaries how confused the modern Vedantists were. As Krishna Mohan Banerjea commented around the middle of the decade:

> Our countrymen [in the Tattvabodhinī Sabhā] are in a false position. They desire to wean their countrymen from the bewitching scenes of a fascinating idolatry, when they dare not condemn it as sinful in itself. . . . The very unity of God, which they profess to uphold, is intimately connected in their sacred writings with pantheistic views, subversive of the foundations of all theism. (Banerjea 1845: 134)

To be fair, some missionaries, like the Rev. Joseph Mullens of the LMS, could at times write approvingly of the way these modern Vedantists set out to actively repudiate ancient Hindu doctrines of the identity of creature and creator. Mullens could likewise endorse attempts to add a more strenuous moral dimension to earlier understandings of Vedānta (Mullens 1852: 131–32). But even granting all this, Mullens was hard pressed to see anything more in this than a hollow Deism. The Rev. Long concurred, choosing to think of Brāhmo theology as a kind of "modified Unitarianism."[21] We know, of course, that Rammohan had been deeply influenced by Unitarianism. The passage from the "Reply to Duff" quoted above also refers approvingly to the Tattvabodhinī message as a species of Unitarianism. Unfortunately, what to the modern Vedantists was a positive dimension of their theology was dangerous error to the missionaries. Trinitarians to a one, the Sabhā's Christian critics found the invocation of Unitarianism to be no endorsement; it merely confirmed the close connection between modern Vedānta and heresy.

Apart from the doctrine of the Trinity, what the missionaries missed in this Unitarian Hinduism was a frank recognition of sin and human fallenness. Most important, the modern Vedantists could offer no theology of atonement. In a word, their Vedānta lacked Christ. Finding this essential core wanting, Duff and his co-religionists were left to chafe at the oft-repeated virtues of "self-reliance" that characterize Tattvabodhinī discourse—diligence, sense restraint, and control of the passions. Even if the Tattvabodhinī group was endeavoring to take these more traditional Hindu virtues and use them to articulate what were innovative perspectives on godly worship, moral rectitude, benevolence, and social responsibility, the missionaries seemed always to return to Duff's stricture against this almost Pelagian emphasis on "self-righteousness" (Duff 1839: 297). Readers of *Sabhyadiger vaktṛtā* may find it useful to consider its discourses from both vantage points. One man's diligent restraint is clearly another man's self-righteousness.

The "halfway house"

That new developments were taking place in Hindu theology the missionaries could scarcely deny. The title of one of Krishna Mohan Banerjea's important essays on modern Vedānta, "Transition States of the Hindu Mind" (Banerjea 1845), aptly captures this sense of change. But for Christian observers, mere change was not necessarily enough. If the end result of such transitions in Hindu theology did not lead the Hindu community to Christ, where might it lead?

In a passage quoted earlier, we saw that Banerjea recognized that the goal of the Tattvabodhinī group was to "wean" the educated youth of Bengal from the errors of idolatrous Hinduism. We also saw that this recognition was emblematic of the missionaries' almost grudging acknowledgment that the inspiration for associations like the Tattvabodhinī Sabhā was a spirit of progress. Thanks to the Enlightenment-based curriculum of schools like Hindu College and to reformist religious initiatives like Rammohan's, young Hindus were increasingly prepared to reject significant aspects of their tradition as irrational or superstitious. The Young Bengal group, of which Banerjea had been so active a member, was clear evidence of this. However, what troubled Banerjea and his missionary colleagues was the idea that the Tattvabodhinī Sabhā might offer educated Bengalis an attractive "halfway house" between rejecting orthodox Hinduism and converting to Christianity (Long 1846: 84; see also Hatcher 1999: 102).[22]

The missionaries had hoped that a modern education would serve as the propaedeutic to conversion. As an Evangelical Anglicist, Duff was a prime mover behind initiatives to use the colonial educational curriculum and the English language to prepare the youth of Bengal for receiving the Gospel.[23] And yet during the 1830s, just as the missionaries saw that the native mind was beginning to reject the centuries-old errors of Hinduism, here came men like Debendranath. These English-educated Hindus now set out to offer a version of Hinduism purged of error. The frustration of the missionaries at such a scenario is surely what stood behind Banerjea's comment from 1840 that the Tattvabodhinī Sabhā had been created as an obstacle to the propagation of the Gospel. No mere descriptive observation, it was rather a register of anxiety. The greatest fear of such Christian observers of Vedantic reform was that the newly opened minds of Bengal's youth would turn for refuge to the illusory security of this seductive halfway house.

Missionary resentment of the Tattvabodhinī Sabhā as a beguiling alternative to conversion was articulated as a critique of modern Vedānta. We have seen how such critiques typically took the form of questioning the authenticity of this newfangled Vedānta. However, another strategy adopted by the missionaries was to accuse the modern Vedantists of pilfering Christian concepts.[24] Sometimes the charge of stealing was conjoined with the claim that these new Vedantins deviated from the truths of their own Hindu tradition. This is what we find in the following indictment penned by the Rev. James Long:

> The scattered rays of Christianity, impinging on *their* minds, in the general irradiation, they fondly mistake for coruscations from Vedantic sources, and proceed to talk and write as Vedantists never talked or wrote before, of *moral* truth and virtue, of God as an object of *moral* as well as intellectual perception and emotion, and the like. The delusion will not last long. (1848: 352; emphasis in the original)

Naturally, members of the Tattvabodhinī Sabhā saw matters differently. In "Vaidantic Doctrines Vindicated," the author expressed astonishment at the charge that the Sabhā had stolen religious truths, replying simply, "we are . . . at a loss . . . to find out wherein we have dressed ourselves out in the borrowed plumes of Christianity" (quoted in Ghoṣa 1981: 107).

What the missionary scorned as a cowardly halfway measure, the Tattvabodhinī group praised as the very inspiration behind their movement. This is the appropriate context in which to read the report cited at the beginning of this chapter. Its statement of the goals of the Sabhā is an indication of the way the Sabhā understood itself and its mission in 1843, if not in 1839. When we look again at the relevant portion of that passage, we can appreciate how it reflects the perceived need to respond urgently to increased Christian scrutiny:

> It was to have been feared . . . that . . . the great body of the people, unshakled [*sic*] from the fetters of superstition, would either imbibe the pernicious principles of atheism, or embrace the doctrines of Christianity, so successfully promulgated by its teachers—a consummation which the members could not bring themselves to look on with indifference, consistent with their regard for the welfare of their countrymen. It was to counteract influences like these . . . that the Society was originally established.[25]

Without using the missionaries' loaded concept of a halfway house, the authors of this report make no bones about suggesting that their religious teachings provide safe passage between the Scylla of abandoned belief and the Charybdis of conversion.

As such, this passage does seem to confirm David Kopf's observation that one of Debendranath's goals in founding the Sabhā was to provide a culturally meaningful answer for Hindus during an age of potentially disruptive and deracinating learning. However, we need to remember that the above passage dates from a period when the Sabhā had begun to consciously view itself as reacting to the perceived threat of Christian proselytizing. It does not reflect the original inspiration for the Sabhā, which was not one of reaction or anxiety. To begin with, Debendranath sought a way to express his religious identity in light of his exposure to Upanishadic theism. It was only as a consequence of the polarizing Vedānta debates of the 1840s that his association would find itself drawn further in the direction of articulating the superiority of Hinduism.[26] One distant repercussion of this gradual shift in the rhetoric of the modern Vedantists would be the emergence of the triumphalist rhetoric of neo-Vedānta around the end of the nineteenth century, again epitomized in the writings of Swami Vivekananda.[27]

The faith of the modern Vedantists

To read the discourses in *Sabhyadiger vaktṛtā* is to pause briefly and observe a diverse group of Bengali intellectuals attempting to outline the norms that should guide their spiritual and moral lives. We may as well carry on calling them modern Vedantists. However, we need to bear in mind that *Sabhyadiger vaktṛtā* in some respects predates such a category, at least as it was deployed in later Christian polemics. In these short discourses, the emphasis is not on confrontation, polemic, or defense. Ironically, for all that later Christian polemicists attempted to sketch the modern Vedānta of the Tattvabodhinī group as a kind of nihilistic pantheism, the discourses in *Sabhyadiger vaktṛtā* reveal a group of intellectuals endeavoring to articulate something like an ethical monotheism. We may wonder at first why the repeated emphasis on diligent moral effort and devotion to a merciful creator God that is so evident in these discourses did not meet with warmer approval from missionaries. The Vedānta debates from the 1840s show us why.

Clearly, one major reason was that the members of the Sabhā felt no need to embrace the missionaries' savior. Viewing this problem from our present vantage point, during an age in which Christian theologians have begun to address more directly the accommodation of Christianity to indigenous forms of worship, one might ponder whether the missionaries might have fared better had they joined cause with the modern Vedantists rather than chosen to fight them. It is a contrafactual question, but it is nonetheless a rather entertaining one to consider. It is entertaining, in part, because at different moments during the nineteenth century, Christian observers had actually hoped to see prominent modern Vedantists—from Rammohan to Keshub Chunder Sen—convert to Christianity. Such conversions never came to pass. And yet, ironically, Rammohan, Keshub, Vivekananda and other major voices of modern Hinduism evinced great interest in Jesus Christ—admittedly always as a great yogi, prophet, or moral examplar and, of course, typically from the standpoint of Vedānta.[28] To a latter-day Rev. Long, this would no doubt only serve to confirm the Vedantist's pechant for pilfering and self-deception. Yet as I have argued elsewhere, it might also suggest how successfully the followers of Rammohan and Debendranath were able to convert their so-called halfway house into a viable spiritual home (Hatcher 1999).[29] The modern Hindu recognition of Jesus was one early sign of their ability to make room in this home for other religions. Rammohan's Brāhmo Samāj and Debendranath's Tattvabodhinī Sabhā, each in their way, played important roles in this process of religious redefinition.

In chapters 6 and 7, I turn to a different set of problems, namely discussion of critical issues concerning the text of *Sabhyadiger vaktṛtā*, in particular the question of authorship. However, it would not be inappropriate at this point for readers interested in the intellectual and theological issues discussed thus far to turn to the discourses of *Sabhyadiger vaktṛtā*, which is translated in its entirety in chapter 8. There they may find evidence of the distinctive Vedantic reflections and exhortations of earliest members of the Tattvabodhinī Sabhā. If the preceding chapters have been successful, then readers should be able to correlate the concerns and rhetoric of these discourses with such issues as the spiritual awakening and theological aspirations of Debendranath Tagore, the parallel (and eventually shared) mission of redefining Vedānta as initiated by Rammohan Roy, and the striking affinity between the theological vision of the Tattvabodhinī group and the worldly interests of its *bhadralok* members. If this proves possible, then it may be hoped that the present translation of *Sabhyadiger vaktṛtā* will contribute to an increased appreciation for the early expression of distinctive themes within the modern articulation of bourgeois Hinduism.

6

The Text of *Sabhyadiger vaktṛtā* and the Problem of Authorship

In the preceding chapters, my goal has been to put the text of *Sabhyadiger vaktṛtā* in its historical and intellectual context. In the remaining three chapters, I turn to the text itself, which is translated in its entirety in chapter 8. To appreciate the full significance of this remarkable text, we need to combine what we know about the genesis of the Tattvabodhinī Sabhā with a thorough analysis of the text itself. As has already been indicated more than once, this text poses real challenges for present-day readers, none more pressing than the question of who was responsible for delivering each of its twenty-one short discourses. On this question, the text itself is all but silent, whispering to us, as it were, only the enigmatic initials of the men who originally created these discourses.

To address the problem of authorship, then, we must confront the enigma of the initials. Our best hope is to establish a method for drawing some reliable connections between these initials and the names of the particular Tattvabodhinī members who composed the discourses. If we can do that much, we shall have good reason to count ourselves lucky, since the sources for doing so turn out to be scarce and often ambiguous. There are some questions we may never answer in lieu of new sources being uncovered: Who edited the volume? Who chose this system of initials? Why? What concerns might have driven the decision to omit any mention of personal names in the text? To all such questions we can at present offer little more than our best guesses. One set of answers might go like this.

It is likely that Debendranath himself had a leading role, both in choosing to produce such a text and in deciding what it should contain. He was, after all, the guiding force behind the Tattvabodhinī Sabhā, a man who came to be known to his friends and associates as the Maharṣi, or "great seer." Given the way his vision shaped so much of the Sabhā's—and then the Brāhmo Samāj's—history, it is hard to imagine his not being involved in the production of *Sabhyadiger vaktṛtā*. As to why the creators of the text chose the system of initials rather than providing names, I already noted in the introduction that, given the tenor of the times in Calcutta around 1839, discretion may have seemed the wisest course. If the analysis developed in this and the following chapter is correct, the authors of these discourses were in many cases prominent members of *bhadralok* society in Calcutta. Religious reform was not the only front on which they were active; a measure of caution in this arena may have been calculated to buy them the continued security they needed to pursue their interests and occupations, perhaps even their family lives. Of course, as I also noted, it may have been the case that the text was produced largely for consumption by members of the Sabhā itself, and, as such, any need for full names may have seemed—at the time—unnecessary. If the former explanation is the more correct, we can certainly sympathize with the editor's concerns; if the latter, we can only lament that the group hadn't been more conscious of posterity. But of course, that's about all we can say. We are left to find our own ways to reestablish a connection between *Sabhyadiger vaktṛtā* and its various contributors. Such will be the burden of chapters 6 and 7.

Why "discourses"?

Before proceeding to analysis of the text, it may be appropriate to pause here and comment on why I have chosen to call the twenty-one short pieces printed in *Sabhyadiger vaktṛtā* "discourses." After all, while the Bengali term *vaktṛtā* may certainly be translated as "discourse," it is frequently rendered as "speech" or "address" or even "sermon." Since these short texts were delivered before the meetings of the Tattvabodhinī Sabhā, why not refer to them as "speeches" or "addresses"? My reasoning is as follows.

Standard English dictionaries such as the *American Heritage College Dictionary*, which I follow here, tell us that a speech is some form of "talk" or "public address." By contrast, a discourse is defined as something like "a formal written or spoken discussion of a subject." While the etymology of the noun "speech" is not fully clear, "discourse" comes into English usage from Latin via Middle English, where it carried the sense of a "process of reasoning."

Thus the Middle English word *discours* could connote the "process or power of reasoning." It is this combination of (1) a formal discussion of some topic and (2) the process of reasoning that one associates with *vaktṛtā* as that term is used in *Sabhyadiger vaktṛtā*.

The discourses in *Sabhyadiger vaktṛtā* represent formal compositions delivered orally before the regular meetings of a voluntary association. They are not speeches, if by that we think of something like a politician's preferred mode of communication; nor are they public addresses, either, since they appear to have initially been delivered solely for the benefit of a particular private association with a clearly defined membership. That they were later published may change their rhetorical status somewhat, but not the context of their original delivery.

Even though it is tempting to view the Tattvabodhinī Sabhā as a religious organization, this may not, in fact, have been the members' initial understanding. After all, a reformist Vedantic religious society already existed—namely, the Brāhmo Samāj. Members of the Sabhā obviously shared an attraction to Vedantic spirituality, but they may not have thought of their raison d'être as one of worship. As such, it is best not to refer to these *vaktṛtā* as sermons (although this translation of *vaktṛtā* can sometimes be found in connection with other works from this period). Most important, the texts printed in *Sabhyadiger vaktṛtā* are not sermons because, while their topic may be overtly theological and their goal roughly homiletic, they were not delivered by persons charged with the regular responsibility of providing a religious message for a particular ecclesiastical body. It is interesting to note, in this connection, that the word used to refer to the formal addresses delivered by Rāmacandra Vidyāvāgīśa before the Brāhmo Samāj—in his official capacity as preceptor (or *ācārya*) of the Samāj—is not *vaktṛtā* but *vyākhyāna*.[1] The latter carries a stronger sense, in particular, of a careful exposition or explanation of a topic. We could say that *vyākhyāna* refers to something like an authorized "exegesis," whereas *vaktṛtā* conveys something like a "reflection."[2]

As discourses, these *vaktṛtā* are thus formal, oral presentations offered by a diverse range of members on a set of topics that express their collective attempt to articulate the goals of their new society. It is just this sense of a group of individuals attempting to articulate—and to reflect on—what they believe has drawn them together that is captured by that other sense of "discourse,"—namely, the process of reasoning. For a good example of this usage of discourse as a kind of close reasoning aloud, one might think of the opening chapter of Daniel Defoe's eighteenth-century novel and the discourse given to Robinson Crusoe by his father in an attempt to persuade the boy not to take to the sea. That his father's discourse was above all understood to be aimed at rational persuasion is captured in the astonishment of the boy's mother who "wondered how I could think of any such thing, after such a discourse as I had had with my father" (Defoe 1961: 11).

That Defoe's fictional discourse was something that took place between father and son suggests a final important dimension of the term as conveying a kind of shared process of reflection. This is precisely what is preserved for us in the discourses of *Sabhyadiger vaktṛtā*—almost a transcript of the shared reflections of this small group as it met to ponder its newfound fascination for Vedānta. In their individual reflections, the speakers adopt different strategies; they echo, but do not mimic, one another. In other words, these discourses do not so much announce the settled conviction or orthodox doctrine of the Tattvabodhinī Sabhā as they speak of the reasoned and open quest for a coherent and meaningful worldview grounded in the basic truths of Vedānta.

Encountering *Sabhyadiger vaktṛtā*

The original Bengali text of *Sabhyadiger vaktṛtā* was published in Calcutta in 1841 by the Tattvabodhinī Sabhā.[3] At thirty-four octavo pages, it doesn't look like much more than a bound pamphlet. The title page (fig. 6.1) bears as a header the Sanskrit mantra (in Bengali characters) that was adopted widely in Brāhmo publications from this period: *ekamevādvitīyaṃ* (God Is One Only without an Equal).[4] A vignette, or printer's ornament, separates this heading from the title of the text, which appears in a slightly smaller Bengali font below, arranged on two lines. The title itself is altogether unassuming: *Sabhyadiger vaktṛtā* (সভ্যদিগের বক্তৃতা), or "Discourses by Members." Beneath this, separated again by a printer's ornament, appear the words "Tattvabodhinī Sabhā," each again occupying a single line. And beneath these words, once again separated by a small printer's ornament, are two lines of Bengali text. The first describes the text as Part One (*prathama khaṇḍa*).[5] The second provides what appear to be the inclusive dates (in the Śaka era) for the discourses, namely "17 Agrahāyaṇa 1761 to 5 Jyaiṣṭha 1762."[6] A final printer's ornament follows, beneath which we are given the place and date of publication (Kalikātā, 1763 [Śaka]). Running across the foot of the title page are the words (in Bengali), "This society was established on Sunday, the 21st of Āśvina, on the fourteenth day of the dark fortnight in 1761 Śaka."[7]

It is somewhat remarkable that no publisher, printing press, author, or editor is anywhere named in the text. If we examine similar Bengali publications from this period, especially those associated with the Brāhmo movement, we find that they often provide far more information. Thus an 1836 reprint

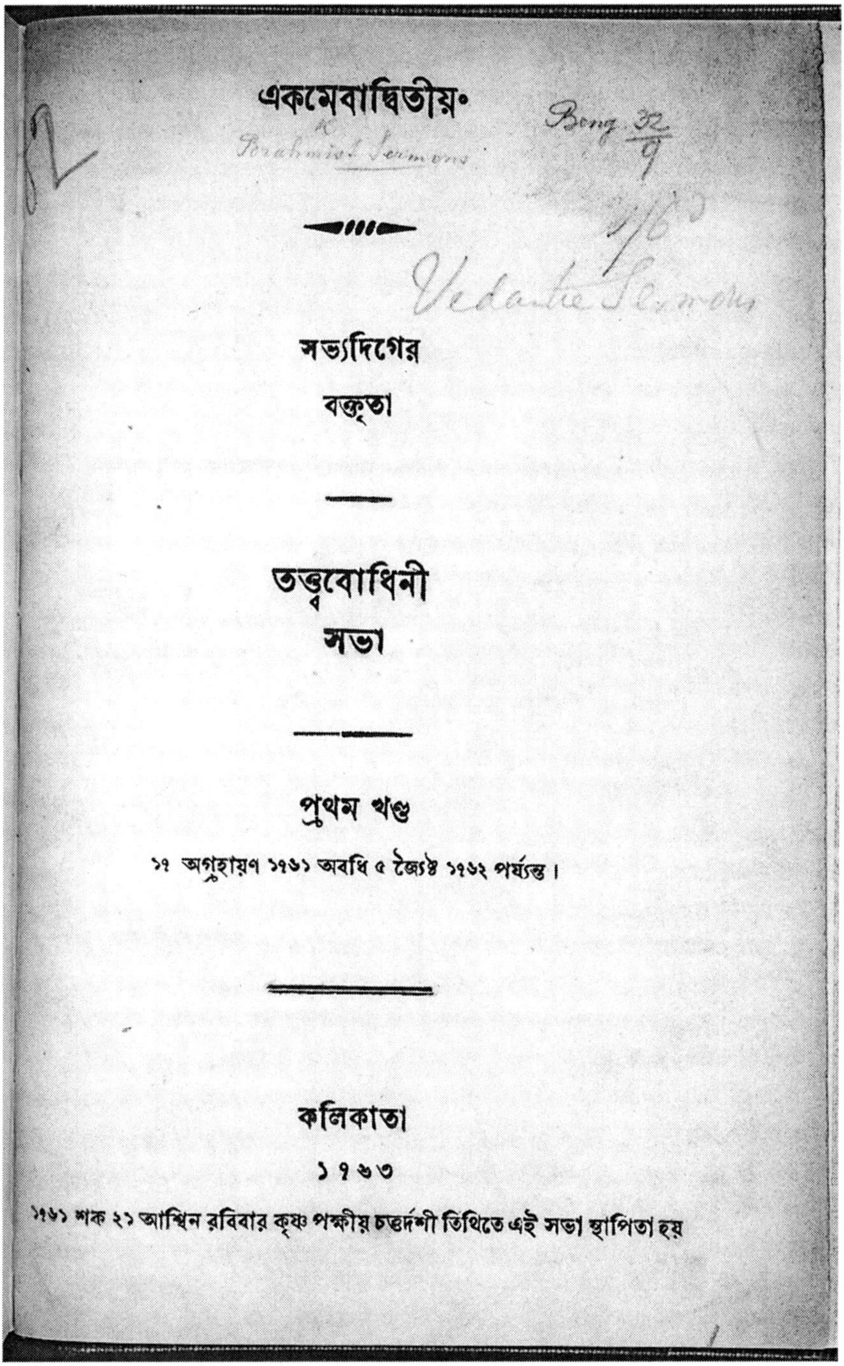

একমেবাদ্বিতীয়ং

সভ্যদিগের

বক্তৃতা

তত্ত্ববোধিনী

সভা

প্রথম খণ্ড

১৭ অগ্রহায়ণ ১৭৬১ অবধি ৫ জ্যৈষ্ঠ ১৭৬২ পর্য্যন্ত ।

কলিকাতা

১৭৬৩

১৭৬১ শক ২১ আশ্বিন রবিবার কৃষ্ণ পক্ষীয় চতুর্দ্দশী তিথিতে এই সভা স্থাপিতা হয়

FIGURE 6.1 Title page of *Sabhyadiger vaktṛtā* (reproduced by permission of the British Library)

edition of Rāmacandra Vidyāvāgīśa's first twelve Brāhmo sermons informs the reader that it was published by the Brāhmo Samāj at the Prajñā Press in Calcutta (Vidyāvāgīśa 1836). Likewise, an English translation of Rāmacandra's second Brāhmo sermon from 1844 includes information that it was published for the Tattvabodhinī Sabhā at the Tattvabodhinī Press (Vidyāvāgīśa 1836). Occasionally such texts indicate not only a publisher and press but also an editor and even information as to where they could be acquired.[8]

Sabhyadiger vaktṛtā is thus rather unusual in this regard. It seems fair to surmise that the Tattvabodhinī Sabhā had not at this time become very sophisticated about its publication program or strategy. The fact that no second part to the work can be found may suggest that what was initially intended to become a longer series of texts never went beyond its initial number. Seen in this light, we should perhaps be thankful that the text provides what information it does. Not only does it identify the scene and dates for the delivery of these discourses at the meetings of the Tattvabodhinī Sabhā, it also documents the date on which the society was created. Additionally, several features help us connect these discourses to broader Brāhmo themes. Such features include the distinctive Brāhmo mantra, *ekamevādvitīyaṃ*, at the top of the title page (which is repeated across the foot of the last page), as well as the Sanskrit phrase that adorns the top of the first page of the text (again in Bengali characters), *Oṃ tat sat*, or "Oṃ, this is the truth."[9]

Apart from these few distinguishing features, there is little else about the book *qua* physical object that merits our attention. However, for all that the object itself is somewhat unremarkable, its contents are of immense interest. Knowing as we do that the Tattvabodhinī Sabhā was established on 6 October 1839, and bearing in mind that the book identifies itself as part one of a collection of discourses for 1839–40, it is in all likelihood the earliest work published by the Tattvabodhinī Sabhā; it is certainly the earliest extant.[10] A cursory glance through the text reveals that it features a range of short discourses of varying length. The initial impression one gets is that a range of different authors are represented in the text. This impression seems to be confirmed by the presence in the right-hand margin, at the end of all but one discourse, of one or two Bengali characters. Though the text provides no guidance as to their meaning, a plausible supposition is that these characters were intended to identify the author of each discourse. Since some of these characters may, even on first inspection, be correlated with the names of major actors within the Sabhā, it is hard for the reader not to feel excited at what the text might therefore contain. For anyone interested in the persistence and transformation of Brāhmo thought in the years following Rammohan's death, the text appears to be a small treasure. Here, so it would seem, we have the chance to read what early—and, most likely, influential—members of the Sabhā were thinking in 1839–40.

It would therefore seem that nothing more is needed than to establish the correlation between these Bengali characters and particular members of the Sabhā in order to realize its potential as a primary source and historical document. But this is easier said than done. While all but one of the discourses appear to be signed with these Bengali initials, this is quite literally all we have to go on. As I have already indicated, *Sabhyadiger vaktṛtā* carries none of the helpful sorts of apparatus we today associate with printed books: no table of contents, no preface, no acknowledgments, no notes, no index, no list of contributors, and no key to its system of abbreviations. There is simply the title page, followed by the twenty-one discourses printed in unnumbered sequence, some of which are dated.

In other words, this text will not give up its secrets easily. It calls for careful analysis. Why do the discourses appear as they do? Who composed them? What role did the composers play in the Tattvabodhinī Sabhā? Thanks to Debendranath's account of the creation of the Tattvabodhinī Sabhā, we do have some information that can guide us as we attempt to make sense of the text. For instance, it will be recalled that Debendranath remarks in his autobiography that anyone attending the early meetings of the Sabhā was permitted to read a discourse before the group, provided it was submitted in advance to the secretary. Furthermore, from his recollection of the third anniversary meeting, it is evident that there were some meetings at which more than one discourse was read. On the basis of this scant information alone, there would seem to be good reason to view *Sabhyadiger vaktṛtā* as a record of the discourses delivered by select members on a range of dates during 1839–40. What more, then, can we say about the text and its creators?

The shape of the text

The title page of *Sabhyadiger vaktṛtā* announces that it contains discourses delivered at meetings held between December 1839 and June 1840. Opening the book, we notice that the first discourse is preceded by the date 17 Agrahāyaṇa 1761 (1 December 1839). This first discourse runs from page one to the middle of page three. The second discourse follows closely upon it, with only three blank lines to suggest a section break; one could be forgiven if one assumed, at first glance, that it was all a single discourse. The second discourse, for which no date is provided, runs to the middle of the fourth page, where it is followed by an obvious section break, indicated by the insertion of a simple decorative printer's ornament. After this follows the third discourse, which is immediately preceded by the date 24 Agrahāyaṇa 1761 (8 December 1839)—that is, one week after the first discourse. The third discourse is rather long, running to the middle of page eight. There it is followed by a fourth discourse, again undated and only demarcated from the third by the addition of some blank lines. The fourth discourse seems scarcely to warrant the name, since it concludes before the bottom of page eight. As occurred after the second discourse, a section break is inserted after it, clearly marked with the same printer's ornament. The fifth discourse follows, preceded by the date 1 Pouṣa 1761 (15 December 1839).

A clear pattern emerges, suggesting that the text is arranged chronologically according to the dates of the Sabhā's weekly Sunday meetings. Judging from the fact that the first date is followed by two discourses, as is the second, it would further seem that the editors have included after each date all discourses—or perhaps only the most noteworthy?—given on that day. For the remainder of the text, there are typically two discourses per day, with the only exceptions being 12 Phālguṇa, 21 Māgha, and 5 Jyaiṣṭha (the last falling in the new year, 1762 Śaka). For each of these dates, only one discourse is printed.

Only two curiosities remain. First, for some reason, the single discourse for 21 Māgha has been inserted between the discourses for 12 and 19 Phālguṇa. If the book is arranged in chronological order, one would have expected any discourses for Māgha (the tenth month in the Bengali calendar) to have been printed before those from Phālguṇa (the eleventh month; for the Bengali calendar, see table 6.1). It is unclear why this break in chronology occurs. It could simply be due to an error in typesetting. In any case, since it does not appear to correspond to any alternative organizational scheme, it seems safe to retain our initial assumption that the organization of the discourses is meant to reflect the progress of meetings throughout the year.

The second curiosity is that the book does not catalogue an entire calendrical year, though it clearly covers slighty more than an obvious half-year period. The text begins in Agrahāyaṇa (the eighth month in the Bengali calendar) and runs through Jyaiṣṭha (the second month of the new year), but it contains no discourses for the months of Caitra (the twelfth month of 1761 Śaka) and Vaiśākha (the first month of 1762 Śaka). Nor is there any indication why this is so. One possibility is that there may have been weeks, even months, during which no discourses were delivered at meetings. Could it even be that meetings were sometimes canceled? Our records for the Sabhā are not com-

TABLE 6.1. The Bengali Calendar

Bengali month	English equivalent
Vaiśākha	April–May[a]
Jyaiṣṭha	May–June
Āṣāḍha	June–July
Śrāvaṇa	July–August
Bhādra	August–September
Āśvina	September–October
Kārtika	October–November
Agrahāyaṇa	November–December
Pouṣa	December–January
Māgha	January–February
Phālguṇa	February–March
Caitra	March–April

Note. Sabhyadiger vaktṛtā provides all dates according to the Śaka Era. The Common Era equivalent may be calculated by adding 78 years (e.g., 1761 Śaka + 78 = 1839 CE). Months conform to the Bengali calendar.

a. The Bengali new year typically commences around the fourteenth or fifteenth of April.

plete enough to allow us to answer such questions, although we do recall that Debendranath was worried about attendence during the first two years. Nevertheless, these two curiosities don't fundamentally impede our ability to understand the discourses. If anything, in lieu of definite information on the editorial choices, we must simply note them and move on. We can at least feel confident about the overall chronological structure of *Sabhyadiger vaktṛtā* and see in it a faithful, if perhaps partial, record of discourses delivered in the first year of the Tattvabodhinī Sabhā.

This leaves us to confront the single greatest puzzle presented by *Sabhyadiger vaktṛtā*: deducing authorship from the minimal information provided by the system of initials used in the text. As I have indicated, each discourse (with one exception) appears to have been "signed" by its author in the right-hand margin using a Bengali character (or, in some cases, two characters). The characters are in the same type font and size as the text and are in no way highlighted. They are, in fact, easy to miss at first glance. However, recognizing these characters is essential to appreciating the significance of this unpretentious little book. Not only does it help us understand why the text is divided into sections as it is, it allows us to go further and identify the authors of these discourses. And it turns out that several of the authors were not just central players in the early Brāhmo movement but were influential figures in the world of nineteenth-century Bengali religion, literature, and social reform.

As I indicate in the introduction, my earliest efforts to establish authorship in *Sabhyadiger vaktṛtā* were focused on just two of its discourses. These two discourses, I originally argued, were written by the well-known Sanskrit pandit and social reformer, Īśvaracandra Vidyāsāgara (for example, Hatcher 1992 and 1996(a)). Up to that point, as far as I have been able to determine, no one even knew of the existence of *Sabhyadiger vaktṛtā*. The attribution of these two discourses to Vidyāsāgara was thus unprecedented and a minor boon to all those interested in the life and work of this complex figure. I remain hopeful that in time these discourses will be included among Vidyāsāgara's collected works (which are regularly reprinted in India and widely available even today).

In the meantime, by now presenting for the first time the entirety of *Sabhyadiger vaktṛtā* in translation, I hope not simply to call renewed attention to my earlier argument but to, in fact, extend it, by attempting to identify the remaining authors represented in *Sabhyadiger vaktṛtā*. As I hope this and chapter 7 will show, in some cases particular authors can be identified with the same degree of certainty as in the case of Vidyāsāgara. However, in other cases, it has to be admitted that definitive evidence is lacking. While it is possible to make reasoned conjectures about authorship, in these few cases we just do not have enough information to reach a firm conclusion. Nevertheless, as will become clear in chapter 7, we can identify the authors of perhaps eighteen of the twenty-one discourses in *Sabhyadiger vaktṛtā*.

The problem of authorship

One of the things that strikes a reader of *Sabhyadiger vaktṛtā* is that it mentions no names, at least none we recognize from history. Apart from passing references to mythic characters like Rama, Yudhiṣṭhira, Duryodhana, and Śaunaka; a few stock characters like heavenly nymphs; and the obligatory mention of ignorant people, wise men, and merchants, the text names no one. The central character is no doubt the Supreme Lord, but as for the names of his *bhadralok* worshipers, the text says nothing. Most frustrating for the historian, the text provides no clearcut information regarding the identity of its several contributors. In rare cases like Discourse Three and Discourse Sixteen, we notice the use of the first-person singular, but we are offered no name to identify the speaker, only a pronoun.[11] In fact, beyond the declaration on the title page that the work was published in Calcutta by the Tattvabodhinī Sabhā in 1843, there are no historical markers to be found in the text. Absent the title page, it seems as if it could have been written almost anywhere, anytime (although the fact of its being a printed text composed in a kind of Sanskritic Bengali with now-archaic verb forms would tend to place it in nineteenth-century Bengal). All of this only adds to the enigmatic quality of the text. Nevertheless, we can find evidence to help us identify the authors represented in the text. That evidence is primarily of two kinds: textual and contextual.

Clearly, the most important textual clue we have—without a doubt, the most intriguing aspect of *Sabhyadiger vaktṛtā*—is the system of initials it employs. Our first goal, therefore, should be to understand the role of these initials in the text. Table 6.2 provides a list of the twenty-one discourses, along with their dates and the corresponding initials found after each discourse. I have taken the liberty of numbering the discourses to make reference to the text more convenient. As is evident from this list, there are several cases where the same initial has been assigned to more than one discourse. The frequency with which each set of initials occurs is indicated in Table 6.3.

To proceed toward the goal of identifying the authors of these discourses, we need to make a series of suppositions, which can then be explored and tested in more detail. These suppositions are:

TABLE 6.2. The discourses of *Sabhyadiger vaktṛtā* with corresponding initials of authors

Discourse	Date	Bengali initial	English equivalent
One	1 December 1839	শ	Ś
Two	1 December 1839	গ	G
Three	8 December 1839	দ	D
Four	8 December 1839	চ	C
Five	15 December 1839	চ	C
Six	15 December 1839	চ গ	C G
Seven	22 December 1839	শ	Ś
Eight	22 December 1839	ভ	Bh
Nine	29 December 1839	শ	Ś
Ten	29 December 1839	র গ	R G
Eleven	5 January 1840	দ	D
Twelve	5 January 1840	অ	A
Thirteen	12 January 1840	ঈ	Ī
Fourteen	12 January 1840	র	R
Fifteen	26 January 1840	দ	D
Sixteen	26 January 1840	ঈ গ	Ī G
Seventeen	23 February 1840[a]	দ	D
Eighteen	2 February 1840	ঈ	Ī
Nineteen	1 March 1840	র	R
Twenty	1 March 1840	n/a[b]	n/a[b]
Twenty-one	17 May 1840	দ	D

a. It is unclear why Discourse Seventeen appears out of chronological sequence.

b. No initial appears after Discourse Twenty.

TABLE 6.3. Frequency of initials in *Sabhyadiger Vaktṛtā*

Initial	Frequency
D	5 discourses
Ś	3 discourses
C	2 discourses
Ī	2 discourses
R	2 discourses
G	1 discourse
A	1 discourse
C G	1 discourse
Bh	1 discourse
R G	1 discourse
Ī G	1 discourse
Unsigned	1 discourse

1. The Bengali characters at the end of all but one discourse should be understood as initials.
2. These initials should be understood as the first letter of an author's name, but not necessarily the first syllable. That is, the Bengali character দ is meant to stand for "D," not "Da," as it would ordinarily be read.
3. These initials should be taken as a shorthand reference to the author's first, or given, name and not to his surname (e.g., Gupta) or title (e.g., Vidyāsāgara). Thus Rāmacandra Vidyāvāgīśa would be referred to as "Rāmacandra," not "Vidyāvāgīśa." His initial would therefore be "R."
4. In cases where we encounter two initials, we have to suppose that the second initial in the pair was added in order to differentiate the author from someone already more commonly associated with the first initial. Thus if "R" were used to refer to Rāmacandra Vidyāvāgīśa, then "R G" must have been created to identify some other individual, whose surname or title begins with the letter "G."[12]

Our first supposition is one that has been invoked several times already in this text. And yet we should test it. Can we be sure that the Bengali characters that follow each discourse are in fact meant to be understood as the initials of the authors? In the absence of any statement to this effect in *Sabhyadiger vaktṛtā,* is there any way to show that such a convention might have been employed in this work?

In nineteenth-century English periodicals the use of initials, as well as the use of pseudonyms, was commonplace. It is not hard to demonstrate that this convention made its way to Calcutta early in the nineteenth century. For instance, in 1820, the Bengal Auxiliary Missionary Society in Calcutta published *A Selection of Hymns for the Use of Native Places of Worship.*[13] Adjacent to the Bengali hymns, in the right-hand margin, are a set of initials indicating a composer for most of the songs.[14] Thus the hymns numbered two to six are attributed to "P. M.," while hymns seven to eleven are attributed to "C. M." This convention is repeated in another book of Christian hymns published by the Baptist Mission Press in Calcutta in 1843, entitled *Dharma gītā.*[15]

Dharma gītā is particularly helpful for two reasons: first, since it was published in 1843, it is nearly contemporaneous with *Sabhyadiger vaktṛtā;* second, it features hymns by two authors—one European, the other native—each of whom is identified in an unambiguous fashion. The European composer was George Pearce, whose songs are signed with the initials "G. P." The native Christian is identified as Rāmakṛṣṇa Kavirāja. Interestingly, the first song in the collection composed by Rāmakṛṣṇa is in fact signed (in Bengali script) "Rāmakṛṣṇa kṛta," which is to say "composed by Rāmakṛṣṇa." However, the very next song, which was also composed by Rāmakṛṣṇa, is signed simply র ক. Clearly this stands for the initials "R. K."

That such a convention was not restricted to Christian publications in Calcutta is demonstrated by an examination of the periodical literature of the time and of the early literature of the Brāhmos themselves. In the case of periodicals, Henry Louis Vivian Derozio, notorious mentor of the rebellious Young Bengal faction, started a journal known as the *Kaleidoscope* in 1829, in the first number of which he printed a poem dedicated to his pupils.[16] The poem is signed with the initial "D." *Kaleidoscope* actually printed a number of letters to the editor during 1829 and 1830 that are signed with initials. A contemporaneous periodical, the *Reformer,* also ran letters over simple sets of initials.[17]

Among the Brāhmo literature from this same period, there is an 1828 edition of Brāhmo hymns entitled *Brāhmasaṅgīta.* This collection includes several hymns, which are identified by a system of initials. In their revision of Sophia Dobson Collet's classic study of Rammohan, Biswas and Ganguly show that the initials "Ni. Gho." (নি ঘো)—which appear in the 1828 edition of *Brāhmasaṅgīta*—were meant to stand for Nilmani Ghosh (Collet 1988: 231n23).[18]

Such evidence suggests that (1) the use of initials had become fairly commonplace in Calcutta among a range of constituencies by the third and fourth decades of the nineteenth century; (2) this convention was shared by Christians, rationalists, and Brāhmos alike; and (3) this system of initials could be used for Bengali, as well as for English, names.

And yet things aren't entirely straightforward. Can we say with certainty how such initials were meant to operate in the case of Bengali names? For instance, in the second supposition above, I suggest that the initials used in *Sabhyadiger vaktṛtā* are meant to refer to the first letter rather than the first syllable of the author's name. What do I mean by making this distinction, and why is it important? Briefly, Bengali (like Sanskrit) is read syllabically; when abbreviating a word, it would be typical to select the first syllable, rather than the first letter. Thus the title Muṇḍaka would be abbreviated "Mu" (মু).[19] What's more, because consonants are always understood (in both Bengali and Sanskrit) to be followed by an inherent short-a vowel unless other vowel marks are added, simply writing ম would communicate to a Bengali reader neither "M" nor "Mu," but "Ma."[20] This explains why the additional vowel sign is added to distinguish "Mu" from "Ma" in the above example.

Learning these rules as they apply to languages like Bengali may seem confusing enough, but when one considers how they may have intersected with accepted English-language customs for abbreviating names, the problems are compounded. There seems, in fact, to have been little uniformity during this period regarding the treatment of initials based on Bengali names. If anything, the rules enunciated above were broken as often as they were applied. For instance, when looking at works like *Dharma gīta*, *Brāhmasaṅgīta*, and *Sabhyadiger vaktṛtā*, we notice that different conventions have apparently been employed for the creation and use of initials. Therefore, understanding what may have been going through the minds of particular Bengali editors will be of great help in decoding the system of initials used in *Sabhyadiger vaktṛtā*.

In *Dharma gīta*, we notice that "Rāmakṛṣṇa Kavirāja" is rendered as র ক. We notice that both first and last names are accounted for, but, interestingly, the appropriate vowel signs in Bengali have not been applied. In Bengali, the name "Rāmakṛṣṇa" begins with the syllable Rā (রা), not Ra (র). Why wasn't the former syllable chosen for the first initial? There are two possible explanations. On the one hand, it could be that among non-Bengali Christians, Rāmakṛṣṇa was known by an anglicized version of his name, such as Ramakrishna (in which the long vowel sign has been dropped). On the other hand, it could be that the editors of this text operated with what we might call an English-language view of initials, whereby the first initial for either "Rāmakṛṣṇa" or "Ramakrishna" (i.e., without diacritical marks) would be "R." When rendering Rāmakṛṣṇa's initials in Bengali, they either ignored, or did not worry about, the vowels. This would suggest, incidentally, that while their choice for abbreviating "Kavirāja," (ক), appears to be correct from a Bengali standpoint (i.e., the syllable "Ka" includes the Bengali inherent short-a vowel), it may not have been intended to stand for "Ka" at all. It may instead have been intended to signify only the first letter of the last name, namely "K." Such nuances of orthography are of immense importance for analyzing *Sabhyadiger vaktṛtā*, as we shall see.

The editors of *Brāhmasaṅgīta*, by contrast, have been somewhat more accurate in choosing their scheme of initials. To take the example from Collet, the Bengali syllables "Ni Gho" are a close approximation of the first syllables of the Bengali name, Nilmani Ghosh. Only close, though, because again they seem to presume familiarity with an Anglicized form of the name (as just given here) and not its correct Bengali form.[21] If one were one to work from the latter, the first initial should technically be rendered "Nī" (নী), rather than "Ni" (নি), since the name is properly Nīlamaṇi.

One begins to see the potential for confusion, with not just two languages in play but with multiple understandings (or misunderstandings) of transliteration coming into conflict. No doubt in English correspondence, Nilmani Ghosh would have been the accepted form to use, rather than Nīlamaṇi Ghoṣa; just as Rāmamohana Rāya came to be known among English-language readers at a very early date as Rammohan Roy (or Rammohun Roy). But if one had to provide initials for such men in Bengali, what choice would one make? Interestingly, when confronting this problem, *Brāhmasaṅgīta* applies no consistent method. While Nilmani's name is rendered "Ni. Gho.," Rammohan's name is rendered in greater faithfulness to the Bengali: "Rā. Mo. Rā."[22]

In view of these concerns, when reading *Sabhyadiger vaktṛtā*—which predominantly employs only single Bengali characters as initials—it seems best not to read the Bengali initials as orthographically accurate transliterations of the first syllable of the authors' names. It seems likely that these Bengali initials referred instead to the Anglicized version of names then becoming popular among English-educated Calcuttans. The best example of this from *Sabhyadiger vaktṛtā* would be the initial দ, which (as demonstrated in chapter 7) is used to stand for the first initial of the Anglicized name, Debendranath Tagore—the widely accepted form of his name since that time.[23]

Within *Sabhyadiger vaktṛtā* there are four instances in which the first syllable of a name is a vowel rather than a consonant. The initial "Ī" is used twice, the initial "A" is used once, and the pair of initials "Ī G" is used once. In the first instance, the editors have without a doubt chosen the long-i character to refer to a name beginning in long-i, or Ī (ঈ); the same is no doubt true for the first initial in the pair "Ī G."[24] Clearly, there would be little sense in using the long-i vowel to abbreviate a name that began in a short-i.

For the initial "A" we need to be careful. Even though it appears in the text as the Bengali short-a vowel (অ), it could conceivably refer either to a Bengali name that in fact begins with a short-a or (in light of our earlier conclusions) to an anglicized version of a Bengali name that really begins in a long-a vowel (आ)—for instance, abbreviating from the anglicized Anandakrishna, rather than the Bengali Ānandakṛṣṇa. Contextual evidence will be our best guide in finally deciding the referent for this particular initial.

The single-vowel initials found in *Sabhyadiger vaktṛtā* also suggest another pattern in the text. Looking at the list of discourses above, we notice that out of twenty-one discourses, only three are identified using a pair of initials (C G, R G, and Ī G). In all other cases (save for the single unsigned discourse), only a single initial is used. Our supposition is that single initials were used in all cases where there was no concern about ambiguity; perhaps these authors were better known or more active in the Sabhā? Whatever the reason, it must be the case that these single initials refer to an author's given name, like Debendranath, rather than the surname. In the three cases where pairs of initials are employed, the second initial must therefore refer to the author's family name or title (as in the case of a pandit) as a further marker of identity. Again, such pairs appear to have been used only in the few cases where ambiguity might otherwise have resulted.[25]

We are now in a position to notice some rather important correlations. Among the most prominent early members of the Tattvabodhinī Sabhā were Debendranath Tagore, Rāmacandra Vidyāvāgīśa, Akṣayakumāra Datta, and Īśvaracandra Vidyāsāgara. Readers will notice that the Bengali initials D, R, A, and Ī appear in the list of discourses above. The very fact that the most discourses in the collection are attributed to D would seem to lend immediate credence to the equation between D and Debendranath, the founder of the association. Likewise, it is tempting to conclude immediately that the intial Ī refers to Īśvaracandra Vidyāsāgara, while Ī G must refer to some other member whose first name began with the same initial.

However, it would be premature to make these claims. We need to find supporting evidence to back up our hypotheses regarding the system of initials. Our best assurance that the aforementioned suppositions are correct is provided when we turn to both internal evidence of style and terminology, as well as to other contextual evidence we can glean from contemporary sources. In a sense, we have already begun to invoke contextual evidence, since we have connected the initials used in the text to the names of certain prominent individuals we know were active in the early Sabhā. However, we need more evidence if we are to conclusively identify the authors of its various discourses. The task in chapter 7 is to provide that evidence.

7

Who Wrote These Discourses?

In chapter 6, I outline an approach for determining authorship of the discourses in *Sabhyadiger vaktṛtā* using as a starting point the enigmatic system of initials employed in the text. By the end of the chapter, we found ourselves in a position to venture some reasoned guesses as to the identity of several of the authors. But to be able to make an attribution of authorship with any real confidence, it is necessary to back up these preliminary guesses with more convincing evidence. In this regard, the best bet for identifying the authors of these discourses is to combine our knowledge of the text itself with a wider range of contextual evidence. There are a variety of places where we might search for clues—for instance, information garnered from membership rosters; other publications of the Sabhā; memoirs and histories of the Brāhmo movement; and reports from other contemporary published sources, be they books, pamphlets, or periodicals. As it turns out, when we examine these supporting materials, we can arrive at rather convincing (if perhaps never absolutely conclusive) attributions for several of the discourses in *Sabhyadiger vaktṛtā*.[1] To be sure, solving the problem of authorship is a cumbersome and uncertain process, and in the end there may well be some who will disagree with my conclusions. Nevertheless, I remain confident that the methods proposed here for establishing authorship are sound, and that if I am unable to achieve complete success in this endeavor, it is only because I currently lack sufficient evidence.

Some conjectures in advance

Because the problem of authorship is a complex one to address, it may help readers to have some sense of the big picture before I plunge into details. Toward that end, I list here in brief the conclusions regarding authorship I hope to substantiate after a thorough review of available evidence. My intention is not to suggest that we merely need to fit what evidence we can find to a set of preconceived conclusions. Rather, at this point, I simply want readers to be able to see in advance what the present inquiry can hope to reveal. Furthermore, it is possible that some readers will have only a passing interest in the details of this investigation. For those readers, I have summarized the relevant information on authorship in Table 7.1.

The purpose of this chapter is to demonstrate with as much certainty as possible the authorship of the discourses in *Sabhyadiger vaktṛtā*. While I cannot always establish authorship with absolute certainty, in many cases I can be very confident about these attributions. Unfortunately, in some cases, attributions must remain tentative; in others I simply have to refrain from drawing any conclusions whatsoever. Table 7.2 arranges data on the discourses according to the degree of certainty we have regarding authorship. For simplicity's sake, it may be best to address the evidence regarding each initial in the order listed in the table, beginning with A and working our way through G (for reasons that will become clear, I consider the single unsigned discourse in connection with

TABLE 7.1. List of authors in *Sabhyadiger vaktṛtā*

Initial: English/Bengali	Author	Discourse number(s)
A / অ	Akṣayakumāra Datta	12, 20[a]
Bh / ভ	Identity uncertain[b]	8
C / চ	Candrasekhar Deb	4, 5
C G / চ গ	Identity uncertain[b]	6
D / দ	Debendranath Tagore	3, 11, 15, 17, 21
G / গ	Identity uncertain[b]	2
Ī / ঈ	Īśvaracandra Vidyāsāgara	13, 18
Ī G / ঈ গ	Īśvaracandra Gupta	16
R / র	Rāmacandra Vidyāvāgīśa	14, 19
R G / র গ	Ramgopal Ghosh	10
Ś / শ	Śyāmacaraṇa Mukhopādhyāya	1, 7, 9

Note: For discussion of the system of initials and evidence supporting the attribution of authorship, see chapters 6 and 7.

a. Evidence is provided in chapter 7 to demonstrate that Discourse Twenty, the single unsigned discourse in *Sabhyadiger vaktṛtā*, was written by Akṣayakumāra Datta.

b. Evidence is lacking to conclusively identify the authors of these discourses.

TABLE 7.2. Attribution of authorship in *Sabhyadiger vaktṛtā*, arranged by degree of certainty

Initial	Author	Discourse
Initials for which attribution is certain		
A	Akṣayakumāra Datta	12
D	Debendranath Tagore	3, 11, 15, 17, 21
Ī	Īśvaracandra Vidyāsāgara	13, 18
Ī G	Īśvaracandra Gupta	16
R	Rāmacandra Vidyāvāgīśa	14, 19
Unsigned	Akṣayakumāra Datta	20
Initials for which attribution is relatively certain		
Ś	Śyāmacaraṇa Mukhopādhyāya	1, 7, 9
C	Candrasekhar Deb	4, 5
R G	Ramgopal Ghosh	10
Initials for which attribution remains uncertain		
Bh	No author identified	8
C G	No author identified	6
G	No author identified	2

the initial A). Neither the same amount nor the same types of evidence is available for every case and, as I have indicated, it is entirely possible that I have overlooked or failed to uncover other kinds of evidence that could aid in this process. Nevertheless, by examining the evidence we have for each set of initials, I hope both to keep the investigation clearly organized and to make the conclusions accessible to those readers who may wish to explore the case of a particular author.

Initials for which attribution is definitive

A (also Unsigned) = Akṣayakumāra Datta

Akṣayakumāra Datta (1820–86; anglicized variously as Aksaykumar Datta, Akkhoy Kumar Dutt, Okhoy Dutta) was nineteen when Debendranath founded the Tattvabodhinī Sabhā.[2] He joined the Sabhā early on and very quickly became a key promoter of its work, taking on several important roles. He was selected to teach geography and science at the Tattvabodhinī Pāṭhaśālā, a primary school founded by the Sabhā in 1840. Later on, Debendranath chose him to serve as editor of the *Tattvabodhinī Patrikā*, the association's journal, which first appeared in 1843. He would hold this post for twelve years. While serving as editor, Akṣayakumāra wrote several important works on natural theology and religion, to which I refer below.[3] Through the *Patrikā*, his writings gained widespread distribution and earned him a prominent place among mid-century Bengali intellectuals.

Akṣayakumāra's dedication to the rational scrutiny of religion and the natural world contributed a special flavor to the publications of the Sabhā. As the Sabhā began to move more vigorously into journalism and public confrontation with Christian missionaries in the early 1840s, Akṣayakumāra would have been the third major voice of the Sabhā alongside Debendranath and Rāmacandra.[4] And his voice is distinctive. Rāmacandra quotes scripture and argues like a pandit, Debendranath sermonizes on morality and the love of God, but Akṣayakumāra always proceeds from a position of scientific empiricism and rational argument. Scriptural proof texts rarely play a part in his writing, and there is little room for emotion. At one point in his autobiography, Debendranath frankly noted that the difference between himself and Akṣayakumāra in this regard was like that between heaven and earth (Tagore 1980: 23).

Somewhat surprisingly, the place to begin in establishing Akṣayakumāra's authorship is with Discourse Twenty, the only unsigned discourse in *Sabhyadiger vaktṛtā*. We begin here, because this discourse happens to have been reprinted in the ninth number of the *Tattvabodhinī Patrikā* for 1844 under the initial "A" (অ).[5] If we can establish that this *Tattvabodhinī Patrikā* essay was composed by Akṣayakumāra, we will have also established the authorship of Discourse Twenty and provided a reference point from which to consider the other "A" discourse. As it turns out, however, the pathway to this proof is a bit roundabout. In fact, we need to back up from the 1844 "A" essay to examine some earlier essays from *Tattvabodhinī Patrikā*.

As we know, the first issue of *Tattvabodhinī Patrikā* appeared in the fall of 1843 (1765 Śaka). At that time, the new journal was under Akṣayakumāra's editorial guidance. Looking over the earliest issues of the journal, we notice there are essays in the fourth and fifth numbers, each from 1843 (for the months of Agrahāyaṇa and Pouṣa), that are signed unambiguously with the initials "A. Ku. D." (অ.কু .দ.; punctuation in original). There are another two essays from the seventh and ninth numbers from 1844 (for the months of Phālguṇa and Vaiśākha) that are signed with the initial "A" (অ).

That Akṣayakumāra might have contributed to the journal so frequently is hardly surprising, given the fact that he was then serving as editor. As for the inconsistency in the system of initials, this should come as no surprise in light of the discussion in chapter 6, where we found that there was wide variability at this time in the use of initials in Bengali publications. In any case, it should be irrefutable that the two essays signed with the set of three initials were written by Akṣayakumāra Datta. Even apart from the matter of the distinctive initials, these two "A. Ku. D." essays also clearly betray Akṣayakumāra's characteristic preference for rational argumentation and a form of evidential theology reminiscent of William Paley.[6] What, then, of the two "A" essays?[7]

The essay from the seventh number of *Tattvabodhinī Patrikā*, published early in 1844, takes issue with Hindu norms of renunciation, making the case that humans have not been created to live in isolation (as a classical Hindu renouncer might), but in social communities.[8] The essay opens with a powerful image. Assuming the absolute necessity of society for human success, the author asks whether there is any chance that a newborn child could survive if torn from its mother's lap and abandoned in the wilderness. Quite apart from the fact that it is signed with the initial "A," this essay is written in Akṣayakumāra's distinctive style. It also foregrounds Akṣayakumāra's preference for natural theology, which is marshaled here to explain how social interaction is part of God's purpose.[9]

The fourth and final essay, from the ninth number of *Tattvabodhinī Patrikā* for 1844, is the same as the single unsigned discourse found in *Sabhyadiger vaktṛtā* (Discourse Twenty). If we are correct in assigning the "A" essay from the seventh number to Akṣayakumāra, then there seems little reason to doubt his authorship of this fourth essay and therefore of the unsigned Discourse Twenty. We are further reassured about this conclusion when we note that the content of this essay remains consistent with Akṣayakumāra's style and theological concerns. A good example is the author's concern to advocate service to others (*paropakāra*), a characteristic theme. This theme is made apparent in such passages as the following: "The omniscient Lord of All has created beautiful laws to encourage us to help one another. In fact, if you think about it, we actually help others when we are diligent about helping ourselves" (*Sabhyadiger vaktṛtā*, Discourse Twenty).

This only leaves us with one question: Why was this single discourse of all the discourses in *Sabhyadiger vaktṛtā* not signed? We will no doubt never know the answer to this question, but once again, considering how much variation there was in the systems of abbreviation employed in early Tattvabodhinī publications, and taking into consideration the fact that the Sabhā was new to the business of publishing, it would hardly be surprising to find evidence of an occasional inconsistency, error, or change in policy regarding attribution. It is also possible that at the time *Sabhyadiger vaktṛtā* was published, no one could recall who had delivered Discourse Twenty. Since we know nothing of the circumstances behind the decision to publish *Sabhyadiger vaktṛtā*, it is impossible to know who oversaw the project or how basic decisions were made about the overall content, organization, or length. We might, in fact, ask whether, by republishing this discourse over the initial "A" in the *Patrikā* for 1844, Akṣayakumāra wasn't in fact attempting to set the record straight.

Be that as it may, it is by beginning with the unsigned Discourse Twenty that we are ironically, but happily, able to triangulate on Akṣayakumāra's identity as an author. What we have thus learned is of immense help when examining the one essay in *Sabhyadiger vaktṛtā* that is signed "A" (অ, Discourse Twelve). It is a short piece, and, on first glance, it might not appear to be the work of Akṣayakumāra, especially since it employs the decidedly more Vedantic-sounding language of "error" and "self-knowledge," while also refering to the Self who is "consciousness and bliss." These are not themes we would typically associate with Akṣayakumāra, especially judging from his later *Tattvabodhinī Patrikā* essays, which tend to trade more in rationalist theology than Vedantic idioms.[10] Nevertheless, even in this discourse we do find the traces of his style and overall concerns.

For instance, Akṣayakumāra's familiar appeal to rational understanding is not entirely absent from Discourse Twelve. That is, the kind of "error" Akṣayakumāra refers to in this essay is less the metaphysical delusion of Vedānta than it is the basic human failure to recognize that the body is not permanent. There is no need to call on scripture to reach this conclusion; observation alone will do. As he argues, all reasonable people will agree that nature is fickle and inconstant. Akṣayakumāra's unique prose style is also felt in the concrete and suggestive analogy he makes between flowers blooming in a garden and the transient nature of human existence. We might note that in the single unsigned discourse, he also employs an analogy from the natural world, conjuring up a busy bee gathering pollen in a garden. At a more textual level, we notice two things. First, both this discourse and the unsigned Discourse Twenty employ the striking and rather distinctive lament, "alas" (*hāy*). Second, both discourses conclude with sentences beginning with the word "therefore" (*ataeva*). If we take this word to be the trademark sign of a rationalist (something like "QED"), it would certainly be consistent with Akṣayakumāra's intellectual disposition. Gathering up such clues, then, it seems there are very good grounds for assigning Discourse Twelve, along with Discourse Twenty, to Akṣayakumāra.[11]

D = Debendranath Tagore

Of the twenty-one discourses in *Sabhyadiger vaktṛtā*, five are signed with the initial "D" (দ). It is the greatest number by a single author, and it would make sense prima facie that these "D" essays were composed by the founder of the organization, Debendranath Tagore. Debendranath went on to take an active role promoting the Sabhā and the broader Brāhmo movement for decades to come. He went on to craft the official Brāhmo "scripture" (Tagore 1975), delivered dozens of discourses and sermons on theism (Tagore 1965), commented on the Upaniṣads (Tagore 1861), and pondered the course of Brāhmoism from its inception under Rammohan (Tagore 1957). Would it surprise us to find that he delivered a significant number of the first discourses before the Sabhā?

Even so, we should seek more definitive reasons for assigning these discourses to him. What follows in this section is a brief review of the evidence supporting the attribution of these "D" essays to Debendranath. We are greatly assisted in this task by the fact that the Indian Institute Library in the Bodleian Library at Oxford University contains a bound set of the *Tattvabodhinī Patrikā* for the years 1843 to 1878. On the inside cover of each bound volume appears a plate that reads: "Presented by Debendra Nath Tagore, June 10th, 1881."[12] Most fascinating of all, in this bound series there are penciled marginal annotations in the form of the Roman initials "DT." These would appear to indicate which of the many unsigned articles in the journal were written by Debendranath. While there is no way to say for certain whose annotations these are, they were most likely made by Debendranath himself, either out of courtesy or vanity. After all, who other than Debendranath would have been able (and willing) to go through the many hundreds of pages of the *Patrikā* and systematically write "DT" in the margin? What we have, then, in the Bodleian edition of the *Tattvabodhinī Patrikā*, are even more initials! But, these initials can certainly help us pin down the authorship of the "D" discourses from *Sabhyadiger vaktṛtā*.

If one begins to read serially through the early issues of *Tattvabodhinī Patrikā*, one finds that four of the five "D" discourses from *Sabhyadiger vaktṛtā* were subsequently reprinted in the journal (which, it will be recalled, began to appear in 1843). Looking at the Bodleian set of the *Tattvabodhinī Patrikā*, one also notices that in all four cases the initials "DT" have been penciled in the margins. The correspondence between the use of "D" to identify these discourses in *Sabhyadiger vaktṛtā* and the marginal annotation "DT" in the Bodleian *Patrikā* leave little doubt that these four discourses were composed by Debendranath. If so, this would account for Discourse Three,[13] Discourse Eleven,[14] Discourse Seventeen,[15] and Discourse Twenty-One.[16]

The only "D" discourse from *Sabhyadiger vaktṛtā* that is not thus accounted for is Discourse Fifteen. The theme of this discourse is the fundamental need to distinguish between what is desirable and what is good. The discourse opens with a quotation from the Kaṭha Upanishad, a Vedantic text that first explored this problem some 2,500 years ago. The text was dear to

Rammohan and was also among those that Debendranath turned his attention to shortly after his awakening (see chapter 2).

As the author of Discourse Fifteen tells us, to follow the desirable is to indulge the passions and thereby lose the path to God. By contrast, to follow the good is to tread the path to ultimate salvation, even if the path may at times be covered with thorns. The author develops this point by narrating an extended scenario in which the worldly householder Śaunaka encounters two heavenly maidens who attempt to lure him onto their respective paths. The diction and style of Discourse Fifteen is quite similar to that found in the other four "D" discourses, and the use of a moralizing narrative is one that Debendranath was to use extensively in his later Brāhmo sermons (Tagore 1909: appendix). Needless to say, the theme of the godly householder was absolutely central to Debendranath's theological vision. For these reasons, it seems reasonable to attribute this last remaining "D" discourse to Debendranath.

This is not the place to attempt an analysis of the way the themes developed in these five "D" discourses relate to the mature writing of Debendranath. However, a separate work dedicated to exploring Debendranath's unique conception of Vedantic theism is surely long overdue. By establishing that he was the composer of these five early discourses, and by providing them in translation, we can hope that someone may take the time to explore in greater detail the genesis and development of his theology.

Ī = Īśvaracandra Vidyāsāgara

Discourses Thirteen and Eighteen in *Sabhyadiger vakt̤rtā* are both signed with the initial Ī (ঈ). While there are relatively few Bengali first names that begin with this vowel (Īśvaracandra and Īśānacandra being among the most common), somewhat surprisingly, there were at least three individuals named Īśvaracandra who were active in the early Sabhā: Īśvaracandra Gupta, Īśvaracandra Nyāyaratna, and Īśvaracandra Vidyāsāgara. Obviously, at first glance and without any help from other evidence, any one of them could have written these discourses. However, we do have other evidence, and as such we can move rather quickly to narrow the field.

We may begin by ruling out Īśvaracandra Gupta as the author of these two discourses. This is not to say that Gupta did not compose anything for *Sabhyadiger vaktr̥tā*. He did. But the following analysis should make it clear that we have far better grounds for believing he actually composed the single discourse that is signed with the rather unambiguous initials "Ī G."

What about Īśvaracandra Nyāyaratna? It turns out there are two good reasons for doubting Nyāyaratna's authorship. The first reason is that at one point in his autobiography Debendranath explicitly criticizes Nyāyaratna for preaching the divinity of Rama from the pulpit of the Brāhmo Samāj. As we know, the Tattvabodhinī Sabhā followed Rammohan in rejecting polytheism, image worship, and all the corresponding myths of Puranic Hinduism (Tagore 1980: 76).[17] For this reason, Puranic deities and modes of worship have no role in the discourses of *Sabhyadiger Vaktṛtā*. And they certainly do not figure in the two "Ī" discourses. Rather, in these we find a consistent appeal to rather standard Brāhmo idioms of rational theism and moral restraint. In other words, there is nothing about these two discourses that would lead us to associate them with Īśvaracandra Nyāyaratna.

The second reason for doubting Nyāyaratna's authorship is that we can in fact identify a later essay written by him and published in *Tattvabodhinī Patrikā* in 1844. This short essay is signed unambiguously with the initials "Ī. C. N." (ঈ চ ন.).[18] The fact that all three initials were used, as opposed to the single initial Ī, may suggest that the editor of *Tattvabodhinī Patrikā* wished there to be no confusion regarding the author of the piece, who must surely have been Īśvaracandra Nyāyaratna. We may likewise infer that he wished to distinguish between Īśvaracandra Nyāyaratna and some other Īśvaracandra.

There can be little doubt that this other Īśvaracandra was Īśvaracandra Vidyāsāgara (1820–91), a figure of immense importance in the intellectual, social, and educational world of mid-century Calcutta.[19] A brahmin by birth, pandit by training, and social reformer by conviction, Vidyāsāgara is renowned for his challenge to brahmanical customs (such as the prohibition on the marriage of Hindu widows) and his contributions to the development of modern Bengali prose. In 1839, Vidyāsāgara was in his final years of study at Calcutta Government Sanskrit College. He would have been nineteen years old, and we can imagine him beginning to move out into the world, making new acquaintances and joining some of the new associations that were beginnning to appear in the city. Vidyāsāgara was involved with the Sabhā at its earliest inception, even if we can't say precisely when he joined (Hatcher 1996a: 230–36). But in light of what we know of Vidyāsāgara's subsequent fame as an author, it is hard to imagine him not playing an active role in the public discussion of Tattvabodhinī ideas.

It turns out that Discourse Thirteen was subsequently reprinted in the *Tattvabodhinī Patrikā* under the initial Ī (ঈ).[20] However, this fact alone still does not help us confirm the identity communicated by the initial. Absent a clear editorial confirmation of Vidyāsāgara's authorship, we have no choice but to turn to other sorts of evidence. It may be best in this case to compare the two "Ī" discourses from *Sabhyadiger vaktṛtā* with Vidyāsāgara's other published writings. Can we find evidence of his distinctive prose style and terminology?

Do we notice the author touching on moral and religious themes that are characteristic of Vidyāsāgara's later writings?

We may begin with two examples of terminology. The Bengali terms *lopāpatti* and *yatheṣṭācāri* both appear in Discourse Thirteen. As it turns out, these are distinctive words in Vidyāsāgara's learned, Sanskritic lexicon. *Lopāpatti* means "destruction" or "disappearance." In Bengali, it would be known as a *tatsama* word—a word that comes directly to Bengali from Sanskrit. If anything, it is a rather technical Sanskrit concept. It would not be found in everyday Bengali usage, even in Vidyāsāgar's day, when Bengali prose was more Sanskritic than it is today. However, it is the kind of word one could expect a pandit like Vidyāsāgara to use. And, sure enough, if one examines his later writings, one finds that Vidyāsāgara uses the word frequently.[21]

The second term, *yatheṣṭācāri*, is another *tatsama* word. It means "one who does as he pleases." Like *lopāpatti*, *yatheṣṭācāri* is not a word that figures prominently in Bengali prose during this period. However, once again we notice that Vidyāsāgara tends to make heavy use of this word in his other writings. In fact, the concept of one who does as he pleases plays a prominent part in defining the limits of Vidyāsāgara's moral worldview. He regularly uses this word (or related forms, like *yathecchācāri* and *yathecchacāri*) to characterize people who indulge their desires instead of living in accordance with the norms of social and religious conduct (Hatcher 1996a: 239). I have attempted elsewhere to flesh out in detail the moral and religious dimensions of Vidyāsāgara's worldview, according to which the diligent restraint of the passions and an ethic of devoted care for others are paramount values. I invite readers to compare these values with the content of Discourses Thirteen and Eighteen to verify for themselves the congruence between these early writings and Vidyāsāgara's later work.

While the question of terminology naturally tends to lead us into consideration of Vidyāsāgara's worldview, we can also segue from terminology to matters of style. The prominence of *tatsama* words like *lopāpatti* and *yatheṣṭācāri* in the two discourses from *Sabhyadiger vaktṛtā* serves to suggest something about the style of these discourses. They read like the work of a pandit rather than the writing of an English-educated graduate of Hindu College, for instance. Terminology aside, these discourses betray the rhetorical techniques of a pandit, notably the use of Sanskrit quotations to bolster an argument. At the same time, these discourses rise above the standard of most pandit writing from this period. Their language is simple, lucid, and engaging. The author also demonstrates the kinds of descriptive skills and creative vision one associates with the work of Vidyāsāgara, who would go on to become one of the nineteenth century's great prose stylists.

As one final piece of evidence, we might select a Sanskrit quotation cited by the author of Discourse Eighteen. This quotation offers tantalizing support for connecting these discourses with Vidyāsāgara. It is a verse from the Bhāgavata Purāṇa (5.1.17). This verse occurs in close proximity to another set of verses in the Bhāgavata Purāṇa about which Vidyāsāgara had composed a Sanskrit poem in 1840.[22] The proximity between the passage on which this poem was based and the single verse cited in the discourse is certainly intriguing, but even more interesting is the fact that both the poem and the discourse were composed at almost precisely the same time, a time when Vidyāsāgara appears to have had the Bhāgavata Purāṇā on his mind (i.e. 1839–40).

Pulling all this evidence together, we might conclude that since (a) apart from Īśvaracandra Gupta and Īśvaracandra Nyāyaratna, there is no other individual who was affiliated with the Sabhā during this period whose name begins with the letter "Ī"; and since (b) these discourses share a distinctive vocabulary and style with Vidyāsāgara's other published writings; and since (c) the content of the discourses also accords closely with Vidyāsāgara's moral and religious worldview; then (d) there are excellent grounds for believing these two discourses were written by Vidyāsāgara. As such, they shed important light on the young mind of a prominent intellectual.

R = Rāmacandra Vidyāvāgīśa

There are two discourses in *Sabhyadiger vaktṛā* signed with the initial "R" (র), Discourses Fourteen and Nineteen. We are fortunate that solid evidence exists to connect these with the Rāmacandra Vidyāvāgīśa (1786–1845), first *ācārya* of the Sabhā and right-hand man to both Rammohan and Debendranath. It will be recalled that it was Rāmacandra who interpreted the Īśā Upanishad for Debendranath, thereby precipitating the latter's spiritual awakening (see chapter 2).[23] We would hardly be surprised, then, to find that Rāmacandra was the author of some of the discourses in *Sabhyadiger vaktṛā*, especially since he had been regularly delivering sermons before the Brāhmo Samāj throughout the 1830s. Nevertheless, in lieu of a direct attribution, we must again advance the evidence to make this case.

We may begin by noting straight away that parallel versions of the two "R" discourses were subsequently published in *Tattvabodhinī Patrikā* above the Bengali initial "R" (র).[24] Both of these later reprints begin with citations from the Upanishads and refer repeatedly to other Sanskrit textual authorities, as was Rāmacandra's wont. After all, Rāmacandra, like Vidyāsāgara, was a pandit. Of all the Tattvabodhinī writers, his writings include the most frequent use of Sanskrit citations. And yet two features serve to distinguish his work from someone like Vidyāsāgara. First is his consistent habit of quoting revealed texts (*śruti*) for authority, notably the Upanishads. Second, those texts he selects, whether revealed or otherwise, tend to mirror the proof texts featured in the writings of his deceased colleague and founder of the Brāhmo Samāj, Rammohan Roy. The same passages from Kaṭha Upanishad, Kulārṇava Tantra, and Yoga-vāśiṣṭha Rāmāyaṇa that were favored by Rammohan appear throughout Rāmacandra's writings.

We are fortunate that from an early date the Brāhmo community made a point of publishing the sermons Rāmacandra had delivered before the Brāhmo Samāj (for example, Vidyāvāgīśa 1844, 1845, and 1849).[25] Indeed, the inaugural issue of *Tattvabodhinī Patrikā* features two sermons delivered by Rāmacandra at meetings of the Brāhmo Samāj in 1843. The editors state clearly in the title of each entry that they are the work of Rāmacandra Vidyāvāgīśa.[26] Reading through all the published versions of these sermons, one quickly learns to detect Rāmacandra's style and spiritual concerns. Stylistically, he is less innovative and engaging than someone like Vidyāsāgara; he exhorts his audience, but he does not enthrall them with creative imagery or evocative word choice. At the level of content, he sticks close to the basic themes of sense restraint and knowledge of the supreme Lord. Not surprisingly, of all the Tattvabodhinī writers, his paraphrase of Vedānta is most reminiscent of Rammohan. When all this evidence is considered, there can be no doubt that the two discourses signed with the initial "R" were composed by Rāmacandra.

I hope that someday scholars will give Rāmacandra's writings the kind of attention they deserve. As I have written elsewhere, he was a crucial bridge linking the worlds of Rammohan and Debendranath. We might even say that were it not for Rāmacandra, not only would the Brāhmo Samāj very likely have perished during the 1830s, but also the Tattvabodhinī Sabhā would almost surely never have been created.

Ī G = Īśvaracandra Gupta

One of the most delightful surprises in *Sabhyadiger vaktṛtā* is to find that it contains a very short piece that we can confidently ascribe to the influential poet and journalist, Īśvaracandra Gupta (1812–59). This is Discourse Sixteen, which is signed with the initials "Ī G" (ঈ গ). As it turns out, Gupta was among the earliest members of the Sabhā.[27] In fact, it was Gupta who first invited Akṣayakumāra to attend meetings with him (Rāy 1885: 44).[28] This was during the Sabhā's very first year, 1839.

Gupta had grown up in Calcutta and had manifested all the markings of a precocious poet while he was still a young man. In his youth, he gravitated to more orthodox expressions of Hindu religion. However, during the 1830s, his attitudes began to shift. By 1838, he had turned his back on the orthodox and had even taken to attacking the conservative Dharma Sabhā. He attacked its journalistic mouthpiece, *Samācāra Candrikā*, through his own journal, *Sambāda Prabhākara*. Alauddin Al-Azad has suggested that the reason for this change in attitude is that Gupta had by this time begun to socialize with the Tagore family of Jorasanko (1979: 31–32).[29] That contact came initially via Debendranath's father, Dwarkanath, who provided assistance and advice to Gupta in his work for the *Prabhākara* (Datta 1968: 121). Through his interaction with the Jorasanko Tagores, Gupta no doubt came to know Debendranath. As a result of his acquaintance with the Tagores, Gupta may have begun to liberalize his views. This would explain his early sympathy with, and interest in, the Tattvabodhinī Sabhā.

The strongest two pieces of evidence for believing Gupta composed Discourse Sixteen—which is really more a benediction than a discourse per se—are (1) that he was active in the Sabhā during its first year, and (2) that the discourse appears above a pair of initials which so clearly correspond to his name. However, we can say more. There is also good textual evidence to suggest that he composed this short piece.

If we examine some of Gupta's other writings, we detect parallels both in content and in style to the discourse found in *Sabhyadiger vaktṛtā*. For instance, the theological content of his *Prabodhaprabhākara* from 1857 parallels the views expressed in the Tattvabodhinī discourses. Admittedly, *Prabodhaprabhākara* is a far longer composition, which takes the form of an extended dialogue on Hindu devotion and philosophy. Unlike the brief "Ī G" discourse, it is composed in both Bengali prose and verse and includes some Sanskrit as well (which Discourse Sixteen does not). Nevertheless, it is a work that inculcates both devotion to a theistic God and a distinctly Brāhmo sort of reverence for God as revealed in his creation (Gupta 1857). This would accord with a report regarding the Second Anniversary meeting of the Sabhā at which Gupta is said to have given a discourse on the need for gratitude and devotion to God (Datta 1968: 123).

The style of *Prabodhaprabhākara* is strikingly similar to that of Discourse Sixteen. Perhaps the most noticeable characteristic of both works is a distinctive use of alliteration. In Discourse Sixteen, the Bengali original contains two lengthy passages of alliteration: *parama padārtha-ke praṇipāta puraḥsara praphullāntaḥkaraṇe pracura prayatna pūrvaka ei prārthanā kari* and *satata svacchanda śarīre susādhu sajjana sahita sadālāpe avasthāna karata*. This kind of extended wordplay may be compared with specimens found in *Prabodhaprabhākara*, most notably a selection from the foreword that reads *ei "prabodhaprabhākara" pustaka prakāśe pravṛttiparavaśa haiyā pracura prayāsa-paripūrita pariśrama o prayatna puraḥsara* (Dāśgupta and Mukhaṭi 1974: 298).[30] Besides the alliteration, there is some obvious shared vocabulary, notably the words *pracura*, *prayatna*, and *puraḥsara*.

Because Discourse Sixteen is more of a benediction than a discourse, we may speculate that at the meeting for 14 Māgha the poet was called on to pronounce a blessing on the assembly and the ongoing work of the Sabhā (as would not be uncommon at such meetings to this very day). While far less substantive than most of the other discourses, this short address may well have been included in *Sabhyadiger vaktṛtā* out of respect for the stature and talent of its composer. A minor piece it may be, but it nevertheless deserves recognition as part of Gupta's overall ouevre.

Initials for which attribution is relatively certain

Ś = Śyāmacaraṇa Mukhopādhyāya

Aside from Debendranath, the author credited with the most discourses in *Sabhyadiger vaktṛtā*—Discourses One, Seven, and Nine—is someone identified with the single initial "Ś" (শ). Identifying the author indicated by this initial is far less straightforward than the cases considered thus far. While records exist for membership in the Sabhā, the earliest extant report dates from 1846, seven years after the creation of the Sabhā and the delivery of these discourses. Similarly, there are no extant reports of the complete membership of the Brāhmo Samāj from the 1830s, a group which likely produced other early members of the Sabhā alongside Rāmacandra Vidyāvāgīśa. Finally, works about the general Brāhmo movement that were composed decades later provide tantalizing clues, but no definitive answers. Most intriguingly, in 1879 G. S. Leonard mentioned the name of Debendranath's brother-in-law, Shama Churn Mukerjea (i.e., Śyāmacaraṇa Mukhopādhyāya), in connection with the early Tattvabodhinī Sabhā (1879: 104). Later still, the Brāhmo historian Śivanātha Śāstrī mentioned a certain Śrīdhara Nyāyaratna as being among a few Tattvabodhinī "preachers" (1911: 93). These names both begin with the character "Ś," but could either of them have been the author of these discourses? Might we not also consider Debendranath's own pandit, the man to whom he first showed the passage from the Īśā Upanishad, Śyāmācaraṇa Bhaṭṭācārya?[31]

Records being inadequate, our conclusions must necessarily be tentative. However, to begin with the Tagore family pandit, Śyāmācaraṇa Bhaṭṭācārya, it seems safe to rule him out for two reasons. First, he appears to be largely absent from the records of the Tattvabodhinī Sabhā.[32] This would be hard to explain were he to have worked closely with Debendranath. By contrast, there are grounds for thinking he may not have been involved with the Sabhā at all: it is quite possible that he was not a particularly progressive pandit; rather, he may have been someone employed by the family not for his advanced religious views but for his ability to meet the family's traditional ritual needs. Second, when Debendranath showed Śyāmācaraṇa the passage from the Īśā Upanishad, the latter dismissed it by saying, "That's all Brāhmo Sabhā stuff" (Tagore 1980: 14). Had he been sympathetic to Brāhmo thought, not only would we expect him to be able to explain the passage to Debendranath, he surely wouldn't have been so dismissive of the passage. This lends credence to the idea that Śyāmācaraṇa Bhaṭṭācārya may have been a fairly conservative ritualist who took no interest in the progressive ideas of the Brāhmos. He would thus seem an odd candidate for membership in the Sabhā.

What, then, of Śrīdhara Nyāyaratna whom Śivanātha Śāstrī includes among the Tattvabodhinī "preachers"? Scanning the earliest issues of *Tattvabodhinī Patrikā*, we do indeed come across a reference to one Śridhara Nyāyaratna in the eighth number of the journal published in the spring of 1846.[33] There we read that Śrīdhara Nyāyaratna was serving as the assistant preceptor (*upācārya*) for the Brāhmo Samāj. The *Patrikā* reports that he delivered a speech to the Brāhmo Samāj in February or March of 1844. His speech began with a passage from Manu's text on *dharma* and went on to explore such brahmanical ideals as the duties of class and life stage (*varṇāśrama-dharma*) and spiritual qualification (*adhikāra*). However, this is the only significant mention of his name in the *Tattvabodhinī Patrikā*, and it is in connection with remarks made before the Brāhmo Samāj rather than the Sabhā. As such, it provides no direct evidence of his membership in or involvement with the Tattvabodhinī Sabhā. Since his name does not appear in later lists of members of the Sabhā, it is hard for us to know anything more about his possible involvement with the Sabhā, especially in its first year. What's more, the theme of this speech to the Brāhmo Samāj does not accord well with the content of the "Ś" discourses, which do not trade in classical brahmanical categories drawn from the *dharma* literature.[34]

This leaves us with Debendranath's brother-in-law, Shama Churn Mukerjea. Here it seems there is a case to make. Unfortantely, even though Leonard commented on Śyāmacaraṇa Mukhopādhyāya's relationship to Debendranath, we know very little about him; we do not even know his precise dates. This is rather surprising, since if he was the author of the three "Ś" discourses, he occupies a more prominent place in *Sabhyadiger vaktṛtā* than either Rāmacandra or Akṣayakumāra. Why is it we know so little about him? After all, the only other significant reference to Śyāmacaraṇa in subsequent histories of the Brāhmo movement comes from Leonard, who also adds that Śyāmacaraṇa had apparently "composed some excellent Brahmic Hymns in Bengali" (1879: 104).[35]

Any further evidence of Śyāmacaraṇa's involvement with the Sabhā must be gleaned from a perusal of materials produced by the Sabhā. In confirmation of the claim that Śyāmacaraṇa was a member of the Sabhā, we find his name listed in 1846 as one of the members of the *Tattvabodhinī Patrikā* publication committee.[36] Scanning the pages of the earliest numbers of *Tattvabodhinī Patrikā*, we learn that Śyāmacaraṇa published a small work entitled "Rational Analysis of the Gospels" in 1845.[37] That same year, *Tattvabodhinī Patrikā* reported that Śyāmacaraṇa attended the annual examination at the Tattvabodhinī school in Bansberia.[38] Finally, we read in an issue of *Tattvabodhinī Patrikā* from 1846 that Śyāmacaraṇa was appointed assistant secretary of the Sabhā.[39]

Most important for our purposes, however, is an essay that appeared in the fourth number of *Tattvabodhinī Patrikā* during its first year of publication, 1843.[40] This essay is signed with the Bengali initials "Śyā. Ca. Mu."—with the Bengali vowel signs clearly indicated (শ্যা. চ. মু; punctuation in original). There can be no doubt these initials belong to Śyāmacaraṇa.

This short essay begins with the sentence, "A man who enjoys sense objects with firmness tastes the nectar of true happiness."[41] As this suggests, Śyāmacaraṇa's concern is to highlight the moral lapses that occur when people indulge their senses, most notably the errors of lying, drunkenness, and jealousy. As a corrective, Śyāmacaraṇa calls on his readers to wake from the sleep of ignorance, to know the true nature of the world, to reflect on the unchanging Lord, and to be ever diligent in restraining the senses. This short piece bears direct comparison with Discourse Seven from *Sabhyadiger vaktṛtā*, which stresses:

> Those who only find delight in the happiness of the senses are unable to understand the highest happiness that is liberation. . . . Those who desire liberation reduce their attachments. . . . Therefore, respected members, be diligent in the kind of practice that holds as nothing the happiness of the senses and attains the highest happiness that is liberation.

We might emphasize, in particular, the way both essays explore the fairly classical Vedantic themes of sense pleasure, ignorance, and liberation. In this respect, the author departs somewhat from the pattern of other discourses, which tend to pair diligent restraint less with the theme of liberation than with the reasoned knowledge of God's laws. In fact, the distinctly Vedantic flavor of the two essays provides us with a sense of Śyāmacaraṇa's unique style and repertoire, which includes a generous helping of quotations from Sanskrit sources, both *śruti* and *smṛti*.

This style and repertoire is worth noting, because we discern something similar operating in a much later work written by Śyāmacaraṇa, his *Cuḍālā Upākhyāna* (Mukhopādhyāya 1877). *Cuḍālā Upākhyāna* retells a story from a classical Sanskrit text that was apparently quite popular among the Brāhmos, the Yoga-vāśiṣṭha Rāmāyaṇa.[42] In *Cuḍālā Upākhyāna* the theme of *tattvajñāna*, or "ultimate knowledge," is clearly prominent. Significantly, this theme is also prominent in the "Ś" discourses. In *Cuḍālā Upākhyāna* as in these "Ś" discourses, *tattvajñāna* refers to knowledge of the one, formless Ultimate Reality, or *brahman*.

On one level, the use of a term like *tattvajñāna* is fairly commonplace and would be insufficient to establish common authorship. After all, the Sabhā's very name enshrines the goal of propagating *tattva*. However, *Cuḍālā Upākhyāna* shares something even more distinctive with the "Ś" discourses in *Sabhyadiger vaktṛtā*. This is the desire to ground ultimate knowledge not simply in the *śāstras* but also in human reason (*yukti*), reason disciplined through restraint of the senses. These are themes that are announced straightaway in Discourse One, the first of the "Ś" discourses. A comparison of Discourse One with *Cuḍālā Upākhyāna* is striking. For instance, in the latter text, Cuḍālā instructs King Śikhidhvaja that austerities, mantras, pilgrimage, and the like are all just a waste of time; all that is required to attain *tattvajñāna* are the teachings of a true guru, the application of one's reason, and the wisdom of the *śāstras*.[43] In Discourse One, this same set of themes is also clearly announced:

> True worship of Brahman consists of restraining the senses and grasping the teaching of the Vedas and Vedānta. It is only by this kind of worship that Brahman is known and liberation attained. On the other hand, if one disregards both reason and the Śāstras and lets one's fickle senses grow strong, one cannot attain the Supreme Lord.

The parallels are striking, not simply between *Cuḍālā Upākhyāna* and Discourse One but also between these two essays and the 1843 essay from *Tattvabodhinī Patrikā* that was clearly attributed to Śyāmacaraṇa. In light of these textual parallels, and in view of Śyāmacaraṇa's active role in the early Sabhā (which obviously included a fair share of writing and editing, given his role on the publication committee), it seems safe to conclude that the "Ś" discourses were indeed composed by him. Still, because we cannot say with absolute certainty that these discourses weren't written by someone like Śrīdhara Nyāyaratna, whom Śivanātha had labeled an important Tattvabodhinī "preacher," this attribution must remain somewhat tentative.

C = Candrasekhar Deb

Discourse Four and Discourse Five are signed with the initial "C" (চ). Although their tenor is largely Vedantic, they differ from the Vedantic discourses of both Rāmacandra and Śyāmacaraṇa. One principal difference is that they quote no Sanskrit authorities. While Rāmacandra writes in the rather formal style of a pandit who throws in proof texts to bolster his claims, and Śyāmacaraṇa might be likened to a popular commentator who plays off the texts he cites, the "C" discourses are short and unadorned; they read something like paraphrase. As a general restatement of the basic Vedantic position, Discourses Four and Five are consistent in their tone and language, and there can be no doubt they are the work of the same author. If our earlier suppositions regarding the system of initials are correct, the common authorship of these two essays is further confirmed by the fact that the editors found it necessary to identify the author of a third discourse in the collection, Discourse Six, by the addition of a second initial, namely "C G."

If the two "C" discourses are viewed as a kind of Vedantic paraphrase, then there is good reason for linking them to the name of Candrasekhar Deb (Candraśekhara Deva, also anglicized as Chunder Sekhar Deb, 1810–79), one of Rammohan's close friends and early Brāhmo associates.[44] It will be recalled that it was Candrasekhar, along with Tarachand Chakravarti, who encouraged Rammohan to create a distinctive place for worship according to the new theology he had begun to promote (see chapter 1 and Collet 1988: 220). Both men had important roles in the earliest Brāhmo Samāj. It is therefore not surprising to find that Candrasekhar and Tarachand also went on to become members of Debendranath's new Tattvabodhinī Sabhā and were to play an active part in its work.[45]

While this is admittedly a small foundation on which to base our attribution, there do seem to be grounds for viewing the "C" discourses as Candrasekhar's attempt to promote the basic vision of his late friend, Rammohan.[46] While the "C" discourses never quote Sanskrit sources, we can nevertheless discern the influence of the very texts that Rammohan had worked so carefully to translate and comment upon, in particular the Upanishads. The author also clearly endeavors to define the proper way to understand such fundamental issues as ignorance, illusion, creation, and the inner controller (*antaryāmin*). And while distinctly Vedantic, these discourses nevertheless distance themselves subtly from the classical system of Advaita Vedānta, just as in the case of Rammohan's writings.[47]

Overall, then, there are adequate grounds for speculating that the "C" discourses are the work of Candrasekhar. Obviously, further concrete evidence of authorship would be required to be able to make this attribution with full certainty. Even so, and in lieu of a certain verdict regarding Candrasekhar's authorship, the "C" discourses nevertheless provide us with valuable evidence of the ways Rammohan's closest followers understood and articulated his message of a reformed Vedānta.

R G = Ramgopal Ghosh

When we turn to Discourse Ten, which is signed "R G" (র গ) there is unfortunately even less evidence to help us identify the author than in the case of the "C" discourses. The very best clue is provided by the initials themselves, since they clearly match the initials for Ramgopal Ghosh (Rāmagopāla Ghoṣa, 1815–68).

Ramgopal was a prominent member of the Young Bengal faction educated at Hindu College under the tutelage of Derozio. He would have to be ranked among the more ardent rationalists who joined the Tattvabodhinī Sabhā in its infancy, sharing more with Akṣayakumāra Datta in this regard than with Debendranath. And like Akṣayakumāra, Ramgopal played an active role in the work of the Sabhā over several years, including serving a three-year term as secretary (*adhyakṣa*).[48] Along with Akṣayakumāra and Debendranath, Ramgopal also joined such liberal associations as the Hindu Theo-Philanthropic Society, which was established in 1843.[49] It would therefore come as no surprise to find that he had delivered discourses at the group's meetings.

When we look at Discourse Ten itself, we notice that it is very short. There is little about it that helps us prove any connection to Ramgopal. Its chief characteristic is its reliance on reasoned observation of creation rather than on scripture or metaphysics, a fact which would certainly fit our expectations of the writings of a commited rationalist like Ramgopal. But this is nearly all we are able to say. Given the clear correspondence between the initials and Ramgopal's name, and taking into account his active role in the Sabhā, we have fairly good grounds for ascribing it to him. This is the most we can say at present.

Initials for which attribution remains uncertain

Bh = Identity uncertain

Discourse Eight, a short passage that opens with two quotations from the Kaṭha Upanishad, is signed with a single initial, the aspirated consonant "Bh" (ভ). Sadly, it is not possible to conclusively connect this discourse with a member of the Sabhā. One name that would fit the single initial is that of

Bhavānīcaraṇa Sen (dates uncertain). Bhavānīcaraṇa is someone we encounter here and there in the records of the Sabhā.[50] Perhaps most important, Debendranath mentions Bhavānīcaraṇa as one of those who were initiated into the Brāhmo path along with him in 1843 (Tagore 1980: 29). This was obviously an important moment in the history of the two associations, but it also occurred four years after the founding of the Sabhā. Whether Bhavānīcaraṇa had joined the group earlier on and could have composed Discourse Eight is something we cannot determine at this point. While we have a report that Bhavānīcaraṇa delivered a sermon at the annual meeting of the Brāhmo Samāj in the spring of 1845, we unfortunately possess no sample from that address to compare with Discourse Eight.[51] What is more, records indicate there were several other early members of the Sabhā who shared this initial. In lieu of any other corroborating evidence, we simply cannot identify the bearer of the intial "Bh."

C G = Identity uncertain

Discourse Six is signed "C G" (চ গ). As noted, the use of two initials in this case must have been intended to distinguish this author from the author of the "C" discourses. And while the presence of two initials should, prima facie, improve our chances of identifying the author, there is in fact little evidence to assist us in this task.

Discourse Six is a mere six sentences long. Intriguingly, a shorter version of this passage, consisting of the first three sentences, was published as an unsigned piece in the inaugural issue of *Tattvabodhinī Patrikā* from 1843. That piece read:

> Of all religions, the most superior consists in knowledge of the Supreme Truth. Therefore, it is absolutely imperative that householders grasp the teachings of the Vedānta Śāstras. For it is by studying the Supreme Truth that the senses, &c., are subdued, one is empowered to live one's worldly life as ordained, and one attains liberation in the next life.[52]

In view of the almost credal tone of this piece and its prominence in the first issue of *Tattvabodhinī Patrikā*, it is tempting to think it was a passage crafted to sum up the essence of Tattvabodhinī thought. But, clearly, it was not written by any of the prominent figures associated with the Sabhā. Who then was this "C G"? Perusal of early sources for the Sabhā turn up no obvious candidate.

There is a slight possibility that "C G" stands for Candraśekhara Gaṅgopādhyāya, one of the authors represented in a much later collection of

Brāhmo sermons (Brāhmo Addresses 1870). However, Candraśekhara remains little more than a name; we know nothing about him, not even his dates. And beyond the initials, there is little to suggest he composed Discourse Six. A comparison of the 1870 tract with Discourse Six reveals no obvious stylistic parallels. And since there were other members of the Sabhā who shared these initials, we really are left without a clue in this particular case.[53]

G = *Identity uncertain*

No evidence exists to determine who wrote Discourse Two, which is signed "G" (গ). The presence of citations from both *śruti* and *smṛti* would suggest perhaps a brahmin or at the least a Sanskrit scholar. The most distinctive thing about the short discourse is that it appears to quote a passage from the Yoga-vāśiṣṭha that was widely cited by Rammohan in his various writings (but for, which no precise citatation can be found). Sadly, as curious as this is, it provides no help in identifying the author of this discourse. Extant records are simply too fragmentary.

Why should we care about authorship?

We should not allow the paucity of evidence in these final three cases to disappoint us regarding what we can know about the authorship of the discourses in *Sabhyadiger vaktṛtā*. Instead, we should marvel that enough evidence exists to conclusively attribute the bulk of the remaining discourses (eighteen out of a total of twenty-one) to individuals with prominent roles in the Sabhā and in Calcutta society more generally. The most exciting thing that emerges from this list is that, apart from the names of Debendranath and Rāmacandra (whom we would fully expect to find represented in these discourses), we can make definitive attributions for three other individuals, each of whom occupies an important place in the history of modern Bengali literature and culture: the rationalist, Akṣayakumāra Datta; the Sanskrit pandit and social reformer, Īśvaracandra Vidyāsāgara; and the poet, Īśvaracandra Gupta.

To find Akṣayakumāra Datta's name in this list should come as no surprise. Alongside Debendranath and Rāmacandra, Akṣayakumāra played an active role in the Sabhā. What surprises us, however, is to see the names of two other individuals not often associated with either religious reform or modern Vedantic theology—namely, Īśvaracandra Vidyāsāgara and Īśvaracandra Gupta. While it has long been known that these two men were associated with the Sabhā, there has hitherto been no evidence that either man wrote or published work in connection with their membership. For scholars interested in the life and work of figures like Vidyāsāgar and Gupta, these attributions should be of considerable interest. And for anyone looking for proof that the Vedantic agenda of the Sabhā provided common ground on which very different types of Bengali intellectual could meet and discourse, *Sabhyadiger vaktṛtā* provides ample proof. It should be a matter of some joy and excitement to find evidence of the early and collective endeavors of such eminent figures in the history of modern Bengal.

8

The Complete English Translation of *Sabhyadiger vaktṛtā*

Oṃ, This is the Truth[1]

Discourses Delivered to the Tattvabodhinī Sabhā on Sunday, 1 December 1839[2] [17 Agrahāyaṇa 1761]

Discourse One

It is not only the Vedānta Śāstras that proclaim the Supreme Lord* to be beyond our senses* and unattainable by our mind* and intellect*.[3] Rather, all the Śāstras—the Smṛtis, Purāṇas, and Tantras—proclaim the Supreme Lord to be so. Even though this basic point may not be evident in every Śāstra, nevertheless we can be certain there are valid means of knowing* that, for instance, the Supreme Lord exists beyond the grasp of our senses. Thus we find it stated in the Vishnu Purāṇa:

> Rūpa nāmādi nirdeśa viśeṣaṇa vivarjitaḥ
> Apakṣaya vināśābhyāṃ pariṇāmārttijanmabhiḥ
> Varjitaḥ śakyate vaktum yaḥ sadāstīti kevalaṃ.[4]

> The Supreme Self* is devoid of qualifications of name and form, devoid of decay and destruction, devoid of transformation, and not subject to birth or sorrow*. The most that can be said is merely, "it is."

Likewise, in the Tantra Śāstra, it is clearly written that the very best worship* is worship of the Supreme Self and that this is the immediate cause of liberation*. Thus, the Kulārṇava Tantra states:

> viditetu pare tattve varṇātīte hyavikriye
> kiṅkaratvaṃhi gacchanti mantrā mantrādhipaiḥ saha.[5]
>
> When it is known that ultimately Brahman is devoid of class and change, all the mantras, along with the divine overlord of the mantras, become servants of the knowledge* of Brahman.

Or to quote another text:

> pare brahmaṇi vijñāte samastair niyamairalaṃ
> tāla vṛntena kiṃkāryaṃ labdhe malaya mārute.[6]
>
> Once the Supreme Brahman* is known, there is no need for laws, just as there is no use for a fan when the southern breeze cools the body.

All these Śāstras—and reason*, too—are perfectly clear. So what is one to say to those who choose to despise them rather than to believe? It is clearly written in the revealed texts*, such as:

> ātmānamevopāsīta.[7]
>
> The Supreme Self alone should be worshiped.

> ātmā vā are draṣṭavyaḥ śroṭavyo mantavyo nididhyāsitavyaḥ.[8]
>
> One should see, hear about, reflect on, and meditate on the Supreme Self.

Humans perform action solely for the attainment of happiness*. It is nothing but a failure of reflection to become attached to the temporary pleasures of the senses, when later one will be plunged into endless suffering*. Serious reflection certainly reveals there can be no experience* of sensory pleasure that is not tinged with suffering. The highest happiness is only found through worship of the Supreme Lord. Valid means of knowing this are found in the following two passages from the revealed texts. The first revealed text is:

> vijñānam ānandaṃ brahma.[9]
>
> Brahman is made of knowledge and its essential nature is bliss.

The second revealed text is:

> brahma veda brahmaiva bhavati.[10]
>
> Who knows Brahman, he alone becomes Brahman.[11]

If on knowing the Supreme Brahman, one becomes Brahman, and if the very essence of Brahman is bliss, then shouldn't we proclaim worship of the Supreme Lord as the cause of the highest happiness?

True worship of Brahman consists of restraining the senses and grasping the teaching of the Vedas and Vedānta. It is only by this kind of worship that Brahman is known and liberation attained. On the other hand, if one disregards both reason and the Śāstras and lets one's fickle senses grow strong, one cannot attain the Supreme Lord. As such, it is necessary to describe how the senses can be restrained. There are five organs of action*, such as the hands and feet, and five organs of knowledge*, such as sight and hearing. These ten senses are under the sway of lust*, anger*, greed*, &c.[12] To subdue lust, anger, &c., one must restrain the hands, feet, and other senses. Conversely, when lust, anger, &c. grow strong, careful effort* to control the senses will be fruitless. If the senses are controlled but greed is not restrained, then no thief will be able to stop stealing. A person who fails to control his lust and anger will suffer all sorts of misfortunes*. However, if he acts with all his senses properly regulated, he gains blessings* in this life and the next*. What's more, if it weren't for our senses, there would be no way to live our lives in this world.

The merciful* Supreme Lord creates* nothing without a purpose*. The origin of a living being* depends on the creation* of lust.[13] The instinct for self-preservation in every person depends on the creation of anger. That people regularly perform their allotted duties* depends on the creation of fear*. That we seek to protect our wives, children, and friends depends on the creation of delusion*. Seen in this way, it is evident that the senses are at the very root of worldly life*. To prevent the predominance of lust, anger, and the other vices, the countervailing virtues of shame*, patience*, &c. were created. Therefore, respected members*, dedicate your lives to the right cultivation of patience, sincerity*, virtue*, truth*, &c. and to the defeat of lust, anger, greed, delusion, pride*, &c. By pursuing the fundamental principles* of the Vedānta and other Śāstras you shall have happiness in this life and liberation in the next. O, Supreme Self, graciously ensure that we do not turn away from the fundamental principles of the Self*, so that we may know you.

[Signed] Ś

Discourse Two

With minds purified by faith*, senses restrained, the passions* of lust, anger, greed, delusion, &c. restrained by the practice* of calmness* and restraint*, diligent* individuals worship the Supreme Lord directly* by following the injunctions of Vedānta. Thereby they attain liberation. In this connection, some people say that householders* are unable to accomplish what Vedānta teaches about control of the senses and restraint of the passions. They say that therefore householders are not fit* to worship the Supreme Lord. However, such people do not consider that in this world* only human beings are able to control* their senses. As such, diligent individuals must necessarily be able to control their senses.

The Supreme Lord has not created a single thing* in this marvelous* world that does not tend toward the collective welfare* of humanity*. All those things that are both separate and distant from the body (like inanimate objects*) and those that are very close to us (like our limbs, digits, forehead, teeth, and senses)—all these things have been created for the enjoyment* and welfare* of human beings. The fruits of the trees relieve hunger and thirst; roots and leaves bring relief from sickness; our teeth are beautiful and assist with eating; and the various senses bring a variety of pleasures* through the observation of sense objects*. The senses are not detrimental to human beings. It is only if they are not subdued* that they become a cause of misfortune. If they are subdued, they are the cause of happiness in this life and liberation in the next. And in order to subdue the hands, feet, senses, &c., it is absolutely essential to restrain the passions like lust, anger, greed, and delusion.

> Satyam āyatanaṃ.[14]
>
> The individual who speaks the truth becomes a support* for knowledge of Brahman.

Therefore, O respected members, purify your minds by subduing your senses and practicing the truth. Externally manifest yourself as the agent, but internally know you are not. May you thereby find happiness in this life and the next. As Vaśiṣṭha instructed Rāmacandra,

> Bahir vyāpāra saṃrambho hṛdi saṃkalpa varjitaḥ
> Kartā bahir akartāntarevaṃ vihara rāghava.[15]
>
> Live your life in this world, O Rāghava, by applying yourself externally to affairs of the world, but without mental intention*; and while

you reveal yourself externally to be the agent, know internally that you are not.

[Signed] G

Discourses Delivered to the Tattvabodhinī Sabhā on Sunday, 8 December 1839 [24 Agrahāyaṇa 1761]

Discourse Three[16]

sasyamiva martyaḥ pacyate.[17]

Human beings are cut down like grain.[18]

The supremely compassionate* revealed texts mercifully seek to dispel the delusion so characteristic of vain human beings—namely, that they will live a long life. Just as we recognize our true appearance* in a mirror, so, too, do we recognize our true nature* in the revealed texts. The reason we think 100 years is an exceedingly long time to live is because few of us live beyond 100. Imagine someone who lived from the Dvāpara Yuga until today: that long-lived individual would view the successive children of Yudhiṣṭhira, Duryodhana, &c., the same way we view the hundreds of successive generations of ants over the period of a few days. Since we are just as short-lived, wouldn't our pride* and vanity* seem laughable to such a person?

O respected members, it is in the nature of time to appear greater or lesser depending on the creature. Five years may seem a very short time to a human being*, but it is a lifespan* to an animal, for whom it is equivalent to 100 of our years. In those five years, an animal goes through childhood, adolescence, and old age. To a creature with a five-year lifespan, five years does not seem trifling. In the same way, we fail to realize that 100 years is a very short time. And so we go about doing wrong, foolishly thinking our lifespans are long.

Even though 100 years is a very short time, if we were certain that we wouldn't die until we reached 100, our pride and vanity would gain just a bit of luster. But there are no guarantees to our lifespan. We should not trust* our breath for even one moment.[19] Is there any guarantee that the life breath* that currently resides in my body will remain until the end of this discourse?[20] And yet even so, what shall we say about those people who, rather than using the few days they are alive to promote the benefit* of humanity, are content causing misfortune?

When we consider time that has elapsed or the time we spend sleeping, we become aware of the true brevity of time. And even though the actions we perform in the present, and the memories we have of various past actions, leave us with a sense of the length of time, if we consider the dream state, we necessarily become aware of how exceedingly brief time is in actual fact. For during a mere instant of dreaming, we may visit all sorts of never-before-seen cities and all sorts of battles, separations, arguments, and reunions. Such travel and such sights would be impossible during the entire lifetime of an individual who is awake.

What I intend to show—namely, that time is very short and that it is only through our actions that time appears lengthy—may be illustrated using the following parable*:

> Once a lame man approached a certain king seeking his protection. The lame man said, "I am a man of great qualities. I shall do whatever the king asks of me." Taking him at his word, the king supported him comfortably with food, clothing, and wealth. But after many days had gone by, the lame man had done nothing for the king. Thinking his protection was proving fruitless, the king decided to send the man away. The lame man learned of this and came to the king while he was bathing. He beseeched him saying, "Your highness has graciously protected me for many days, but no opportunity has arisen for me to demonstrate my learning. This troubles me greatly. Therefore, if it pleases your majesty, summon your ministers so that I may give you an example of my unprecedented learning." The king agreed to this request, and the royal messenger notified his ministers.
>
> When they arrived, the lame man announced, "Let his highness be submerged in the water!" The king submerged himself briefly in the water. When he raised his head, he found a great river in flood. Neither his ministers nor the lame man were anywhere to be seen. Alone and distraught, he climbed onto the riverbank. Finding no clothes, he cast off his bathing garments. Nowhere could he see a tree in whose shade he might retire for a while. Burning beneath the midday sun, he set off on foot to seek some human settlement. It wasn't until evening that he found one, now overwhelmed by hunger and thirst. He noticed various sweetshops open for business. He had no money, but he could not bring himself to beg. He was stricken with grief. He lamented falling into these dire straits simply by offering to protect a vile cripple. After begging for a bit of sustenance, he spent the entire night on the ground weeping. Finally,

he became so desperately hungry that he agreed to work as a servant for a trader*.

In this way he acquired a bit of something with which to begin trading on his own. With time and great effort, he eventually earned enough wealth to become a respected figure in the region. He married the beautiful daughter of a trader. Before long, his wife gave birth to seven sons and seven daughters. But as fate would have it, his trading business began to decline. His wealth was all but destroyed. Soon he had so little left that it became difficult to safeguard his children.

Finding himself unable to feed and provide for his family, and overcome by mental anguish, he threw himself in the water to drown. However, when he could hold his breath no longer, he raised his head out of the water. And lo, the king found himself in the very place where he had been bathing, with his ministers standing all around wringing their hands. And the vile cripple was there as well. The king cast an angry look at the lame man and said, "Listen here, cripple, how dare you subject me to so much suffering for so long!" The lame man answered him, "But your highness, you were only underwater for an instant before you surfaced. These ministers saw the whole thing. Don't be angry, I pray."[21]

O respected members, surely you can appreciate from this story my contention that time appears long because of our action alone. This earth* is our abode for only a very short time. Every day, in little ways, we draw closer to death*. Therefore, you should be diligent in those practices that will bring blessings* in the next life.

The Lord* creates nothing without a purpose. Many shudder at the very mention of death. But if there were no death, our misery* would know no limit. There are so many diseases that bring unbearable misery, and which no amount of medicine can cure. It is precisely because death exists that we are able to transcend such misery. If sick and suffering individuals never died, the thought of their misery would just as equally become a source of misery for us. This is why on earth death is itself our savior* from such afflictions* as sickness*, grief*, fear, and shame*.

If, from the time of creation until now, no human being had ever died, there would never be enough crops to stave off hunger. The pride and conceit* of the wealthy* would know no bounds. And there would be no end to the evil deeds* done in this life for the sake of sensual pleasure*.

The merciful Supreme Lord has allotted to human beings a lifespan of 100 years to rescue them from all this misery. If it were decreed that death could only come after these 100 years had passed, human beings would be extremely unhappy*. They would know the very day of their death. So even though the Supreme Lord grants human beings a 100-year lifespan, he nevertheless claims lives at random. We never know for sure when death will come or just how long we might live. What is remarkable is that even though there is no certainty about life*, human beings nevertheless cherish the hope* that they will live* for many a day. Trusting in this hope, they attend thoughtfully to their respective duties. Without this trust in life, in fact, there would be no way to carry on the affairs of the world. Would farmers plant their grain if they could not hope to enjoy the fruit? Would merchants send the delights of their country—like grain, &c.—to other countries if there were no possibility of receiving a reward* for their efforts*? The Lord has implanted in our hearts* this trust in life. Even when we are afflicted by disease—even when we are ground down, emaciated and aged—we hold death at bay. We devote ourselves to performing the duties of worldly life as best we can. O respected members, consider in what marvelous ways the all-powerful* Supreme Lord uses his myriad powers* to sustain this world. If there were any relaxing of his law*, the world would be completely destroyed.

Therefore, make an effort to know the Supreme Lord through everything he has created for our happiness, so that you may be rescued from all hardship and become immersed in eternal happiness.

[Signed] D

Discourse Four

Of all the ways to worship the Supreme Lord, knowledge alone is the best. A diligent individual finds happiness in this world and liberation in the next through the pursuit of such knowledge—which consists of examining the marvelous works* of this world and of learning the manifest* and essential* characteristics of the creator* in nature* as taught by the beneficent Vedānta.[22]

Just as the sound "a" is contained within all the consonants from Ka to Kṣa, so, too, does the Supreme Self, who is comprised of knowledge, pervade all things at all times in its essential nature as the inner controller*.[23] The Supreme Self exists in the mind, intellect, &c., by virtue of having Being* as its very support*, and it is by intellect that one judges all actions* on this earth as good or bad. There is no other repository of mercy than he who mercifully bestows on us this wonderful intellect. It is through the laws of this merciful Supreme Lord that a child is born after spending ten carefree months in its mother's womb; and it is by his laws that young children are nourished with milk produced from the blood and fluids of the mother's breast. It is our continual prayer to the Supreme Lord who is this repository of mercy that through his grace we might attain ultimate knowledge*.

[Signed] C

Discourses Delivered to the Tattvabodhinī Sabhā on Sunday, 15 December 1839 [1 Pouṣa 1761]

Discourse Five

The Supreme Lord, who is creator, preserver*, and destroyer*, pervades everything through his essential nature. This is because the Supreme Lord is the inner Self* of all beings*. There can be no attainment of this inner Self by means of the senses, which correspond to natural sense objects, such as form, taste, smell, sound, and touch. Which is to say, there is a Supreme Lord who is one without a second* and who is the inner Self. He is other than all perceptible things like human beings, beasts*, the sun, moon, trees, creepers, &c. And this Supreme Lord cannot in any way be attained through the senses. Everything, including human beings, is the work of his magical power* and is therefore false*. Only the inner Self, the one Supreme Lord, is unchanging* and real*. However, a great-souled* individual endowed with faith should use reason to firmly establish in his mind the true meaning of Vedānta, the great teacher. By continually practicing the discipline of the Self*, he alone will come to know that nothing exists apart from the Self—just as there can be no butter without milk. A child who sees only milk is unable to experience the butter. So, too, an individual who lacks discrimination* is unable to attain the creator because all he sees is creation.

This much can be said: The Supreme Lord in his essential nature is consciousness*.[24] Consciousness is that by which one has awareness* of all objects. The senses, memory, doubt, resolve, indecision, &c., depend on consciousness. Many have realized the essential nature of consciousness as something pure*, awakened*, and liberated* which is grasped when one separates consciousness from the various senses, from memory*, doubt*, resolve*, and indecision*. One cannot know what a flower smells like if one has only been told about it by someone else. Neither can one experience the essence* of consciousness as separate from the senses, &c., merely by being told about it.

Some individuals are unable to conceive of the Supreme Self whose essential nature is consciousness. They imagine him in a worldly fashion as being equivalent to an embodied* being caught in the round of birth and death*. However, they fail to recognize that there could be no creation of a body—a body made up of bones, blood, flesh, and endowed with limbs and digits—if there were no elements* like earth, water, fire, wind, and ether. If one wished to say that the unchanging Supreme Lord was embodied, one would have to hold that the elements created by the Supreme Lord had in fact preceded him. But it is completely untenable that the elements precede the creator of the elements. Therefore, it goes completely against reason to hold that the Supreme Lord is an embodied being caught in the round of birth and death.

Some individuals say that wind is ultimate reality*; some say the ether, some say fire, and some say water. But such people do not recognize that the creation and preservation of the world cannot come about through wind alone, or fire alone, or water alone, or ether alone. It is only through the conjunction of these various elements that creation and preservation come about; and it is through their dissolution that destruction occurs. After all, is it possible that the creation of this world comes about from wind, fire, water, or ether alone? Bear in mind that the five elements are by nature simply matter*. How could this multifarious world be sustained by them? According to whose plan* do the limbs and digits of this body occupy their appropriate places? If it is food that creates bone, flesh, semen, and blood, then by what fundamental cause* is it ordained* that such food will be created on earth for the sustenance of the body? What scheme ensures that humans are born from humans, beasts from beasts, insects from insects, trees from trees? Is it even remotely possible that such amazing results are caused by matter alone?

This being the case, abandon the false hope that the creator and ordainer* of all beings can be perceived through the senses like wind, fire, or the earth. Make a careful effort to know—according to the teachings of Vedānta, which are a thousand times more beneficial than your father and mother—the Supreme and Ultimate Reality, whose essential nature is consciousness, who is beyond speech and thought, who is the breath of breath, and thought of thought, that you may find fulfillment.

[Signed] C

Discourse Six[25]

Of all religions, the most superior* consists in knowledge of the Supreme Truth*. Therefore, it is absolutely imperative that householders grasp the teachings of the Vedānta Śāstras. For it is by studying the Supreme Truth that the senses, &c., are subdued, one is empowered to live one's worldly life as ordained, and one attains liberation in the next life. By the will* of the Supreme Lord, the Tattvabodhinī Sabhā was established to further this noble cause. For this we thank him, and render repeated obeisance to him in body, mind and speech. We pray* that he may grant the Sabhā a long life.

[Signed] C G

Discourses Delivered to the Tattvabodhinī Sabhā on Sunday, 22 December 1839 [8 Pouṣa 1761]

Discourse Seven

That this society was established for the pursuit* of ultimate knowledge makes manifest our great fortune insofar as it is through ultimate knowledge that the highest happiness of liberation is obtained.

People blind from birth are unable to experience the happiness that comes through seeing the blessings of the world. However, if they had eyes to rescue them from the torments of blindness, they would surely be able to know. Bound as we are to this round of birth and death, we cannot know what ultimate happiness is like. But if we could vanquish our senses, we would cease to suffer, and then we would certainly be aware. Just consider how in deep sleep*—when our eyes, ears, &c., as well as desire, anger, greed, &c., have ceased from their respective actions—we delight in the highest happiness.

Those who only find delight in the happiness of the senses are unable to understand the highest happiness that is liberation. Due to the fickleness of the mind, they feel happy or they suffer, but it is really only a falsely imagined* happiness or sorrow. Mistaking greater power for greater happiness, they grow ever more addicted to power*; seeking ever more wealth, they grow agitated and suffer all manner of afflictions.

Those who desire liberation reduce their attachments. They are satisfied* with very little wealth. They devote their entire life to knowing the

Supreme Self, who is the creator.[26] And so they find happiness in this life and the next.

Therefore, respected members, be diligent in the kind of practice that holds as nothing the happiness of the senses and attains the highest happiness that is liberation.

[Signed] Ś

Discourse Eight

> Aśabdamasparśamarūpamavyayaṃ tathārasaṃ
> Nityamagandhavacca yat
> Anādyanantaṃ mahataḥ paraṃ dhrūvaṃ
> Nicāya taṃ mṛtyu mukhāt pramucyate.[27]

> A person is freed from death who knows the Supreme Self devoid of sound, touch, color, taste, or smell, that neither grows nor decays, that is beginningless, endless, and eternal, and completely separate from material reality*.

> Eṣa sarveṣu bhūteṣu gūḍātmānaprakāśate.
> Dṛśyatetvagrayābuddhyā sūkṣmayā sūkṣmadarśibhiḥ.[28]

> Although this Supreme Self pervades everything from Brahma down to inanimate matter, it is not revealed to those without knowledge; rather, this Supreme Self is obtained by the subtle and firmly established intellect of all wise men* of subtle vision.

From the aforementioned revealed texts, it is evident that the Supreme Lord who is without attributes is beyond all our senses. It is only deluded* and ignorant individuals with faulty reasoning* who doubt the existence of the Supreme Lord because it is beyond perception*.

And yet, if you consider how even a single body is fashioned purposefully*, it is evident that there must be a creator who has so precisely* fashioned this body with its limbs and digits. Notice how the five elements—earth, water, fire, wind, and ether—remain marvelously consistent from our birth right up to our old age, thus sustaining our body. Were any one of these five elements to grow stronger or weaker, the body would cease to exist. It would be equally impossible for naturally inanimate matter* like the five elements to remain constant without a single, all-powerful ordainer. Therefore, renounce all faulty reasoning and seek to know the Supreme Self who protects living beings through his control over the five elements, &c.

[Signed] Bh

Discourses Delivered to the Tattvabodhinī Sabhā on Sunday, 29 December 1839 [15 Pouṣa 1761]

Discourse Nine

Happiness comes only through knowledge. If one plants seeds in the soil, plants and trees will grow. Once we have this kind of knowledge, we can produce vegetables, flowers, and fruit. Enjoying them, we are happy. Once there is knowledge, we can use fire to prepare raw, undigestable vegetables for our enjoyment. We can ward off cold weather by using our knowledge of the fleece of various animals to fashion beautiful clothing. Through knowledge, we think nothing of the mighty waves of the ocean. Traveling at will from country to country, we gather learning and wealth. And so we become happy. We quell the various afflictions of disease by knowing how to administer beneficial medicines. Through the power of knowledge, we come to know that the Supreme Brahman—who is consciousness—is beyond our senses.[29] We come to know that he creates, sustains, and destroys the world. We come to know that the entire world, animate and inanimate, relies on him. And we come to know that it is through fear of him that the sun, moon, and stars unceasingly travel their ordained paths. Knowing this, we are happy, taking care to live our lives just as he has ordained.

Without knowledge, there is the possibility for all sorts of sorrow born from error. Sniffing a foul-smelling flower after mistaking* it for a lotus causes sorrow. Ruining one's crops because ignorance* prevented one from planting seeds in the proper fashion causes affliction. If one cannot accurately diagnose a disease* and mistakenly administers the wrong medicine, think how much potential for harm there is. And how much misfortune* befalls a kingdom when its laws are instituted in error?

As long as ignorant and misguided* people mistakenly say there is no Lord and no afterlife, they are deprived of happiness. It is like someone who mistakenly says there is no ruler when in fact there is. Such a person violates the law and winds up being punished. The same goes for someone who mistakenly says there is no Lord and no afterlife. Such a person is tainted by the sins* of various evil deeds and eventually meets with misfortune. Not being able to remember the Supreme Lord—who is our savior and refuge*—when confronted by some fear or anxiety is only to have one's fears redoubled. One mistakenly thinks there is no afterlife. One mistakenly thinks that at death the Self is destroyed. With every passing day, one grows more sorrowful at the thought of death. Then, on the day of one's death, one plunges into a sea of hopelessness.

Those great-souled individuals who put away error know that because of the mind and the senses all sorts of entities appear as if they truly existed, whereas in actual fact everything is Brahman. Thus the revealed text:

> Brahmaivedaṃ viśvaṃ idaṃ variṣṭhaṃ
> Idaṃ variṣṭhaṃ varatamaṃ brahma eva idaṃ viśvaṃ samastaṃ jagat.[30]
>
> Brahman alone is the superlative; it becomes this entire universe.

Therefore, he who has ultimate knowledge looks on this whole world with equanimity. Shunning all partisanship, he performs all his worldly actions in accordance with the Lord's laws. And knowing that the merciful Supreme Lord is the ordainer of everything, he is not overcome with grief for wealth, sons, &c. Instead, because he recognizes that he is the protector of his wives and children, he does not think the less of supporting them. Knowing that the all-pervading Supreme Lord dwells within, this great-souled individual performs no evil action, but instead is diligent in the pursuit of those things that are beneficial to himself and others.

[Signed] Ś

Discourse Ten

One only has to examine the whole of creation to see that this world was not created solely for suffering.[31] If the Supreme Lord had wanted us to be miserable, he certainly could have made it so—making what I ate bitter, what I heard rude, what I smelled foul, and what I saw frightening.[32] But creation is not like this, as we discover when we observe how the compassionate Supreme Lord creates a variety of fruits and roots at different seasons and in different lands solely for our gustatory pleasure;[33] how he creates a variety of beautiful, tender flowers for our visual, tactile, and olfactory pleasure; how he creates a variety of lovely sounds for our auditory pleasure. It is abundantly clear that he creates all these things for our pleasure. This being so, what should we say to someone who pays no attention to the One who has created all these things for our happiness but chooses instead to waste his time in food, entertainment, jokes, and curiosities?

[Signed] R G

Discourses Delivered to the Tattvabodhinī Sabhā on Sunday, 5 January 1840 [22 Pouṣa 1761]

Discourse Eleven[34]

Na vittena tarpanīyo manuṣyaḥ.[35]

Man is not satisfied by riches.

An ignorant* person looks at a mountain from afar and because of the sun's rays perceives it to be covered with all sorts of delightful gems. In the same way, a person under the sway of sense objects gazes at unearned riches* and imagines them to promise endless possibilities for happiness. And yet, no sooner do those riches come to him by dint of countless afflictions than he is left unsatisfied*. Driven by a longing for happiness, he once again grows agitated to acquire more riches. This kind of thirst* for sense objects can never be overcome through riches.

The business of life* is by and large accomplished because this thirst for sense objects finds no cessation*. Motivated by this longing for wealth, farmers and artisans produce huge amounts of the finest fruits and foods and a variety of the finest garments; seeking ever-greater power, they call on merchants to ship those goods from one country to another. Here we sit in this one place, satiated* with all kinds of goods* from different countries. Seeking ever-higher levels of advancement, government officials carefully perform their respective duties, while we pass our time without fear of thieves or other villains. Wise men, desiring greater glory, expend great energy preparing a variety of books for the welfare of the country, by means of which we all gain knowledge and fulfillment.

So it is that some individuals promote the welfare of the country for the sake of gaining wealth, power, glory, &c. But wiser and happier still than these people are those who pray for wealth and power solely in order to promote the welfare of the country.

[Signed] D

Discourse Twelve

This entire world and all its inhabitants are under the sway of a mighty delusion. They make the error of thinking that this inconstant* world is permanent. In their thirst for happiness, they chase after empty, evil deeds like a mirage. Self-knowledge* is forsaken.

Alas, such is the error* of ignorant people! They do not recognize that they are like a flower that blooms in the garden in the morning. It sways in the soft, cool breeze, delighting the entire garden with its wonderful fragrance. But just as this flower will soon fade and dry out, so, too, do men, who are endowed with youth and the good looks that engender pride. Men who are celebrated by the world for their various glories meet their demise at some random* time, thanks to the force of fickle and inconstant nature. Therefore, those who know the body to be inconstant and random in this way will abandon their affection* for evil paths and reflect* on the Self whose essential nature is consciousness and bliss*.[36] These are the people who earn a reward* whose very nature is an incomparable, eternal* happiness.

[Signed] A

Discourses delivered to the Tattvabodhinī Sabhā on Sunday, 12 January 1840 [29 Pouṣa 1761]

Discourse Thirteen[37]

It is difficult to say what sort of misfortune may befall us when the mighty passions like lust and anger overwhelm our intellect and bring our senses under their sway.

Consider how bad* it is for us and for others when even one of the passions—such as anger—grows strong. Iron undergoes a change when exposed to fire and is thereby able to burn other things. In the same way, human beings are transformed by anger and are led to harm* other people. Fire reduces lovely things like clothes and ornaments to ash. In the same way, all the human virtues are destroyed by anger, only to be replaced by all the vices*. When anger grows strong, the senses are fully enlisted in doing wrong to ourselves. Our ears do not heed good counsel, our eyes look on our closest friends as enemies, and our speech becomes improper. We notice time and time again that anger causes us to lose the ability to discern what benefits or harms the Self. It even causes us to destroy our dearest children and friends. Because of anger, we shame and slay our most revered parents and teachers. Because of anger, human beings are even capable of suicide. When we are taken over in this way by anger, we completely lose touch with worldly concerns*, ultimate concerns*, wealth, people, respect, our servants, and our advisers.

Likewise, when we fall prey to lust, we view our parents, brothers, wives, and children as if they were enemies. And those people who are in fact ill-disposed toward us seem to be our friends. We consider it proper to associate with selfish people* and despise the company of good people*. Unrestrained in our fancy for pleasure, we consume all sorts of intoxicating substances. We wear out our bodies, which are plagued by all sorts of diseases on account of our appetites.[38] Under the rule of lust, we are prepared even to destroy our own life.

When lust grows strong, so, too, does greed. We fail to recognize as evil those deeds we perform in our quest for the very wealth that fuels our wastefulness. Eventually, we turn to theft and robbery, and we suffer lifelong from the effort to conceal our evil deeds. We suffer mental torment for as long as we live, knowing that if we are found out we could be imprisoned or sent into exile.

When we are completely overcome by delusion, we make the mistake of thinking this world is permanent; we become overly attached to impermanent things like children, friends, wives, wealth, and so forth. Eventually, even the slightest loss plunges us into a sea of grief. The person who is blinded by delusion finds it difficult to spend money simply to feed himself, never mind to benefit others with his wealth. Such a person is completely destroyed, both in this life and the next.

When all the passions are thus roused, it is possible to cause incredible misfortune. However, if we are able to subdue them, we can bring an end to suffering and attain happiness. Remaining firm and steadfast at the first onslaught of the passions, we can easily subdue them. But if we think we can calm them by feeding them, not only will they not be calmed, they will grow in strength:

> Najātu kāmaḥ kāmānāmupabhogena śāmyati
> Haviṣā kṛṣṇavartmeva bhūya evābhivardhate.[39]
>
> One cannot restrain lust by feeding it the objects of lust, just as one cannot put out a fire by adding clarified butter; it only grows stronger.

The Supreme Lord has given us the power to subdue the passions in this manner; he has not given this power to beasts. Therefore, if we do not use all our means* to restrain* our passions, we are no better than beasts.[40] However, the Supreme Lord has not granted us so much power that we are able once and for all to destroy lust, anger, &c. If all the passions were destroyed once and for all, it would be difficult for us to carry out the duties of worldly life.

Without lust, there would be no bonds of love with our wives and children. Without an object of our love, we would cease to exert ourselves in caring and providing for others; we would go about listless and confused, doing false deeds. Caring only to find some way to feed our own stomachs, and deprived of all the other pleasures of life, we would descend even lower than the beasts.

Without anger, there would be no shame. All of a sudden, everyone would be stealing. Children, servants, and wives, &c., would not live as they ought to. How could the duties of worldly life be carried out in such a situation?

Without selfishness, there would also be no friendship on earth. No one would share in the suffering and happiness of others; no one would lift a hand to help anyone else. People would scarcely feel it necessary to care for their wives and children.

Therefore, respected members, be diligent in steadfastly controlling lust, anger, &c., and reflect on their proper functioning, that you may find salvation* from all misfortune.

[Signed] Ī

Discourse Fourteen[41]

> Ānandaṃ brahmaṇovidvān na bibheti kutaścana.[42]
>
> Once he knows the Supreme Brahman whose essential nature is happiness, a man of the world is never afraid.

From the revealed text quoted here, it is evident that the essential nature of the Supreme Self is supreme happiness*. If one worships him, there is nothing to fear. However, not all men are engaged in His worship. Instead, they are addicted to the impermanent and partial happiness that comes from sense objects. As a result, they reap a variety of afflictions.

Everyone wishes in his heart* for nothing but unending happiness, with not a trace of sorrow remaining. Under the sway of such a wish, men will give their all in a careful effort to secure happiness and bring an end to sorrow. But what they don't know is that happiness is never attained, nor sorrow ended, by means of sense objects. So many people expend enormous effort and time amassing wealth. They travel to distant countries, they traverse the ocean, they follow the commands of proud and wealthy individuals, and they suffer rebuke when their obedience falls even the slightest bit short. Eventually, they reach their appointed hour, overcome by old age and death. Then there are those who have copious wealth and various avenues for enjoyment, but who are unable to enjoy it because of illness. Still others are wracked with grief at being separated from their wife or troubled at the loss of their son. Some are distraught by worries about wealth, or politics, or rain, or drought. Others still are troubled by the lack of such things.

The moment someone fails to find satisfaction from his wife and sons, he turns against them and becomes hostile. Disagreements with brothers over worldly concerns threaten a man's physical and mental health, lead him to squander his wealth, and eventually bring utter ruin.[43] The more such a man's family prospers, the more his sorrow increases. When a man lives alone, he need only look after himself. As a result, his troubles are minimal. When he marries, he assumes the responsibility for another person. Sons, daughters, grandsons, and granddaughters come next, and soon he must care diligently for several people. How can a man be happy in such conditions? In a big family, it is unlikely that everyone will be healthy all the time, and so such a man must consult with a doctor daily. His family's suffering troubles him, and the need to provide medicines is cause for distress. Should anyone in the family be foolish or stubborn or resort to evil deeds—like theft or adultery—he suffers endlessly. And if the miscreant is brought before the law, his sorrow is only compounded. This is why in such a world, it is impossible for us either to find uninterrupted happiness or to completely banish sorrow by means of sense objects. Nor will we have any means of doing so as long as we live. And so a man should consider what the world is really like, give up his attachment* to it, and worship the Supreme Lord.[44] This is all one need do to calm one's worldly concerns. Blessed Vaśiṣṭha has said:

> Parijñānenasarpatvaṃ citra sarpasya naśyati
> Yathā tathaiva saṃsāraḥsthita evopaśamyati.[45]
>
> As long as one does not know that the snake is painted, then the painted snake is taken for a snake. And so at the sight of it, a person is frightened. But once one knows it is painted, it is no longer taken for a snake. In the same way, once one knows the true nature of the world, the world is automatically calmed.

O, how deluded we are! There is a single Overlord* of the world, who is greater than all men. When properly worshiped by the mind alone, he is pleased and is thereby prepared to bring us to him*. And yet while this Supreme Lord exists and is fit for our worship, we engage in the worship of some ordinary man who is the moderately generous overlord of a few villages. According to the Kulārṇava:

> Sopanābhūtaṃ mokṣasya manuṣyaṃ prāpya durlabhaṃ
> Yas tārayati nātmānaṃ tasmāt pāpatarotrakaḥ.[46]
>
> Who is more sinful* than the individual who seeks not his own salvation* after having attained that hard-to-obtain human birth that is like a stairway to liberation?
>
> prāptvācāpyuttamaṃ janma labdhvācendriya sauṣṭhavam
> na vettyātmahitaṃ yastu sa bhavedātmaghātakaḥ.[47]
>
> He who does not know his own good after gaining this precious human birth and perfect health commits suicide.

O Supreme Lord, we have fallen into this sorrow-filled world through the power of your creative will*. Surrounded in our family by wife, son, grandson, and granddaughter, we suffer many afflictions. Be content this very day to rescue us from these afflictions.

> Eko bhavāmisma bhavehamādau
> Dārairathobhausma bhavāva āvāṃ
> Vayaṃ bhavāṃo vahavaḥsma
> Putraistvanmāyayādyāpi vibho prasīda.[48]

[Signed] R

Discourses Delivered to the Tattvabodhinī Sabhā on Sunday, 26 January 1840 [14 Māgha 1761]

Discourse Fifteen

> Anyacchreyonyadutaiva preyaste
> Ubhe nānārthe puruṣaṃ sinītaḥ
> Tayoḥśreya ādadānasya sādhu
> Bhavati hīyaterthādyau preyovṛṇīte.[49]
>
> What is good* is one thing and what is desired* is another. Because the good and the desired bear two different rewards, each man is enjoined to his own ceremonies*. Of these two, the individual who

chooses the good finds blessings, while the individual who chooses the desired falls short of the supreme goal of human life*.

Early one morning, the great soul Śaunaka—still just a young man—went wandering.[50] Lost in reflection on such things as the ultimate versus the trivial, good versus bad, righteousness versus unrighteousness, happiness versus sorrow, duty versus prohibition, he entered absentmindedly into a grove.[51] Eventually, he found himself at the foot of a mountain. Moving somewhat unsteadily because of the uneven path, he looked up and saw the mountain before him. From it, two heavenly nymphs were descending. Śaunaka noticed that they were coming toward him, so he stopped and waited for them. As they came closer, he saw that they were both young and beautiful, though they differed in their age, comportment, and dress. The elder of the two approached him modestly; her eyes were downcast, and she stepped gingerly. She wore no ornaments, and her whole face beamed with maternal affection. The younger nymph wore elegant clothes and was adorned with a variety of ornaments. She smiled as she approached him, displaying her varied charms. She cast her glance this way and that, then gazed at him from the corner of her eye. Impelled by an innate exuberance, she quickly overtook the first nymph and called out, "I say, my dear Śaunaka, why do you suffer so, as if you were drowning in worry? It pains me to see your sorrow. Why don't you put worry and grief behind you. Follow me down a path that is covered in fragrant flowers and shaded by groves of trees from whose branches sweet bird calls are ever ringing. Travelers on this path never grow weary. They are charmed* by happiness alone."

Śaunaka's heart was filled with wonder by these charming*[52] words. He asked, "Who are you? What is your name?"

"My name is the Desired One, and those who follow me spend all their time in happiness. And she who comes behind me is called the Good One. Unfortunate souls who follow her decree have no end of sorrow."

At this, the first maiden drew closer, moving softly as was her nature. She said, "O Śaunaka, I come for your welfare, drawn by your many virtues and your faith. Do not be like those ignorant people who are fooled by the words of the Desired One; follow me instead. True, it is possible that if you take my path you will encounter some difficulties at the outset. But the more you enter into this path, the more your happiness will increase. Eventually, when you reach the end of the path you will find an inexpressible* happiness that is beyond all change. However, I make one difficult demand: No one may accompany me who hasn't defeated the armies of the Desired One, those soldiers of lust, anger, greed, &c. You are intelligent*; reflect on this, and act as you should."

The Desired One listened to all this, and then said with a laugh, "Listen to all these difficult and grievous things the Good One asks you to practice, Śaunaka. She is the only one who knows anything about such unobservable, inexpressible, unchanging happiness. If she was truly interested in your welfare, she would never ask you to wage war against my allies—lust, anger, and greed. Isn't it astounding that when complete happiness can be found by catering to lust &c., any sensible person would deliberately seek suffering by waging a war that is sure to bring countless afflictions? It is inconceivable that an intelligent person would pay attention to such fiendish and grievous words.

"Only fools give up present happiness in the hope of a happiness that cannot be perceived. My dear Śaunaka, how happy you will be if you join me. You will live in a golden palace adorned with gems and pearls, and lie in a bed adorned with all kinds of fragrant flowers. Think how delighted you will be when you are surrounded by all your ministers, and the southern spring breeze blows all through the day as you listen to the sounds of cuckoos and other birds who have arrived on the gentle southern breezes. How satisfied you will be, tasting the sweet nectar of the finest fruits available for your enjoyment, and sipping cool, perfumed waters. How enchanted you will be by the pleasant songs sung for you by any number of gorgeous heavenly maidens, who will surround you on all sides. What sensible person would give up all these pleasures to follow the path offered by this miserable Good One, who really dispenses sorrow?"

The Good One was saddened by the younger nymph's attempt to use such arguments to bring Śaunaka under her power. Feeling compassionate*, she said to the Desired One, "How like you it is to show no mercy toward this virtuous and trusting young man, but to egg him on to evil behavior that will only plunge him into a sea of sorrow. We know it is impossible to go on enjoying the kinds of sensory pleasures you depict, since the senses decay through indulgence. That's why we grow agitated if we listen constantly to musical compositions or sweet birdsong. Endlessly indulging our lust only makes us ill. Furthermore, we know there is no sensual happiness that comes without the experience of sorrow. One is only driven to eat fruits, &c., if one is tormented by hunger; the body is only refreshed by a drink of water after first being tormented by thirst; lying down feels good only when one is overcome by sleep. Therefore, Desired One, what you call the happiness of the senses is always mixed with sorrow.

"Śaunaka, think about it, were you put on this earth solely for sensory pleasure? Isn't it possible you could do something to benefit this world? Think of all the benefits provided by this tree. By its fruit, creatures satisfy their hunger and thirst; birds find happiness in its shelter; animals find rest in its shade; its leaves cure all sorts of illness and satisfy the hunger of countless animals. So, too, do all things—the wind, water, fire, moon, sun, and stars—work to benefit the world. Following this universal law you, too, were created to respect your father and mother, love your neighbors, work for the welfare of the government, rescue people from the torment of suffering, provide religious instruction to your son and students, and give knowledge to the ignorant. This is the Lord's law, and if you try to defy it out of a desire for sensual happiness, you will instantly fall into a sea of affliction. Don't be fooled by the sweet-sounding but poisonous words of the deceitful, untrustworthy Desired One. Know that you are the one in control,[53] and begin to perform your duties as best you can in keeping with the Lord's laws so that you may be happy in this life and the next."

As soon as he heard these beneficial words of the Good One, the great-souled Śaunaka understood. Defeating the armies of the Desired One—lust, anger, &c.—he followed the Good One and gained happiness in this life and liberation in the next.

Therefore, respected members, give up the Desired One and seize the Good One so that you may be blessed.

[Signed] D

Discourse Sixteen

My heart overflowing with delight, I bow down before the Supreme Substance that takes the form of the mystic syllable Oṃ—by whose will all the Vedas and Śāstras, the sun, the stars, humans, animals, and the five elements themselves are created—and I pray that the respected members of the Tattvabodhinī Sabhā will enjoy good health and will spend their time in beneficial discourse with good people of the holiest character, and by tasting the nectar of the knowledge of the highest reality, will instantly be liberated from the three fires of existence and find fulfillment.

[Signed] Ī G

Discourses Delivered to the Tattvabodhinī Sabhā on Sunday, 23 February 1840 [12 Phālguṇa 1761]

Discourse Seventeen[54]

Nāvirato duścaritānnāśāntonāsamāhitaḥ
Nāśānta manasovāpi prajñānenainamāpnuyāt.[55]

> The Self cannot be obtained by the intellect of one who does not desist from evil deeds, who has not pacified the fickle senses, whose mind is not concentrated, and whose mind has not calmed all desire for the fruits of action.

The Lord has created everything. In order to preserve his creation, he has arranged it so that every individual thing works for the welfare of all other things. Everything he has created assists others in some way—the sun by its heat, the trees by their fruit, and the rivers and streams by their water. Likewise, the Supreme Lord has created humans for the welfare of others.

Were humans not to help one another, the world would instantly collapse. If fathers and mothers did not nourish and care for their children, then how would the frail bodies of the young be protected? The Supreme Lord has instilled affection in the hearts of human beings to protect these young ones.[56] Were it not for this love, how would we know it is our duty to nourish and care for our children? Were it not for such love, the birth and death of our children would bring no more sense of gain or loss than the birth and death of a fly or an ant. Truly, how could the world carry on if we didn't make some careful effort to protect our children? To ensure the well-being* of the world, the Lord has created affection so that we will devote our full attention to nourishing and caring for our children.

We gain a better awareness that such affection has been created for the protection of living things when we take animals as an example. Animals have no intellect, and yet how beautifully they care for their offspring because of this affection! Let a stronger animal attempt to harm her offspring, and a mother will do all she can to chase it off. She will spare no effort in protecting her offspring. And the mother's affection remains constant for as long as her offspring need milk and support. As soon as they no longer need her care, her affection also disappears.

Human beings live long lives. They require the care of others. This is why affection for our children lasts all through our lives. Humans would have no way to stave off hunger without the special effort and assistance of others. Unlike animals, human beings cannot survive by eating grass from the fields or leaves from the trees. Human beings need clothing to ward off the cold. Unlike animals we have not been provided with thick coats to ward off the cold. In order to avoid countless afflictions, human beings need homes. We are not able to live in caves and other such places as animals do. There are so many things we need. If our affection were only temporary, as in the case of animals, our suffering here on earth would know no end. This is why the Supreme Lord has granted us the ability to feel affection for our children all through our lives.

If he has created affection so we will protect our relationships with our sons, grandsons, and granddaughters, he has created mercy* for the welfare of all. Just as there can be no affection for sons and grandsons in the absence of a relationship, the same is true for mercy. Is it not true that as soon as we witness the suffering of someone who has no eyesight, we feel mercy? The Supreme Lord has created this kind of sentiment*—which suffers at the sight of another's suffering—so that human beings will liberate others from sorrow. Thus, if we were to see someone cutting off the hand or foot of someone else with a saw, we would immediately feel pain and would do everything in our power to keep this wicked person from such an awful act. Because of mercy, evil people are simply unable to inflict suffering on people in a settled society. Should they try to cause someone pain, other people will make a careful effort to rescue that person from their evil hands. Were it not for this mercy, even if we had the strength to rescue someone from sorrow, we would have no inclination to do so. Mercy is such that we will even set aside our own welfare in order to rescue a person from sorrow. Without mercy, we would not make the slightest effort to rescue a blind person if we saw him lose his way and fall into a well. Mercy is such that we will instantly rescue someone from the ocean, without worrying whether it might do us harm.

The Lord has made love, mercy, affection &c., the law of our hearts. Clearly, we have been created solely for the welfare of others, and anyone who works for the welfare of another finds happiness by following the divine law*.

We call any action that injures another an evil action. The Lord has created shame, revulsion, fear, &c., to discourage human beings from evil action.

We try to conceal any action we know is evil, because we would suffer shame were we to reveal it. Yet no matter how hard we try to hide our evil actions, they will not remain concealed. We may find the courage to persist in evil as long as we think we can hide our actions. But once we realize that our evil actions will be revealed—and that once revealed they will cause suffering and shame—we abandon evil.

The mere sight of an evil person causes revulsion*, just as does the sight of something putrid. We find no satisfaction in the company or the conversation of such a person. Something made from diamonds, silver, or gold tends to show corrosion all that much more. Likewise, evil actions are all the more evident in a person of learning, wealth, and high station. No matter how virtuous* or powerful* he may be, someone who does evil cannot be considered anything other than repulsive. Respected members, consider how effectively this revulsion deters evil action.

The Lord created fear in the minds of human beings so that evil people are unable to resort to evil deeds. And if they do evil, they live in fear lest it be revealed. If it is revealed, they must abandon their wife and children out of fear of the government. Renouncing the civilized world, they wander from forest to forest without the means even to feed themselves. Nor are they free of fear even there, since the mere rustling of leaves frightens them into thinking of the authorities.

Such are the sorrows that follow from evil action. The possibility of doing great harm to creation causes great mental distress, whereas the possibility of doing lesser harm causes less distress. The merciful Supreme Lord neither punishes serious evil lightly nor minor evil seriously. This is why revulsion, shame, and fear are greater or lesser in accordance with the degree of evil action.

Of all the evil actions, there is none worse than murder. This is why someone who commits murder suffers terribly. If the Supreme Lord didn't cause a special kind of sorrow in the hearts of human beings to act as an obstacle to this kind of evil, humans would kill one another out of the slightest anger, hatred, or pride. There would be absolutely no means to protect the world.

While people who are the vilest miscreants are likely to become accustomed to the suffering induced by evil deeds, even they cannot overlook the sorrow that accompanies murder. A person who commits this evil deed is so lost to reason that they seem unable even to save their own life. Those who are guilty of other evil deeds are careful to conceal their evil from the authorities, but those who are guilty of murder aren't just careful. They are positively zealous. But as long as they go without punishment, they can find no liberation from sorrow in this life.

These are the sorts of sorrow that come from doing injury to others. If being diligent in benefiting others brings a special kind of inner satisfaction*, then, clearly, the chief law of the Supreme Lord is that we should benefit others. This being the case, is anyone fit to worship the Supreme Lord who defies his chief law? Surely, then, we will never obtain Ultimate Reality merely by wisdom*; we must first forsake evil.

[Signed] D

Discourses Delivered to the Tattvabodhinī Sabhā on Sunday, 2 February 1840[57] [21 Māgha 1761]

Discourse Eighteen[58]

Restraint of the senses is an absolutely essential aid in the worship of God, because without restraint of the senses there can be no steadiness of mind:

Indriyānāṃ vicaratāṃ viṣayeṣvapahāriṣu
Saṃyame yatnamātiṣṭhedvidvān yanteva vājinām.[59]

The learned person should take care to restrain all the senses, which are led astray by sense objects, in the same way that a charioteer takes care to restrain his horses.

The best charioteer abandons a bad road and sets his horses on a good road. Likewise, an intelligent person abandons sense objects that occasion error and fixes his senses on those that do not. A blind charioteer cannot distinguish a bad road from a good one and falls into a pothole. In the same way, people who are swayed by lust, anger, &c., fall into difficult straits because of their inability to distinguish vice from virtue. So if the senses are to be restrained, we must first overcome the passions. If the passions are not overcome, there can be no restraint of the senses, be it in the forest or in the home. If the passions are overcome, restraint of the senses will always be possible, no matter what the conditions.

Bhayaṃ pramattasya vaneṣvapisyāt
Yataḥ sa aste saha ṣaṭsapatnaḥ
Jitendriyasyātmaraterbudhasya
Gṛhāśramāḥ kiṃnu karotyavadyaṃ[60]

An impassioned person feels fear even in a forest, since such a person is always accompanied by the six passions; and yet what harm can the householder's life do to the wise person who has conquered the passions and is self-possessed?[61]

This is why it is as pointless to go to the forest to conquer the passions as it is to go there in search of sense objects.

The householder's life is approved by the Supreme Lord. Why renounce it and go to the forest to seek him? In any case, one cannot seek the Supreme Lord while living alone in the forest, since concerns about food cause mental agitation. In the householder's life, even while supporting the lives of children and friends, we are able to study scripture and meditate without hindrance.

It must be said, to those who worry that in the householder's life one's mind is unsettled by association with so many people—and who thus think that the solitary life of the forest is the best—that it is simply not possible for a person who has not learned concentration to quell the disturbances of the mind simply by living in the forest. After all, the mind is unsettled at the mere sound of mosquitoes. And yet, if one's mind is not disturbed in the midst of a beautiful, sweet-smelling forest full of multicolored birds and dangerous beasts like tigers and bears, why might this be? It is because even amid throngs of people, the concentrated person is alone:

> Ādāvanteca madhyeca jano yasminnavidyate
> Yenedaṃ satataṃ vyāptaṃ sadeśo vijanaḥ smṛtaḥ.[62]
>
> As long as one focuses on the ultimate reality of the Supreme Self, which has no persons either in its beginning, middle, or end—that is, which is One only[63]—and which is everywhere and always present, then even amid throngs of people one is alone.

God has not given beasts the power of speech. He has given it to us so that we may grow in knowledge through our association with one another. Therefore, if we do nothing but live in the forest like beasts, saying nothing, then how do we differ from them? Blessed Manu, compiler of all knowledge, has written:

> Yasmāttrayo 'pyāśramiṇo jñānenānnenacānvahaṃ
> Gṛhasthenaiva dhāryante tasmāt jyeṣṭhāśramo gṛhī.[64]
>
> Because the other three stages of life are supported daily by food and learning given by those in the householder's stage, it is truly the householder's stage that is the best.

Consequently, we must worship the Supreme Lord while maintaining the life of the householder so that we shall have blessings in this life and the next.

[Signed] Ī

Discourses Delivered to the Tattvabodhinī Sabhā on Sunday, 1 March 1840[65] [19 Phālguṇa 1761]

Discourse Nineteen[66]

> Sarvaṃ khalvidaṃ brahma tajjalāniti śānta upāsīta.[67]

This phenomenal world* that we perceive with our senses verily has Brahman as its essential nature, and for this reason it is from Brahman that the world arises, persists, and perishes. Substances like earthen vessels are made from clay, with clay as their basis. They resolve back into clay when broken. All such substances are really nothing but clay. In this connection, we find the following in the revealed texts:

> Yato vā imāni bhūtāni jāyante yena jātāni
> Jīvanti yat prayastyabhisaṃviśanti.[68]
>
> The world arises from Brahman, finds its persistence in Brahman as its basis, and resolves back into Brahman when it dies. Thus the phenomenal world is not something other than Brahman; after restraining one's senses, one should worship Brahman.

From the above revealed texts it can be seen that the Supreme Lord is the cause of the world. And when one witnesses his splendid effects, one must recognize that he possesses a splendid power. After all, nothing is ever created from something that does not itself have the power to make another thing.[69] And this, too, is found in the revealed texts:

> Vicitra śaktiḥ puruṣaḥ purāṇaḥ.[70]

Therefore, the inexpressibly splendid power of the Supreme Lord must be acknowledged. In the philosophy of Vedānta, this power is called such things as nescience*, illusion*, nature*, &c.

Even though the individual Self* is in essence the Supreme Self, a sense of individuality* appears due to nescience. And so the heart's sense of religion is beset with countless desires, and one performs all kinds of desirable and prohibited actions.[71] In consequence, one enjoys the fruits of heaven or hell. From what positive and negative karma remains, one is born again and performs more action and enjoys more fruit as a result of this remaining karma. In this way, just like a clock or a potter's wheel, one wanders deluded—sometimes in a lofty world, sometimes in a middling world, sometimes in a nether world—thinking of oneself as sorrowful or joyful, happy or satisfied. Having attained heaven* through one's actions, one begins to fear that when their karma decays they will fall. One is distraught upon assuming a heavenly body and suffers when the time comes to fall. Upon arriving in a middling world, one enters the darkened womb of one's mother, which causes personal distress. After all, what can compare to the distress one undergoes at the time of birth? From then on, one is unable to move; one is dependent on others and nearly always sick. And who hasn't experienced the suffering that comes with being forced to learn once one reaches the age of five? Afterward, as a young man, one goes through great trials to earn money in order to build a house and a garden. Then one has children and begins to worry. One starts saying, this is my house, this is my garden, this is my wife, this is my son, this is my daughter, this is my grandson, and so forth. Later on, the tiger of time grabs one's shoulder in his teeth, and look out! What in anyone's present experience can suggest such grief? And yet, this much is worth considering. One feels profound misery at being separated from a son or a wife or one's wealth. But this is nothing compared to the grief that comes from knowing that ultimately one will be separated from all of this—from knowing one will never again see one's wife, son, home, garden, &c. This is why we must never forget the Self, but through mindfulness* should know its essential nature if we are to be rescued from this sorrow.

[Signed] R

Discourse Twenty[72]

It is necessary to help one another as best we can, since it is difficult to face any task without the help of others. We would not even have these clothes we put on every day were it not for the collective work of a multitude of friends. Spinners create thread on their wheels using cotton grown by farmers; weavers carefully make cloth from this thread. It is by means of such collective help that we acquire all our goods and produce. The Supreme Lord has not given the power to help one another merely to human beings; he has given the ability to help one another to all things, conscious and unconscious, like beasts, birds, worms, and insects. No action on earth would proceed were it not for this power to help one another. Consider the little bee that wanders through the garden gathering bits of nectar from various flowers, and who builds a marvelous house with the help of others; there is no way such things could be accomplished by a single bee. Were it not for the power of attraction*, which causes every minute atom* of creation to be drawn into relationships with other atoms, there would be no way to preserve creation.

The omniscient* Lord of All has created beautiful laws to encourage us to help one another. In fact, if you think about it, we actually help others when we are diligent about helping ourselves. When people engage in profit*-making businesses*, then other people in all sorts of countries profit in a variety of ways. The wheels on a wagon each revolve around a single hub, yet they allow us to travel to other buildings or towns. Likewise, when people set out to help themselves, they can also help others in any number of ways.

Lo, what an amazing purpose there is behind the deeds of the most utterly Supreme Lord. Should he destroy one thing, he gives shelter to another. A droplet may be lost in the fathomless waters of the ocean, but by mingling with the waters of the ocean it contributes to the flow of the rivers and streams. A body composed of the five elements perishes. It dissolves back into the five elements. Thereby it contributes to the production of trees and plants. The flowers and fruit born from these trees and plants benefit all sorts of animals, birds, and human beings.

Therefore, respected members, be especially diligent in protecting the chief law of the Supreme Lord. By undertaking to help others to the best of your ability, may you also be blessed.

[Unsigned]

Discourses Delivered to the Tattvabodhinī Sabhā on Sunday, 17 May 1840[73] [5 Jyaiṣṭha 1762]

Discourse Twenty-One[74]

> Yasminsarvāni bhūtāni ātmaivābhūdvijānataḥ
> Tatra ko mohaḥ kaḥśoka ekatvamanupaśyataḥ.[75]
>
> When a knower understands that all living beings are in fact the Self, and when he looks upon all things as one, then there can be for him no grief or delusion.

Is there a single member of this Society who doesn't know how much the world is helped by business? Through their varied efforts, merchants determine what sorts of essential goods are wanting in various nations*. Then they diligently set about producing the various goods that will address these needs. In this they are capable—at one and the same time—of helping both their own nation and foreign nations. They provide continual support to the farmers and craftsmen of their own nation* who grow bountiful corn and fruits and who make all sorts of clothing and jewelry. And by distributing this corn, fruit, clothing, and jewelry to other lands where they are needed, they increase the general welfare. It is by the very grace of these merchants that we have come to live in the one place where all these delightful goods are prepared, here on the shore of the mighty ocean. Right now, as I deliver this very discourse, how many merchants from how many nations are busily working to promote our happiness?

Do you suppose it is the case that all these merchants have gone into business merely to work for our happiness? Do all the sea captains brave the ocean waves out of a desire for our well-being? This cannot be so. It is practically a universal truth that people exert themselves out of a desire to increase their own wealth, reputation, and fame. Most people are so caught up in the work of accumulating wealth that they scarcely pause to consider whether it helps or harms the general populace. There are very few people on this earth who act simply out of a desire to help the general populace. Those individuals who seek the well-being of the general populace are the true votaries* of the Supreme Lord, and they alone can be called rich.

We only truly find pleasure in the company of someone whose actions reveal a desire for our happiness. It is impossible to find pleasure in the company of anyone who desires otherwise. This is why, if we are invited to a friend's house to listen to a singer or a speaker who has been hired for the occasion, we take no pleasure in the company of the singer or the speaker. We do not feel obliged to them, because they do not desire our welfare. They sing or speak only out of a hankering for wealth. But we do find pleasure in the friend who, out of a desire for our happiness, undertakes to hire that singer or speaker; to such a one we are certainly obliged. And this is why those who make an effort solely for the welfare of others are cherished by all and are always worthy of gratitude. How can we cherish someone and show them our gratitude if they don't give a moment's thought to helping the world, but are fixated only on acquiring wealth?

Someone who performs a helpful deed without intending to never deserves a reward. Prisoners of the state do all sorts of services for the general populace, like constructing roadways, but since such acts don't reflect their own intention*, we never reward them with wealth or praise.[76]

Conversely, someone who performs a harmful act without intending it should never be punished. If a man driving a carriage were to strike someone and kill him, that man should not be punished, since he never intended to kill that person.

Therefore, respected members, it is only through intention that men are guilty or blameless. We cannot know a person's intentions until he performs an action; once he does so, and we know his intentions, we can apply the appropriate punishment or reward. If we don't know someone's intentions, we cannot know if they are righteous or unrighteous. And therefore we may not be able to decide whether to reward or punish them. But the omniscient Supreme Lord knows every desire of their heart. No unrighteous person escapes punishment, and no righteous person goes without reward. This is why it is essential that we guard our intention according to the law![77] We must always be on guard, lest there be any intention to do evil.

People who only make an effort to accumulate wealth are not always able to help others; their wealth may even come from doing harm to others. How astounding it is that for the sake of fleeting wealth, people can become addicted to evil and thereby sink into an ocean of sorrow.

Those who have a mind only for doing things to help others will never exert themselves to acquire wealth through evil actions. They are as satisfied in helping others as rich people are in accumulating wealth. While people who help others are happy if wealth comes their way, they do not suffer at its loss. Even if they have no wealth, they do their best to help through other means. They always exert themselves with care, whether by keeping good company, providing counsel, quelling sorrow, treating illness, or bestowing knowledge. Such great-souled men are indeed wealthy, and they alone are the true votaries of the Supreme Lord.[78]

Those who follow the teaching of the revealed text quoted at the outset of this discourse, who look upon the whole world as the Self, and who overcome the grief and delusion of this dreadful illusory world—they alone are able to set aside their own interests and work for the welfare of all.

[Signed] D

God is One Only without an Equal[79]

Appendix 1

Note Regarding the Translation

In preparing this translation, I have tried to be both accurate and consistent, staying as close as possible to the language of the text. For instance, even if a sense of English style might have suggested adopting a more creative use of synonyms, I have tried to render Bengali terms the same way in every instance (unless otherwise indicated in the notes and glossary). While I fear this may have resulted in a rather wooden translation, I nevertheless feel confident that the translation I have produced will serve as a useful guide to the terminology and style of the original Bengal discourses. I hope that nonspecialists will be able to read the text without too much aggravation, while specialists may be able to see through my translation to the original.

That said, I have made one or two minor changes to the formatting of the discourses, principally to provide easier visual access to the text. For instance, I have made the headings within the text somewhat more descriptive, whereas the original text simply provides dates (for more on dating, see below). Likewise, I have added rubrics that serve to number the discourses in sequence, a feature not found in the original. This latter change has been made principally in order to make reference to the discourses in the rest of this work more convenient. At the end of each discourse, I have also added in brackets the word "Signed" before the initials that appear in the original. This is to call attention to the role these isolated characters have in the text. For information on the system of initials used in *Sabhyadiger vaktṛtā*, and for my attempt to identify the individual authors of these discourses, readers should consult chapters 6 and 7.

Quotations from Sanskrit sources (which appear in Bengali script in the original) are scattered throughout the text of *Sabhyadiger vaktṛtā*. I have transcribed these just as they appear in the original, rendering words and compounds as they are found in the original—although I have reduced certain duplicated consonants, adopting *sarva* instead of *sarvva*, for example. Wherever necessary, I have noted discrepancies from received versions in the notes. In the interest of readability, I have treated these Sanskrit passages as block quotations, introducing line breaks for verse couplets where appropriate. The authors of the discourses provide their own Bengali translations (or in many cases paraphrases). I have chosen to translate the authors' Bengali translations of the originals rather than the original Sanskrit itself, since this allows us to appreciate how these authors understood a particular passage. I have also in most cases treated these glosses as block quotations, though they are not set this way in the original text. While the authors of these discourses do not provide citations for these passages (apart from an occasional reference to *śruti* or to the title of the work in question), I have tried to provide this information in the notes wherever possible. For a list of all texts cited, readers may consult appendix 2.

Multiple authors are represented in *Sabhyadiger vaktṛtā*, and understandably there is some subtle variation in style among the various compositions (although the vocabulary is almost entirely drawn from Sanskrit and the terms of address are largely formal and abstract). I regret it if my translation goes too far in flattening out the subtle differences from author to author, although hopefully even in translation readers will be able to detect the difference in cadence, idiom, and tone between individual authors.

One Sanskrit convention widely adopted by these authors is the use of the suffix *–ādi* at the end of lists to suggest what English-language speakers communicate using the Latin term et cetera. Because this convention is shared by all the authors, and because in English-language works of the same era one routinely finds the abbreviation "&c.", I have adopted the latter convention here in preference to the oft-used and potentially tiresome phrase "and so on."

Within the body of the translation, I have used an asterisk (*) to indicate the first occurrence of words or phrases that are listed in the glossary, along with their Sanskrit or Bengali equivalents. As I have noted, every attempt has been made to be consistent in translating terminology.

Appendix 2

List of Texts Cited in *Sabhyadiger vaktṛtā*

The authors of the discourses collected in *Sabhyadiger vaktṛtā* frequently cite Sanskrit passages from revealed texts (*śruti*) or other traditional texts (e.g., *smṛti, itihāsa*, and *tantra*) to amplify and lend authority to their presentations. *Sabhyadiger vaktṛtā* provides no detailed citations, but every effort has been made to identify these Sanskrit passages so that interested readers may consider the range and type of sources drawn on by members of the Tattvabodhinī Sabhā to articulate their vision of religion and morality. In some cases—for instance, a piece of gnomic verse in Discourse Eighteen and a verse purportedly from the Yoga-vāśiṣtha Rāmāyaṇa in Discourse Two—it has proven impossible to find a direct textual reference. Citations from Sanskrit sources are given by book, chapter, and verse as appropriate.

Passages from Śruti	Discourse number
Bṛhadāraṇyaka Upanishad	
1.4.8	1
2.4.5	1
3.9.28	1
Chāndogya Upanishad	
3.14.1	19
6.2.1	Benediction
Īśā Upanishad	
7	21
Kaṭha Upanishad	
1.6	3
1.27	11
2.1	15
2.24	17
3.12	8
3.15	8
Kena Upanishad	
4.8	2
Muṇḍaka Upanishad	
2.2.11	9
3.2.9	1
Taittirīya Upanishad	
2.4.1	14
3.1	19

Passages from other Sanskrit sources	Discourse number
Bhāgavata Purāṇa	
5.1.17	18
Kulārṇava Tantra	
1.16	14
1.17	14
9.21	1
9.28	1
Mahābhārata	
1.693.6	13
Manu Smṛti	
2.88	18
3.78	18
Viṣṇu Purāṇa	
I.2.10b–11	1
Yoga-vāśiṣṭha Rāmāyaṇa	
2.18.41	14
Unattested	2
Śaṅkara's Commentary on Muṇḍaka Upanishad	
2.2.11	9
Gnomic verse (oral circulation)	
Not applicable	18
Unknown sources	
Unidentified	14
Unidentified	19

Appendix 3

Glossary of Key Terms Used in the English Translation

This glossary provides translation equivalents for some of the more technical, curious, or possibly ambiguous terms and phrases in my translation of *Sabhyadiger vaktṛtā*. Words and phrases in the translation that appear in the glossary are marked with an asterisk (*). Wherever possible, an attempt has been made to translate Bengali (or Sanskrit) terms using only a single English term (e.g., *sukha* is always rendered "happiness"). However, there are cases in which multiple Indic terms bear a similar meaning (e.g., *śocanā* and *śoka* are both translated "grief"). Likewise, there are cases in which a single Indic term can bear multiple English meanings (e.g., *dharma* may be translated "law" in one context, "virtue" in another, and "righteousness" in yet another).

Because of the predominance of Sanskrit loan words in these Bengali discourses, terms have been transliterated following Sanskrit spellings.

Action	Karma (*see* Duty)
Affection	Anurāga, sneha
Affliction	Kleśa (*see* Distress, Trouble)
All-powerful	Sarva śaktimān
Anger	Krodha
Atom	Paramāṇu
Attachment	Āsakti
Attraction	Ākarṣaṇa
Awakened	Buddha
Awareness	Cetana, bodha
Bad	Manda
Basis	Adhiṣṭhāna

Beast	Paśu
Being	Sattā
Beings	Bhūta
Benefit	Hita
Beyond perception	Apratyakṣa
Blessings	Śubha, maṅgala, kalyāṇa, kuśala
Bring us to him	Svapada pradāna
Business	Vāṇijya
Business of life	Lokayātra
Calm, calmed	Śānta
Calmness	Śama
Careful effort	Yatna
Cause	Kāraṇa
Ceremony	Anuṣṭhāna
Cessation	Nivṛtti
Charmed	Mohita
Charming	Mohajanaka
Compassionate	Karuṇāmayī
Conceit	Abhimāna
Concentrated	Samāhita
Consciousness	Caitanya
Consciousness and bliss	Cidānanda
Control	Śāsana
Create	Sṛṣṭi karā
Creation	Sṛṣṭi
Creative will	Māyā
Creator	Sṛṣṭikartā
Death	Mṛtyu
Deep sleep	Suṣupti
Deluded	Mūḍha
Delusion	Moha
Desired	Preyas
Destroyer	Layakartā
Diligent	Yatnavān, yatnaśīla
Directly	Sākṣāt
Discipline of the Self	Adhyātmayoga
Discrimination	Viveka
Disease	Roga
Distress	Kleśa (*see* Affliction, Trouble)
Divine law	Aiśvarika niyama
Doubt	Saṃśaya
Duty, duties	Karma (*see* Action)
Earth	Pṛthivī
Effort	Pariśrama
Elements	Pañcabhūta (*see* Five elements)

Embodied	Śarīraviśiṣṭa, śarīrī
Enjoyment	Tuṣṭi
Error	Bhrama, bhrānti
Essence	Bhāva
Essential (characteristic)	Svarūpa (lakṣaṇa)
Eternal happiness	Nityasukha
Evil deeds	Kukarma, duṣkarma
Experience	Anubhava
Faith	Śraddhā
False	Mithyā
Fashioned	Nirmitta
Faulty reasoning	Kutarka, dustarka
Fear	Bhaya
Fit	Yogya
Five elements	Pañcabhūta (*see* Elements)
Fundamental principles	Tattva
Goal of human life	Puruṣārtha
Good	Śreyas
Good people	Śiṣṭajana
Goods	Dravya
Grace	Anugraha
Great soul	Mahātmā
Greed	Lobha
Grief	Śoka, śocanā
Happiness	Sukha
Harm	Aniṣṭa karā
Heart	Manas (*see* Mind), Antaḥkaraṇa
Heaven	Svargaloka
Help	Upakāra (*see* Welfare)
Hope	Āśā
Householder	Gṛhastha
Human being	Manuṣya
Humanity	Loka
Ignorance	Ajñāna
Ignorant	Ajña
Illusion	Māyā
Imagined	Kalpita
Inanimate matter	Jaḍapadārtha (*see* Matter)
Inanimate objects	Sthāvara
Inconstant	Anitya
Indecision	Vikalpa
Individual self	Jīvātmā
Individuality	Jīvabhāva
Inexpressible	Anirvacanīya

Inner controller	Antaryāmī
Inner self	Antarātmā
Intellect	Buddhi
Intelligent	Buddhimān
Intention	Icchā
Knower	Jñāni
Knowledge	Jñāna
Law	Niyama, dharma
Liberated	Mukta
Liberation	Mukti, Mokṣa
Life	Jīvana
Life breath	Prāṇa vāyuḥ
Lifespan	Āyuḥ
Live	Jīvana dharaṇa
Living being	Jīva, prāṇi
Lord	Īśvara
Lord of all	Sarveśvara
Lust	Kāma
Magical power	Māyā
Manifest (characteristic)	Taṭastha (lakṣaṇa)
Marvelous	Acintanīya
Material reality	Mahat-tattva
Matter	Jaḍapadārtha
Means	Upāya
Memory	Smṛti
Mental intention	Saṃkalpa
Merchant	Vāṇik (*see* Trader)
Merciful	Dayāvān, dayāmaya
Mercifully	Kṛpā kariyā
Mercy	Dayā
Mind	Manas (*see* Heart)
Mindfulness	Manodhāraṇa
Misery	Yantranā
Misfortune	Amaṇgala, aniṣṭa, durgati
Misguided	Bhrānta (*see* Error)
Mistake	Bhrama (*see* Error)
Nation	Deśa
Nature	Prakṛti
Nescience	Avidyā
Of their own nation	Svadeśīya
Omniscient	Sarvajña
One without a second	Advitīya
Ordained	Niyamita
Ordainer	Niyantā

Organs of action	Karmendriya
Organs of knowledge	Jñānendriya
Overlord	Adhipati
Parable	Itihāsacchala
Passion	Ripu
Patience	Kṣamā
Phenomenal world	Prapañcamaya jagat
Plan	Tātparya (*see* Purpose)
Pleasure	Sukha
Power	Śakti, aiśvarya
Powerful	Aiśvaryavān
Practice	Sādhanā (*see* Pursuit)
Pray	Prārthanā Karā
Precisely	Yathāyogya
Preserver	Sthitikartā
Pride	Dambha
Profit	Lābha
Pure	Śuddha
Purpose	Tātparya (*see* Plan)
Purposefully	Tātparyarūpe
Pursuit	Sādhanā
Random	Aniścita
Real	Satya
Reason	Yukti
Reflect	Cintā karā
Refuge	Śaraṇa
Rescue	Uddhāra
Resolve	Saṃkalpa
Respected members	Sabhya mahodayerā
Restrain	Damana karā
Restraint	Dama
Revealed Text	Śruti
Revulsion	Ghṛṇā
Reward	Puraskāra, phala
Riches	Vitta
Round of birth and death	Saṃsāra
Salvation	Trāṇa, paritrāṇa
Satisfaction	Tṛpti
Satisfied	Santuṣṭa
Satiated	Parituṣṭa
Savior	Trāṇakartā
Self	Ātman
Selfish people	Yatheṣṭācārī
Self-knowledge	Ātmabodha
Sense	Indriya

Sense objects	Viṣaya
Sensual pleasure	Indriya sukha
Sentiment	Maner bhāva
Shame	Apamāna, lajjā
Sickness	Roga
Sincerity	Ārjjava
Sin	Pāpa
Sinful	Pāpī
Sorrow	Duḥkha (*see also* Suffering)
Subdued	Vaśībhūta
Substance	padārtha
Suffering	Duḥkha (*see also* Sorrow)
Support	Ādhāra, avalambana
Supreme Brahman	Parabrahma
Supreme happiness	Paramasukha
Supreme Lord	Parameśvara
Supreme Self	Paramātman
Supreme Truth	Paramārtha
Supremely compassionate	Paramakāruṇika
Thing	Vastu
Thirst	Tṛṣṇā
This life and the next	Ihakāla o parakāla
This world, next world	Ihaloka, paraloka
Time	Samaya, kāla
Trader	Vaṇik (*see* Merchant)
Trouble	Kleśa (*see* Affliction, Distress)
True appearance	yathārtha svarūpa
True nature	yathārtha svabhāva
Truth	Satya
Trust	Viśvāsa
Ultimate concern	Paramajñāna
Ultimate knowledge	Tattvajñāna
Ultimate Reality	Brahman
Unchanging	Nitya
Unhappy	Asukhi
Unsatisfied	Asantuṣṭa
Valid means of knowing	Pramāṇa
Vanity	Abhimāna
Vice	Doṣa
Virtue	Guṇa, dharma
Virtuous	Guṇavān
Votary	Upāsaka
Wealthy	Dhani
Welfare	Upakāra (*see* Help)

Well-being	Maṅgala (*see* Blessings)
Will	Icchā (*see* Intention)
Wisdom	Prajñā
Wise men	Paṇḍita
Without a purpose	Vyartha
Without a second	Advitīya
Works	Racanā
World	Jagat, saṃsāra, loka
Worldly	Laukika
Worldly concern	Viṣayajñāna
Worldly life	Saṃsāra
Worship	Upāsanā, ārādhanā

Notes

INTRODUCTION

1. I borrow this phrase from the title of Tithi Bhattacharya's recent study (2005). I comment more on the significance of the *bhadralok* in chapter 4.

2. A comprehensive and up-to-date account of the place of the *Patrikā* in the intellectual history of colonial Bengal has yet to be written, though a chronological summary can be found in Sen 1979. Information from the *Patrikā* informs several studies of this period, as in Damen 1988, Kopf 1979, and Hatcher 1996a.

3. For a discussion of Vedānta's significance in contemporary Hinduism, see Hatcher 2004.

4. A rough pronunciation equivalent for the title would be *Shúb*-bho-di-ger *Bók*-tri-ta (with stress falling on the first syllable of each word and the "g" pronounced as in "golf").

5. On the semantics of *vaktṛtā*, see chapter 6.

6. My conclusions were first presented in Hatcher 1992, which also included translations of the two discourses by Vidyāsāgara. The same conclusions, but not the translations, were restated in chapter 9 of Hatcher 1996a.

7. My discussion of these modern Vedantists here and in chapter 5 is informed in part by the perspective I articulated in chapter 5 of Hatcher 1999.

8. Use of the concept of the middle class in this case is not without its theoretical difficulties; see Lutgendorf 1997, Joshi 2001, and Ahmad and Reifeld (n.d.).

9. For an earlier version of her argument, see Waghorne 1999.

10. Hatcher 1996a seeks a model for understanding the uniquely Bengali articulation of the norms of industriousness, while Hatcher 1996b

explores the influence of this revolution on the lives and activities of Sanskrit pandits. The latter issue is one I hope to explore in more detail in the future.

11. Elsewhere (Hatcher 2006) I have explored how the religious needs of Debendranath and the Sabhā worked to create a collective memory of Rammohan as "founder."

12. We need to be careful when speaking about neo-Vedānta. There are subtle variations, running from the theistic varieties associated with Rammohan and the Tattvabodhinī Sabhā to the modified Advaita Vedānta of Vivekananda and Radhakrishnan to the synthetic philosophy of K. C. Bhattacharya, developed in explicit conversation with modern European thought (on the last of which, see Burch 1976).

13. While Wilhelm Halbfass (1988: 222) calls attention to the idioms of "new" and "modern" being applied to Vedānta in the first half of the nineteenth century, he makes too rapid a transition from the age of Rammohan to the later nineteenth century when neo-Hinduism more properly comes into being.

14. For example, Pennington 2001: 583–85. See also Pennington 2005.

15. I thank Gyan Pandey for suggesting this way of viewing *Sabhyadiger vaktṛtā* (after a lecture I delivered at Emory University in September 2005).

16. For an example of Rammohan's defense of reason alongside scripture, see his "Reply to a Gosvāmin" (translated in Killingley 1982: 40).

17. In at least one place that Halbfass may not have noticed, Rammohan does refer to the direct experience (*sākṣāt anubhava*) of the supreme (*Bhaṭṭācāryer sahita vicāra*, Roy 1973: 120).

18. Halbfass argues that Debendranath took his idea of *ātmapratyaya* from the Upanishads and that he used this concept to speak of "intuition," whereas it had originally indicated "non-dualist presence of absolute consciousness" (1988: 224).

19. Debendranath twice uses the word "merciful" to refer to *śruti* (see Discourse Three in chapter 8).

20. For works that touch on the Sabhā's later history and significance, see Kopf 1979, Sen 1979, Damen 1988, and Halbfass 1988.

21. More than one colleague has remarked on this way of interpreting the text's use of initials. I especially thank Paul Courtright and Tom Lutze for encouraging me to consider this possibility.

22. It has long been thought that Vidyāsāgara's earliest written work was a life of Krishna that was composed in Bengali in 1842, went unpublished, and was subsequently lost to posterity. His first extant published work has therefore long been taken to be his *Betala Pañcaviṃśati* from 1846. The present work, however, provides two short discourses that date from 1840, fully six years before *Betala*. In the case of Debendranath, apart from unsigned articles in the *Tattvabodhinī Patrikā*, his earliest published work is *Brāhmo Dharmaḥ* from 1850. Again, *Sabhyadiger vaktṛtā* changes this picture, since it includes five discourses that are ten or more years earlier than this. These discourses are earlier even than anything he may have written for the *Patrikā*, all of which remains largely overlooked.

23. The Tattvabodhinī Sabhā published versions of the first sermons that Rāmacandra delivered before the Brāhmo Samāj beginning at its inception in 1828

(Vidyāvāgīśa 1849; Vidyāvāgīśa 1844 is an English translation of Rāmacandra's second sermon before the Brāhmo Samāj).

24. It is disappointing that my earlier arguments (in Hatcher 1996a) on behalf of Vidyāsāgara's authorship of two of these discourses have generated no such discussion.

CHAPTER 1

1. For an overview of the life of Rammohan Roy, see Collet 1988. Chapter 8 of Hatcher 1996a provides a sketch of the transition from Rammohan's worldview to that of the later Tattvabodhinī Sabhā.

2. For an exploration of Rammohan as "founder" and "father," see Hatcher 2006.

3. On Rammohan's debt to Islamic thought, see Collet 1988: 32.

4. See Rammohan's introduction to *Precepts of Jesus: The Guide to Peace and Happiness* (1820) in Roy 1906: 485.

5. "Second Appeal to the Christian Public in Defence of 'The Precepts of Jesus'" in Roy 1906: 566.

6. For an interpretation that stresses Rammohan's appeal to a Vedic golden age, see Kopf 1969.

7. For discussons of Rammohan's Vedānta, see Killingley 1976, Hatcher 1996a, and Robertson 1995.

8. Relevant here are Rammohan's *Vedānta Grantha,* which he titled in English "The Resolution of All the Veds," and his related exposition of Vedānta in *Vedāntasāra,* or "Abridgement of the Vedant." The latter has long been thought to have been based on the *Vedāntasāra* of Sadāndanda, but Bruce Robertson has plausibly suggested it is really "an original monograph" by Rammohan that owes no direct debt to Sadānanda (1995: 83).

9. "The Brahmunical Magazine, or the Missionary and the Brahmun," no. 4 (1823), in Roy 1906: 198.

10. See the short editorial piece in the *Tattvabodhinī Patrikā* from 1847 (no. 50 [1769 Śaka], p. 107), in which we are provided with an early statement of the evolution of Rammohan's earliest religious association, the Ātmīya Sabhā, into the Brāhmo Samāj. Compare Collet 1988: 220 and Śāstrī 1983: 103.

11. On the name Brāhmo, see the comments of the Rev. Joseph Mullens: "They call themselves Brāhmas . . . that is 'worshippers of Brahma,' the one supreme God of the Hindus: and their religion, Brāhma Dharma: i.e. 'the religion of the worshippers of Brahma.' I would suggest, therefore, that in our English idiom their system should be called Brāhmism: and themselves Brāhmists or Brāhmas" (1852: 111).

12. Killingley (1993: 12) notes that while Rammohan arranged to republish some of his books on Vedic monotheism in England, he did not come forth with editions of his anti-trinitarian works, perhaps (as one contemporary observed) out of discretion for the established religion of his host country.

13. On Rāmacandra, see Bandyopadhyay 1973 and Sinha 1993: 135–39. For an attempt to situate his work in relation to that of Rammohan, see Hatcher 1996a: ch. 8.

For a brief discussion of the controversy over his dismissal from the Sanskrit College, see Hatcher 2005.

14. These facts are reported in a short life of Rāmacandra published in *Tattvabodhinī Patrikā* (1 Vaiśākha 1767), as quoted in Bandyopādhyāy 1973: 68.

15. For reports of upper-caste Hindu members of Young Bengal buying meat kebabs from a Muslim vendor and eating them in plain view, see Śāstrī 1983: 172.

16. For more on these developments, see Pennington 2005.

17. David Kopf refers briefly to the work of the Sabhā in updating and revitalizing Rammohan's message (1979: 157).

18. Following Rammohan's lead, the group sought intentionally to dissociate their Upanishadic Vedānta from the non-dualism associated with the classical school of Advaita associated with Śaṅkara (Tagore 1980: 24).

CHAPTER 2

1. For an examination of the relationship between Rammohan, Rāmacandra, and Debendranath, see Hatcher 1996a: ch. 8.

2. On Dwarkanath, see Kling 1976. One of Dwarkanath's contemporaries commented rather uncharitably that "Dwarkanath is a great merchant more ready to do a thing to gain popularity amongst Europeans rather than starting anything himself" (letter from Ramkamal Sen to Horace Hayman Wilson, dated 18 April 1840; British Library Mss Eur E 3015/66–68).

3. On occasion, I cite passages from the English translation of *Ātmajīvanī* (Tagore 1909). It is also worth comparing Rajnarain Bose's essay, "Brāhmadiger sādhāraṇa sabhā" (Bose 1871: 91–106), which includes a short version of the founding of the Tattvabodhinī Sabhā. Rajnarain, who was a close associate of Debendranath in the later Brāhmo movement, also clearly links the origin of the Sabhā to Debendranath's spiritual awakening.

4. In his autobiography, Debendranath uses the term *pramāṇa*, which is the technical term for "valid means of cognition" in most Indian philosphical systems. Readers will find this term used in the opening discourse in the present translation of *Sabhyadiger vaktṛtā*, although there the "valid means of cognition" of God are said to be the sacred scriptures of Hinduism. This raises an important point noted in the introduction to this volume: in *Sabhyadiger vaktṛtā* the argument from personal experience receives little attention (figuring only in Discourse Five). That Debendranath went on to emphasize experience in his autobiography (written many years after publication of *Sabhyadiger vaktṛtā*) may be understood in part by the fact that Debendranath eventually rejected the authority of revelation and substituted what he was to call the testimony of the "pure, unsophisticated heart" (Tagore 1909: 161). For more on this, see chapter 3.

5. This term, which means something like "knowledge of the essentials," has something of a Tantric ring to it. It was used on occasion by Rammohan and is invoked by more than one of the authors represented in *Sabhyadiger vaktṛtā*.

6. Later, Debendranath attended Hindu College, the very epicenter of progressive, English-medium education so closely associated with the birth of skepticism and the revolt of Young Bengal.

7. For an independent investigation of these developments, see Hatcher 2006.

8. In Bengali: *e to sab brāhmo sabhār kathā*. In early documents, the Brāhmo Samāj was often referred to as the Brāhmo Sabhā. In the published English translation of Debendranath's autobiography, the line is rendered, "This is all about the Brāhmo Sabha" (Tagore 1909: 15), which is a bit misleading since the passage isn't technically "about" the Brāhmo movement at all.

9. There is reason to believe that the page Debendranath had found was in fact torn from an edition Rammohan had made of this Upanishad (Tagore 1980: 169), which is plausible since we have seen that after his death Rammohan's library had been stored at the Tagore mansion.

10. The relevant phrasing in the original Bengali is *satyadharma pracāra* (Tagore 1980: 15).

11. Later, Debendranath published an edition of the Īśā, Kena, Kaṭha, Praśna, Muṇḍaka, and Māṇḍukya Upanishads along with his own commentary (Tagore 1861).

12. Later, the group made use of rooms provided by Dakṣiṇarañjana Mukhopādyāya in Simuliya, North Calcutta. See *Tattvabodhinī Patrikā*, part 3, no. 31 (1 Phālguṇa, 1767 Śaka), p. 261.

13. Notice the title page of the original Bengali edition of *Sabhyadiger vaktṛtā*: "This society was established on Sunday, the 21st of Āśvina, on the fourteenth day of the dark fortnight in 1761 Śaka."

14. Compare Tagore 1980: 17. The original couplet is attributed to Vyāsa and was quoted by Rammohan Roy in his *Bhaṭṭācārya sahita vicāra* (Roy 1973: 119). It reads:

> rūpaṃ rūpavivarjitasya bhavato dhyānena yadvarjitam
> stutyā nirvacanīyatā khilaguro dūrīkṛtī yanmayā
> vyāpitvañca vināśitaṃ bhagavato yastīrthayātrādinā
> kṣantavyaṃ jagadīśa tadvikalatādoṣatrayaṃ matkṛtam.

15. See *Tattvabodhinī Patrikā*, part 2, no. 10 (1 Jyaiṣṭha 1766 Śaka), p. 73, where we are told that *sabhāte sabhyerā īśvaropāsanā viṣayaka vaktṛtā kariten*.

16. Compare this with the Rev. Mullens' description: "The special *aim* of the Tattwabodhini Society, as recorded in its own papers, is to make 'known the Religion of Brahma'; to induce men to believe that religion, and practise what they believe" (Mullens 1852: 5; emphasis in original).

17. For discussons of Rammohan's Vedānta, see Killingley 1976 and 1981, Hatcher 1996a, and Robertson 1995.

18. See chapter 1, note 8.

CHAPTER 3

1. As noted in the annual report of the Sabhā for 1844 (*Tattvabodhinī Patrikā*, part 2, no. 10 (1 Jyaiṣṭha 1766 Śaka), p. 73.

2. This figure is taken from Ghoṣa 1963: 14–15. Ghosh reports that, by 1859, membership was nearly 800. This accords roughly with the Rev. James Long's report from July of 1849 that membership was around 600 (CMS Archives, University of Birmingham, Long 185/117, p. 10). Figures on membership can be found in the published reports of the Tattvabodhinī Sabhā, though we lack these for the earliest years (Tattvabodinī Sabhā 1846, 1848, 1850, and 1854).

3. For an early Bengali biography of Radhakant, see Caṭṭopādhyāya 1867; Raychaudhuri 1988 contains a helpful chapter on Bhudeb.

4. Ghosh refers as well to Bhudeb Mukhopadhyay, but it is difficult to establish details of his membership. It does not appear he had joined the Sabhā in its first year. Moreover, a later report does not list his name among members (Tattvabodhinī Sabhā 1854).

5. Some of the men mentioned here are among the authors we can identify in *Sabhyadiger vaktṛtā*. In those cases, further details regarding their involvement with the Sabhā are found in chapter 7.

6. As Biśvās notes, many of the Young Bengal group had admired the work of Rammohan Roy and had become members of the early Brāhmo Samāj (1958: 34).

7. In Bengali, *nirākāra, caitanya-svarūpa, sarvagata, vākya maner atīta* (Tagore 1980: 19).

8. "Report of the Tuttuvoadhinee Subha, 1843–1844" in *Tattvabodhinī Patrikā*, part 2, no. 13 (Bhādra 1766 Śaka), pp. 103–4.

9. Tagore 1980: 76.

10. The title page of *Sabhyadiger vaktṛtā* reads (in Bengali): "This society was established on Sunday, the 14th day of the dark fortnight, in the month of Āśvina, in the year 1761."

11. *Tattvabodhinī Patrikā*, part 2, no. 9 (1 Vaiśākha 1766 Śaka), p. 72.

12. On January 23, 1830 (11 Māgha 1752 Śaka), meetings of the Brāhmo Samāj were shifted to a new building on Chitpur Road in north Calcutta. This date marked a new level of organization and self-awareness for the group, as is evidenced by the signing of the Brāhmo Trust Deed. This document testified to Rammohan's desire to create a public form of worship open to all people "without distinction" and dedicated to worship of the "Immutable Being who is Author and Preserver of the Universe" (quoting from the Trust Deed, as cited in Collet 1988: 435).

13. One later Tattvabodhinī author praised the date as a "joyous holy day" (*ānandajanaka pavitra divasa*) (*Tattvabodhinī Patrikā*, part 1, no. 103 [1 Phālguṇa 1773 Śaka], p. 146).

14. *Tattvabodhinī Patrikā*, part 1, no. 1 (1 Bhādra 1765 Śaka), p. 1.

15. Quoted in Damen 1988: 34.

16. Compare Benoy Ghosh (1973: 17–18), who commented on the transformation of the Brāhmo Samāj in 1843 from a mere association into a religious organization (*dharmagoṣṭhī*).

17. For his comments in context, Kopf 1979: 163.

18. To adopt a concept from Terdiman 1993.

19. In Hatcher 2006, I attempt to apply the insights of communal memory studies, especially the work of Danièle Hervieu-Léger, to the question of how the Sabhā's act of remembering Rammohan served to achieve its integrity over time as a religious movement. As Hervieu-Léger has written, an elective fraternity (such as the Tattvabodhinī Sabhā) can become a religious association when it "finds . . . a representation of itself that can incorporate the idea of its own continuity" beyond the immediate context that brought members together (2000: 152).

20. Quoting from an English-language statement of beliefs found in *Tattvabodhinī Patrikā* part 2, no. 16 (1 Agrahāyaṇa, 1766 Śaka), pp. 125–27. Incidentally, this may explain why certain prominent members of the Sabhā, notably Vidyāsāgara, eventually chose to dissociate themselves from the group. Membership initially demanded little or no religious commitment, but this changed once the Sabhā became overtly Brāhmo. On Vidyāsāgara's role in the Sabhā, see Hatcher 1996a: ch. 9.

21. See *Tattvabodhinī Patrikā*, part 2, no. 9 (1 Vaiśākha 1766), p. 66, where Rammohan is referred to as the *sthāpanakartā*, or "founder" of the Brāhmo Samāj.

22. "Report of the Tuttuvoadhinee Subha, 1843–44," *Tattvabodhinī Patrikā*, part 2, no. 13 (1 Bhādra 1766), pp. 103–4.

23. Tattvabodhinī Sabhā 1846: 1–2. Interestingly, the first Indian biography of Rammohan appeared around this same time. Writing in the *Calcutta Review* for December 1845, Kishorychand Mitra cast Rammohan in the role of cultural progenitor, remarking that Rammohan "was evidently the first who consecrated, so to speak, the Bengali language" (quoted in Majumdar 1983: 279).

24. *Tattvabodhinī Patrikā*, part 3, no. 40 (1 Āgrahāyaṇa 1768), p. 382; emphasis in original.

25. Biśvās 1956: 47. The textual expression of this new identity came in 1850 in the form of Debendranath's new Brāhmo "scripture," entitled simply *Brāhmo Dharmaḥ* (Tagore, 1975).

26. Quoting from Tagore 1957: 2.

27. The date of Debendranath's formal adoption of the Brāhmo path (7 Pouṣa) would in time become an important liturgical date for Brāhmos.

28. Referring to Keshub's remarks in the *Indian Mirror* (1 January 1865), see Damen 1988: 30.

29. Quoting from Basu 1940: 126–27.

30. Quoting from Basu 1940: 127–28.

31. It is worth noting that the Trust Deed of the Brāhmo Samāj, the document that appears to enshrine the founder's vision, was first published in the *Tattvabodhinī Patrikā* in 1850 (Roy 1906: 213).

32. David Kopf has speculated that Debendranath dissolved the Sabhā in 1859 in order to curtail the increasing influence within the association of the so-called atheists, like Akṣayakumāra Datta and Īśvaracandra Vidyāsāgara (Kopf 1979: 58–59). In light of our analysis, this seems too simplistic.

33. Rabindranath took up editing the *Patrikā* in 1911. For comments on his essays and editorials, see Kopf 1979: 299–304.

34. For a generous selection of material from the *Tattvabodhinī Patrikā*, see Ghoṣa 1963. Whenever possible, parallel passages from *Sabhyadiger vaktṛtā* appearing in later numbers of the *Patrikā* are indicated in notes to the translation in chapter 8.

CHAPTER 4

1. If anything, all too often the Brāhmo Samāj is taken as a shorthand for modern Hinduism during this period (Hatcher 2001).

2. A forerunner in this respect is Babb 1986; see also Waghorne 1999 for an earlier version of her argument. Lutgendorf 1997 gives due recognition to the potentially amorphous quality of the "middle class" as an analytic category. For a recent attempt to consider this category in a comparative fashion, see Ahmad and Reifeld n.d.

3. Sumanta Banerjee describes the common "outward manifestations" of the *bhadralok* as: "(i) residence in a 'pucca' house, either through ownership or renting; (ii) attention to one's sartorial style in public; (iii) use of a chaste Bengali that was being shaped from the middle of the nineteenth century; and (iv) a noticeable knowledge of English language and manners" (1989: 54).

4. Mukherjee notes that while *bhadralok* was largely a Hindu group, caste status was not in fact a basic requirement (1977: 31).

5. Echoes of Antonio Gramsci are particularly evident in the work of Asok Sen 1977; for a similar set of conclusions, see De 1977.

6. Parimal Ghosh notes that "somewhere along the way, caste/origin ceased to matter less [sic], and conduct, which was taken to be an attribute of achievement, became important." He goes on to argue that the colonial *bhadralok* lived a "dual life" characterized by norms of civility, on the one hand, and the energetic quest for wealth, on the other. He suggests that the key to their success was to create a "dreamworld" based on shared "belief in a code of conduct." Threatened with despair, they retired to this dreamworld "where a radical posture can be reconciled with a humdrum existence" (2004: 248).

7. Compare Swapna Banerjee's comment that the "self-image of the bhadralok as members of a new political class was shaped by the aspiration to be a member of the 'educated middle-class' . . . , or *sikkhita sampraday* (educated community)" (2004: 6).

8. In the same document, Bentinck notes that he "will only be following, not preceding the *tide of public opinion* long flowing in this direction" (quoted in Ahmed 1976: 140; emphasis added).

9. The group has been called a curious combination of modern voluntary association and traditional caste tribunal (Mukherjee 1977: 54).

10. It has been estimated that by 1876 at least 200 other voluntary associations of a similar nature were formed in Calcutta (Sanyal 1980: 14).

11. On the idea of "affinity," see Weber 1958: 27.

12. One of the deficiencies of the earlier work of David Kopf on the Brāhmo Samāj was his overly simplistic invocation of "Puritanism" as an explanatory category. As I have argued elsewhere, a model of cultural encounter that envisions European ideas

being unloaded and distributed in Calcutta like so many commodities is inadequate to capture the unique dynamics of cultural "convergence" (Hatcher 1996a).

13. For an investigation of these schoolbook societies and the creation of Bengali educational literature, see Hatcher 1996a: part 2.

14. As Steven Lindquist kindly pointed out (email communication, 5 August 2006), the image of the mirror is used fairly extensively in the Upanishads in connection with self-knowledge (see Bṛhadāraṇyaka 2.1.9 and Chāndogya 8, for instance).

15. Of the Tattvabodhinī group, the keenest proponent of Mandeville's view of society was Akṣayakumāra Datta, who alludes to the "Fable of the Bees" in his own writing (Majumdar 1934: 130).

16. The theology of the group places great weight on arguing from perception and the evidence of cause and effect, as in the following passage:

> Lo, what an amazing purpose there is behind the deeds of the most utterly Supreme Lord. Should he destroy one thing, he gives shelter to another. A droplet may be lost in the fathomless waters of the ocean, but by mingling with the waters of the ocean it contributes to the flow of the rivers and streams. A body composed of the five elements perishes. It dissolves back into the five elements. Thereby it contributes to the production of trees and plants. The flowers and fruit born from these trees and plants benefit all sorts of animals, birds, and human being. (Discourse Twenty)

According to this theology, God is the wise and purposeful creator, who has brought into existence a marvelous world of order, proportion, and lawfulness. Our duty is to know God through this order and to strive to conform to his purpose by following his laws.

17. For a contemporary reflection on applying Weber's insights to the Indian middle class, see Waghorne 2005: 13–16.

18. Consider Discourse Four, where we read that it is "through the laws of this merciful Supreme Lord . . . [that] a child is born after spending ten carefree months in its mother's womb."

19. The use of the concept *rāja-daṇḍa* (or royal punishment) makes it clear that such punishment is delivered by human political authority. Compare Discourse Fourteen, where we are told that the miscreant is "brought before the law" (*rāja-dvāra*). This emphasis on what Weber might have called the "rational structures of law" seems to further confirm the emergence of bourgeois norms of civil life (1958: 25).

20. In this respect, these discourses shed important light on the process whereby *dharma* came to be naturalized in colonial Bengali religious discourse, a process to which Wilhelm Halbfass had earlier called attention (Halbfass 1988: 334–35; Hatcher 1996a: 251).

21. That a certain tension remains between innate *dharma* and external *niyama* is made clear in Discourse Seventeen, where we read that "anyone who works for the welfare of another, finds happiness in following the divine law (*aiśvārika niyama*).

22. They are, literally, "yoked to *yatna*" (*yatna yukta*).

23. There was a dark side to the *bhadralok* cultural project as well. Sumanta Banerjee (1989: 144–45) has demonstrated how the bourgeois project of "strict ritual and stiff restraints" had devastating consequences for many exuberant forms of popular culture (e.g., poetry, song, theater). In the eyes of the *bhadralok*, such popular entertainments were "annoying, wasteful, immoral and even dangerous" (199).

CHAPTER 5

1. Or, to give its full Bengali title, *Satya dharma sambandhīya vividha prastāve pracārita upadeśa kathā*.

2. The reprints of Rammohan's works were published by Annadaprasad Banerji in 1839, as reported in the *Calcutta Courier* for January 6, 1840 (see Chakravarty 1935: 141). I would like to thank Dermot Killingley for calling this reference to my attention (personal communication, October 16, 2006).

3. Speaking as a new convert, Banerjea's fears in this regard may have been somewhat higher.

4. "Report of the Tuttuvoadhinee Subha, 1843–44," *Tattvabodhinī Patrikā*, part 2, no. 13 (1 Bhādra 1766), pp. 103–4.

5. Ali cites a "Circular Letter of the Tattvabodhinī Sabhā," published in the *Calcutta Christian Advocate* in February of 1840 (Ali 1965: 17). I have not seen this "Circular Letter," but the fact that even this document was published after the formation of the Sabhā lends credence to the notion that opposing the Gospel may not have been the primary purpose of the Sabhā at its inception.

6. The students were Mahendralal Basak and Kailas Chandra Mukherji (Ali 1965: 70).

7. At the beginning of the twentieth century L. S. S. O'Malley recorded some curious observations about the school, confirming that it had been established in 1843, "close to the river." He adds that it had been founded by the Tattvabodhinī Sabhā of Calcutta, which he tells us was "the original name of the modern Adi Brahma Samaj." Clearly, the Tattvabodhinī Sabhā had not been the original name of the Brāhmo Samāj, but insofar as that branch of the Samāj that was revived by Debendranath was in later years dubbed the *ādi*, or "original," Samāj, O'Malley was in a sense half right. He goes on to say that the school had flourished with an enrollment of 200 boys. Then he adds that, because "some of the boys became Vedantists, many parents withdrew their sons from the school." This is a curious remark, which may again reflect a half truth insofar as there may have been some resistance by more orthodox Hindu families to have their children exposed to Debendranath's progressive religion. But one wonders how much O'Malley's comment is shaped by the very anti-Vedānta rhetoric of the missionaries that we need to explore. One measure of the atmosphere of interreligious struggle at the time can be had from O'Malley's further comment that in later years the Rev. Duff purchased a "perpetual lease" on the school and its grounds for Rs. 6,000. Here Duff established a mission school that survived well into the last quarter of the nineteenth century (O'Malley 1985: 253).

8. Ali 1965: ch. 2 provides a useful sampling of Christian anxiety regarding the increasing role of groups like the Sabhā in opposing missionary work in Calcutta.

9. Commenting on the work of the twentieth-century neo-Vedantin, K. C. Bhattacharya, George Burch noted that "Neo-Vedanta has developed in the favorable cultural environment formed by the struggle for political independence, the religious revivals of the Ramakrishna Order and Brahmo-samaj, and the Bengali literary renaissance. . . . Neo-Vedanta is not a doctrine to be accepted or rejected but a way of thinking capable of indefinite development and variation" (1976: 2). For contemporary perspectives on the place of neo-Vedānta in Orientalist and postcolonial constructions of modern Hinduism, see King 1999 and Hatcher 2004.

10. It would take us too far afield to review here the extended debate over Vedānta conducted between missionaries like Duff on one side and the Tattvabodhinī group on the other. In any case, this debate has been summarized well by others (for example, Ali 1965: ch 2; Biśvās 1956).

11. In Bengali, this sense of "newfangled" is captured by the use of the term *ādhunika* to describe these Vedantins (Banerjea 1903: 343). That this was only a "so-called" Vedānta is made clear in the same work (299).

12. Yet another charge was that the Vedas, being the special preserve of the brahmins, were not equally accessible to all believers (Biśvās 1956: 255–56).

13. Letter dated 8 March 1855 from Lacroix to the Rev. A. Tidman of the London Missionary Society; LMS Archives, School of Oriental and African Studies, University of London, Correspondence, North India, Box 9.

14. Banerjea's curious argument in this regard was later rejected by the anonymous author of *Remarks on Rev. K. M. Banerjia's Lecture on Vedantism by a Hindu* (Calcutta, n.p., 1851). The author cites a definition of Vedānta by the medieval Jain lexicographer, Hemacandra: *vedāntaḥ syādupanisat*, "Vedānta should mean Upanishad."

15. *India and India Missions* is a lengthy and overdetermined work that involves far more than a critique of Vedānta. However, insofar as it highlights some of the key themes in the missionary critique, it helps us appreciate how heated the debate over Vedānta would become during the 1840s.

16. In an earlier work, I referred to these words in order to portray Duff as a kind of "Evangelical Anglicist" who could usefully be distinguished from a missionary like William Carey, who is better viewed as an "Evangelical Vernacularist" (Hatcher 1996a: 59–60).

17. One dividend of postcolonial/postorientalist perspectives on this period is that we are able to see how frequently the construction of religion or debates over an "Oriental other" are, in fact, reflections of internal disputes within Western European Christendom (for example, King 1999: ch. 1).

18. The essays appeared, respectively, in *Tattvabodhinī Patrikā*, part 2, no. 14 (1 Āśvina 1766 Śaka) and no. 19 (1 Phālguṇa 1766 Śaka). They are reprinted in Ghoṣa 1981: 89–114. It is quite possible that they were penned by Rajnarain Bose (Rājanārāyaṇa Basu, 1826–99), an influential Brāhmo who was active in the Sabhā

beginning sometime in the early to mid-1840s. This is how I have listed them in the bibliography (Bose 1844 and 1845).

19. Readers interested in a breakdown of the major elements of the point/counterpoint as revealed in the Tattvabodhinī response to Duff will want to consult the useful analysis in Biśvās 1956: 253–59.

20. This fixation on pantheism persisted unabated for decades, as attested by Banerjea's lengthy overview of Hindu philosophy from 1861. In this work, Banerjea argues for the necessary connection between materialist pantheism and immorality (Banerjea 1903: 294–300).

21. Quoting from Long's papers in the CMS Archives, University of Birmingham, Long 185/117, p. 10.

22. Compare this fascinating entry from Long's personal journal from 1849: "Called at the Tatwabodhini Sabha, the centre of Deism in Calcutta; it has 600 members, who each pay 4 annas monthly for its support. They form the important party in Calcutta who have [renewed?] Hinduism and have taken up a kind of half-way house between Christianity and Hinduism" (CMS Archives, University of Birmingham, Long 185/117, p. 10).

23. On Duff as an Evangelical Anglicist, see note 16 above. Gauri Viswanathan 1990 explores the theme of colonial education, especially the emerging canon of English literature, as a secular means to promote the Christian agenda in India.

24. Among the evidence of such borrowing, the Rev. James Long listed such "nowise ambiguous" practices as "*sermonizing* and *lecturing* in the religious meetings of the body, outward tokens of religious reverence adopted from the Christians, such as bending the head and covering the face with the hand in prayer, or in listening to the Vedic scriptures" (1848: 352; emphasis in the original). Kopf (1979: 157) seems to accept in large part the accusation that the Brāhmos generally borrowed from Christian theology.

25. Quoting the "Report of the Tuttuvoadhinee Subha, 1843–44," *Tattvabodhinī Patrikā*, part 2, no. 13 (1 Bhādra 1766 Śaka), p.103.

26. Reaching its high point in Rajnarain Bose's address from 1794 Śaka, "Hindudharmer śreṣṭhatā," or "The Superiority of Hinduism" (Bose 1872).

27. On the relationship between neo-Vedānta and contemporary Hindu thought, see Hatcher 2004.

28. For a representative example of the twentieth-century neo-Vedānta perspective on the Gospel, see Prabhavananda 1964.

29. The Hindu defense of Vedānta from charges of pessimism, pantheism, abstractionism, and immorality continued unabated into the twentieth century, as evidenced by such works as Mukerji 1983.

CHAPTER 6

1. See Vidyāvāgīśa 1849 (*Parameśvarer upāsanā viṣaye prathamāvadhi saptadaśa vyākhyāna*), which contains the first seventeen of his sermons before the Samāj (the first dating from 1828). There was great fluidity in the use of such terms during this

period, however, since the indigenous (and in this case largely Sanskritic) semantic field was beginning to converge with notions current among such groups as Christian missionaries, government officials, and colonial educators. Thus, when Rāmacandra's *vyākhyāna* were translated into English, they were called "discourses." See Vidyāvāgīśa 1844 (*Second Discourse on the Spiritual Worship of God*).

2. Some further validation of this distinction may be inferred from the fact that when important leaders of the Brāhmo community (like Rāmacandra and, later on, Debendranath) spoke before the meetings, their talks were called *vyākhyāna*, while the addresses of others—like Rajnarain Bose—were called *vaktṛtā* (Bose 1855 and 1871).

3. The only known copy can be found in the Asia, Pacific and Africa Collection (formerly the Oriental and India Office Collection) of the British Library, London [shelfmark: 14123.d.4.(9)]. The text can be found at the end of a small volume, bound by the library, containing a number of separate works associated in one way or another with the Brāhmo movement.

4. This is one of the so-called great sayings (*mahāvākya*) of the Upanishads and can be found at Chāndogya Upanishad 6.2.1. Rāmacandra Vidyāvāgīśa glosses this mantra as: *jagater kāraṇa parabrahma eka-i mātra dvitīya rahita hayen* (Vidyāvāgīśa 1849: 23). I have followed the English translation of the mantra favored by early Brāhmos (Vidyāvāgīśa 1844).

5. While the work is entitled Part One, I have been unable to ascertain whether a Part Two was ever published.

6. See the catalogue of printed Bengali books at the British Library, which notes: "A collection of sermons delivered by different members of the Tattvabodhinī Sabhā, a society for Theistic reform, from 21 Dec 1839 to 4 June 1840." However, these dates—provided by an earlier British Library cataloguer—do not seem to correspond to the actual dates of the discourses (for which, see chapter 8).

7. On the title page of the British Library copy, someone has penned "Brahmist Sermons" under the header. To the right of this is written an old shelfmark (Beng 32/9). Beneath this, and in a larger hand, offset toward the outer margin, is written "Vedanta Sermons." The verso of the title page bears the old stamp of the British Museum (where the British Library was originally housed).The final page of the text has been stamped with the accession date of 9 April 1866.

8. As in the case of an edition of seventeen of Rāmacandra's sermons edited by Annadaprasad Banerji, which included the notice that copies could be acquired from both the Calcutta and the Telinipara Brāhmo Samāj (Vidyāvāgīśa 1849).

9. This is the same layout one finds in other Tattvabodhinī publications from this time, such as *Varṇamālā*, a spelling book from 1844 (Tattvabodhinī Sabhā 1844).

10. An extensive review of Bengali holdings in libraries in India and in the United Kingdom, as well as a review of secondary literature, has produced no reference to any earlier publications by the Sabhā. This is not surprising, however, given the date of *Sabhyadiger vaktṛtā*.

11. Discourse Sixteen is really little more than a short benediction. However, the case of Discourse Three is more interesting, since analysis suggests it was written by Debendranath Tagore (see chapter 7), the very man whose autobiography not only

provides valuable insight into this period but also ranks as one of the first important self-narratives in modern Bengali literature.

12. One might have anticipated a pattern whereby single initials were used within the text until the point when an author appeared whose first initial had already been assigned to a previous author. At that point, two initials would have been employed. Within *Sabhyadiger vaktṛtā* this pattern does apply for the sets of initials "C" (Discourses Four and Five) and "C G" (Discourse Six), as well as "Ī" (Discourses Thirteen and Eighteen) and "Ī G" (Discourse Sixteen). But it does not apply to the set "R" (Discourses Fourteen and Nineteen) and "R G" (Discourse Ten), where "R G" is used before the single initial "R."

13. This work is available in the British Library.

14. The use of initials is not completely consistent throughout. Some hymns are identified by numbers (e.g., "7's"), while a small number of hymns (i.e., numbers twenty to twenty-six) are identified as "Native." In at least one case, the margin is left empty.

15. This work is available in the British Library.

16. The poem provides a nice illustration of the sentiment that inspired the rational skepticism of the Young Bengal group. It begins:

> Expanding, like the petals of young flowers,
> I watch the opening of your infant minds,
> And the sweet loosening of the spell that binds
> Your intellectual energies and powers. (Quoted in Chattopadhyay 1978: 5)

17. For examples, see Chattopadhyay 1978: 45, 83, 115, 165. Other letter writers employed the device of pseudonyms, writing under such names as Amicus, the Wanderer, and Rusticus (Chattopadhyay 1978: 127, 170, 177).

18. A later edition of *Brāhmasaṅgīta* (1861) includes this system of initials. A copy can be found in the library of the School of Oriental and African Studies in London.

19. Interestingly, one of the authors in *Sabhyadiger vaktṛtā* refers to this convention to make an analogy: "Just as the sound 'a' is contained within all the consonants from Ka to Kṣa, so too does the Supreme Self, who is comprised of knowledge, pervade all things at all times in its essential nature as the inner controller " (Discourse Four).

20. The way to indicate a consonant alone is to write it with a *virāma* or "stop" sign, as in ম্, which should be read as "M" (though there is no uppercase in Sanskrit or Bengali).

21. For a similar pattern of using anglicized (or, more properly, romanized) names, see the list of members of the Society for the Acquisition of General Knowledge from the early 1840s. Here names are alpabetized using the first initial of the Bengali first name, understood in its anglicized version. Thus for 1843, we find listings for Calachand Sett (i.e., Kālācāṃd Śeṭh), Chintamoy Day (i.e., Cintāmaya De), and Debendro Nauth Tagore (Chattopadhyay 1965).

22. A further example of the latitude taken with such schemes is found in Śyāmacaraṇa Mukhopādhyāya's schoolbook, *Key to Rijupatha Part III* (1879), where

the editor signs his Bengali preface "Ś.C.M." (শ চ ম), where a reader would expect "Śyā. Ca. Mu." (শ্যা চ মু). This text is available in the British Library.

23. A good example of this practice from the latter part of the nineteenth century would be Romesh Chunder Dutt (Rameśacandra Datta), who published a survey of Bengali literature under the initials of his anglicized name, which he rendered phonetically, "Ar, Cy, Dae" (Dutt 1877).

24. In the case of the "G," we continue to face a number of possibilities. Given the lack of conventional rules, and assuming it represents a family name, it could stand for Gaṅgopādhyāya, Gupta, or Ghosh.

25. It is worth noting, in support of this supposition, that the majority of Bengali surnames do not begin in vowels. Furthermore, from available records, it seems that among the early members of the Tattvabodhinī Sabhā, there were none whose family names began with a vowel.

CHAPTER 7

1. Some guidelines to consider when attempting to prove authorship of unsigned or pseudonymous works are provided by Dermot Killingley, who suggests there are four types of evidence one might consider: (1) Evidence found in other works written by the author himself, which prove common authorship; (2) the presence of distinctive ideas; (3) signs of a distinctive style; and (4) references found in contemporary accounts (1993: 13).

2. For background on Akṣayakumāra, see Hatcher 1996a and Rāy 1885.

3. Amiya Kumar Sen sees two basic strands of thought represented in the Sabha: Vedānta and Deism. If it was Rāmacandra who promoted the former, "Akshay Kumar Dutt was responsible for disseminating arguments from design among his contemporaries" (1979: 15).

4. On Akṣayakumāra's rational theism and role in the Sabhā, see Hatcher 1996a: 220–30.

5. *Tattvabodhinī Patrikā*, part 2, no. 9 (1 Vaiśakha 1766 Śaka), pp. 70–71.

6. The essays in question are in *Tattvabodhinī Patrikā*, part 1, no. 4 (1 Agrahāyaṇa 1765 Śaka), pp. 25–27, and *Tattvabodhinī Patrikā*, part 1, no. 5 (1 Pouṣa 1765 Śaka), p. 40. Of these, the earlier essay exhorts the reader to know God (the cause, *karaṇa*) by examining the handiwork of his creation (the effects, *kārya*). The later essay focuses on the need to restrain our passions. It begins with the line, "Youth is a very difficult age, as all the senses are robust" (*yauvana ati viṣama kāla, ei kale indriya samudaya balavān hay*).

7. It should be noted that long ago, Rachel van Meter Baumer argued for Akṣayakumāra's authorship of these two "A" essays (Baumer 1975: 90).

8. *Tattvabodhinī Patrikā*, part 1, no. 7 (1 Phālguṇa 1765 Śaka).

9. One of Debendranath's initial concerns about appointing Akṣayakumāra to edit *Tattvabodhinī Patrikā* was that Akṣayakumāra seemed to harbor a slight sympathy for the ideal of the renouncer (Tagore 1980: 23). But Debendranath tells us he was so impressed by Akṣayakumāra's style that he chose to go ahead and appoint him editor. Since *Tattvabodhinī Patrikā* adopted the normative position of Debendranath in

opposition to renunciation, this essay could be seen as Akṣayakumāra's attempt to demonstrate conclusively that he had accepted Debendranath's position. Readers of *Sabhyadiger vaktṛtā* will find arguments against renunciation in a variety of discourses (see, for instance, Fourteen, Seventeen, and Eighteen in the present translation).

10. One might well ask whether this Vedantic language gives us a hint of the "early" Akṣayakumāra, the one Debendranath initially worried might be a bit too traditional in his views about renunciation.

11. Going further afield, we could note how the author's use of the word *yauvana* in this discourse is mirrored in the opening line of the essay in *Tattvabodhinī Patrikā*, part 1, no. 5 (1 Pouṣa 1765 Śaka), p. 40: *yauvana ati viṣama kāla.*

12. The Indian Institute Library was opened in 1883. Prior to its opening, the Oxford Sanskritist Monier Monier-Williams had sent out an appeal for donations to support the new collection. The Indian Institute Librarian, Dr. Gillian Evison, has confirmed for me that the volumes were most likely donated to the library in response to this request, and that they carry the distinctive Indian Institute bookplate, as opposed to Monier Williams's personal bookplate (email communications from 31 July and 4 August 2006).

13. Reprinted in *Tattvabodhinī Patrikā*, part 2, no. 16 (1 Agrahāyaṇa 1766), pp. 129–32.

14. Reprinted in *Tattvabodhinī Patrikā*, part 2, no. 20 (1 Caitra, 1766 Śaka), pp. 153–54.

15. Reprinted in *Tattvabodhinī Patrikā*, part 2, no. 18 (1 Māgha 1766 Śaka), pp. 145–47.

16. Reprinted in *Tattvabodhinī Patrikā*, part 2, no. 14 (1 Āśvina 1766), pp. 108–9. The *Tattvabodhinī Patrikā* version omits the Sanskrit verse and Bengali paraphrase found in *Sabhyadiger vaktṛtā* and begins instead with the lines that follow: *vāṇijya dvārā loker yādṛś upakār haiteche, tāhā ei sabhār madhye ke nā jñāta āchen?*

17. This point is confirmed by Śivanāth Śāstrī in his *History of the Brāhmo Samaj* (1911: I, 98).

18. The essay is titled "Vidyāmodinī Sabhā" and appears in *Tattvabodhinī Patrikā*, part 2, no. 20 (Caitra, 1766 Śaka).

19. The evidence presented in this section draws on my earlier treatment of this matter in Hatcher 1996a: 230–40.

20. *Tattvabodhinī Patrikā*, Part 1, no. 7 (1 Phālguṇa 1765 Śaka), pp. 55–56.

21. Examples are in his *Bhrāntivilāsa*, *Bahuvivāha*, and *Vrajavilāsa*, as well as in his introduction to *Ślokamañjarī* (for detailed citations, see Hatcher 1996a: 238n78).

22. His poem concerned the austerities of King Agnīdhra (Bhāgavata Purāṇa 5.2.1–23). It was written for an examination at Calcutta Sanskrit College in 1840 (Hatcher 1996a: 239–40).

23. For a sketch of Rāmacandra's life, see Gautam Niyogi, "Paṇḍita Rāmacandra Vidyāvāgīśa mahāśayer jīvanī," in Vidyāvāgīśa 1977: 131–78.

24. Discourse Fourteen appeared in *Tattvabodhinī Patrikā*, part 1, no. 6 (1 Māgha 1765 Śaka), and Discourse Nineteen appeared in *Tattvabodhinī Patrikā*, part 2, no. 17 (1 Pouṣa 1766 Śaka).

25. Rāmacandra's Brāhmo Samāj sermons have been reprinted in Vidyāvāgīśa 1977.

26. *Tattvabodhinī Patrikā*, part 1, no. 1 (1765 Śaka), pp. 2–3.

27. Bhavatoṣa Datta provides evidence from contemporary sources to show that Gupta joined the Sabhā on 4 December 1839 and remained a member until 1848 (Datta 1968: 121–22).

28. Debendranath provides a brief account of the early involvement of Gupta and Akṣayakumāra (Tagore 1980: 17). Akṣayakumāra apparently became a member on 28 December 1839 (Datta 1968: 122).

29. This view finds support in Dāśgupta and Mukhaṭi 1974: x–xi.

30. Compare *vicitra vyāpāra vyūha* and *camatkārakara cittaghaṭita citrakalpana* (Dāśgupta and Mukhaṭi 1974: 292).

31. There could well be other candidates, since the initial "Ś" is common in Bengali names. Thus, *Tattvabodhinī Patrikā* refers to a certain Śyāmacaraṇa Basu being present for a ceremony in 1845, but we know nothing else about him.

32. One curious exception is *Tattvabodhinī Patrikā*, part 2, no. 19 (1 Phālguṇa 1766 Śaka), which lists the names of those who delivered discourses at the annual meeting of the Brāhmo Samāj in 1844. Among those listed is one Śyāmacaraṇa Bhaṭṭācārya (pp. 149–51). Could this be the Tagore family pandit? Even if it were, it doesn't seem to be evidence enough to conclude he was active in the affairs of the Tattvabodhinī Sabhā. In all likelihood, it was someone who shared the same name (not all that unusual in this case) with the Tagore family pandit.

33. *Tattvabodhinī Patrikā*, part 1, no. 8 (1 Caitra 1765 Śaka).

34. As we search for evidence of Śrīdhara Nyāyaratna's involvement in the Sabhā, we also come across records for another Śrīdhara, namely Śrīdhara Vidyāratna. This Śrīdhara served both as assistant preceptor (*upācārya*) for the Brāhmo Samāj around 1845 (*Tattvabodhinī Patrikā*, part 3, no. 31 [1 Phālguṇa 1767 Śaka]) and assistant preceptor for the Tattvabodhinī Sabhā around 1847 (*Tattvabodhinī Patrikā*, series 2, part 1, no. 46 [1 Jyaiṣṭha 1769 Śaka]). But judging from entries appearing in the *Tattvabodhinī Patrikā*, this Śrīdhara did not become active in the Sabhā until after 1845. This would rule him out as a possible author of these discourses.

35. Curiously, Śyāmacaraṇa's initials do not appear in connection with any of the hymns in the popular collection of Brāhmo hymns published from Burdwan (*Brahmasaṅgīta* 1861). An earlier edition of theistic hymns, probably published by the Sabhā itself, provides no indication of authorship for many of the hymns (*Gītāvalī* 1846).

36. This information can be found in the earliest extant report of the Sabhā (Tattvabodinī Sabhā 1846).

37. The book was apparently based on the work of Carlyle (*Tattvabodhinī Patrikā*, part 3, no. 29 (1 Pouṣa 1767 Śaka), pp. 245–48).

38. *Tattvabodhinī Patrikā*, part 3, no. 30 (1 Māgha 1767 Śaka), p. 256.

39. *Tattvabodhinī Patrikā*, part 3, no. 42 (1 Māgha 1768 Śaka), and no. 43 (1 Phālguṇa 1768 Śaka). The latter issue also records that he donated some books to the Sabhā (p. 459).

40. *Tattvabodhinī Patrikā*, part 1, no. 4 (1 Agrahāyaṇa 1765 Śaka), p. 32.

41. The Bengali reads: *ye puruṣa dhairya dvārā viṣaya āsvādana kare, sei sukha svarūpa madhu bhoga kare.*

42. This text is cited in two of the discourses in *Sabhyadiger vaktṛtā.*

43. *Tapasyā japa dāna tīrthaseva vrataniyamādi karma sakala kevala kālyāpanārtha mātra hay, sadguru haite upadeśaprāpti nija buddhi yukti o śāstradṛṣṭi dvārā ye tattvajñāna lābha hay* (Mukhopādhyāya 1877: 25).

44. While we know that a certain Candranātha Rāy (whose first initial would fit the present case) spoke at the Third Anniversary meeting of the Sabhā (see chapter 3), we know nothing about this individual, his membership, or his role in the group.

45. For instance, see *Tattvabodhinī Patrikā*, part 3, no. 23 (1 Āṣāḍha 1767 Śaka), where both men are listed among the patrons of a new Hindu charitable school (pp. 185–87). The annual report for 1768 Śaka (Tattvabodhinī Sabhā 1846) shows that Candrasekhar was then serving as secretary of the Sabhā, while the report for 1772 Śaka lists him as a member of the publications committee of *Tattvabodhinī Patrikā* (Tattvabodhinī Sabhā 1850). In the 1854 report, he is listed as a member (Tattvabodhinī Sabhā 1854).

46. According to the editors of Collet (1988: 98), Candrasekhar published "Reminiscences of Rammohan Roy" in *Tattvabodhinī Patrikā*, no. 351 (1 Agrahāyaṇa 1794 Śaka), pp. 139–40.

47. Rammohan occasionally published tracts under the names of other Brāhmos. One such tract, "Answer of a Hindu to the Question—'Why do you frequent a Unitarian place of worship . . . ?'," was published under the name of Candrasekhar (Robertson 1995: 53). In some cases, the question of Rammohan's authorship has been a vexing one. Rammohan's authorship of a tract against idolatry, published in the name of Braja Mohan Deb (1843), was accepted by Hay 1963 but was later questioned by Halbfass (1988: 520n57). Could writings published under Candrasekhar's name have been composed by him? Was Candrasekhar able to mimic the style and concerns of Rammohan?

48. According to Ghoṣa (1981: 203), Ramgopal is listed as having donated funds to the Tattvabodhinī Pāṭhaśālā in *Tattvabodhinī Patrikā*, part 2, no. 18 (1 Māgha 1766 Śaka). For further evidence of his activities, see the following: *Tattvabodhinī Patrikā*, part 2, no. 19 (1 Phālguṇa 1766 Śaka); *Tattvabodhinī Patrikā*, series 2, part 1, no. 45 (1 Vaiśākha 1769 Śaka); and Tattvabodhinī Sabhā 1848.

49. The *Friend of India* notified its readers that the Hindu Theo-Philanthropic Society was a group of "Vedantists" from the Tattvabodhinī Sabhā (Biśvās 1956: 252).

50. Bhavānīcaraṇa appears several times in *Tattvabodhinī Patrikā*: *Tattvabodhinī Patrikā*, part 3, no. 21 (1 Vaiśakha 1767 Śaka); *Tattvabodhinī Patrikā*, part 3, no. 31 (1 Phālguṇa 1767 Śaka); and *Tattvabodhinī Patrikā*, part 3, no. 35 (1 Āṣāḍha 1768 Śaka). He is also listed as a member of the Sabhā in 1854 (Tattvabodhinī Sabhā 1854).

51. *Tattvabodhinī Patrikā*, part 2, no. 19 (1 Phālguṇa 1766 Śaka).

52. *Tattvabodhinī Patrikā*, part 1, no. 1 (1 Bhādra 1765 Śaka). Compare Discourse Six in chapter 8 of this volume.

53. The 1854 report, for instance, lists a member by the name of Candraśekhara Ghoṣa (Tattvabodhinī Sabhā 1854). We have no information regarding when he might have become a member of the Sabhā.

CHAPTER 8

1. Hindu texts often begin with benedictory words, in this case the Sanskrit phrase *oṃ tat sat*. This mantra was used widely by the wider Brāhmo community. In one of his works, Rammohan points out that in the Bhagavadgītā, this mantra is used to indicate Ultimate Reality or *parabrahman* (Roy 1973: 339).

2. The original text provides only the date of 17 Agrahāyaṇa 1761 [Śaka era]. I have added the more descriptive header and translated the dates to assist readers. For information on translation, see appendix 1. For the Bengali calendar, see table 6.1.

3. Words and phrases marked with an asterisk (*) appear in the glossary.

4. Viṣṇu Purāṇa 1.2.10b–11. The text cited contains two minor variations from the verse as found in *Viṣṇu Purāṇa* (1986: 9–10).

5. Kulārṇava Tantra 9.21. The text cited contains a minor variation from the verse as found in *Kulārṇavatantram* (2002: 203), which begins *vidite parame tattve* instead of *viditetu pare tattve*. The passage quoted here is cited by Rammohan Roy in the preface to his translation of the Īśā Upanishad (Roy 1973: 75), which was reprinted in *Tattvabodhinī Patrikā*, part 1, no. 1 (1765 Śaka), p. 7. In his preface, Roy writes, "The Upanishads plainly show that the Supreme Lord is one alone and everywhere present" (*upaniṣader dvārā vyakta haibek ye parameśvara eka mātra sarvatra vyāpī*).

6. Kulārṇava Tantra 9.28. This passage is also cited by Rammohan Roy in the preface to his translation of the Īśā Upanishad (see note 5).

7. Bṛhadāraṇyaka Upanishad 1.4.8. The text should read: *ātmānam eva priyam upāsīta*. See Olivelle's *Early Upanishads* (1998: 48).

8. Bṛhadāraṇyaka Upanishad 2.4.5.

9. Bṛhadāraṇyaka Upanishad 3.9.28.

10. Muṇḍaka Upanishad 3.2.9.

11. Though the Bengali reads *brahma*, I write "Brahman" to avoid confusion with the classical deity and demiurge, Brahmā. While the Upanishadic context should make it clear that it is Brahman that is being referred to, the use of the compound *parabrahma* in the next sentence removes any doubt that the author refers to the absolute, or "supreme," Brahman.

12. I have chosen to translate *kāma* as "lust" rather than "desire" since the authors of these discourses are typically concerned with the unrestrained, and therefore dangerous, passions (like *krodha* and *lobha*). When they speak of *kāma*, they do not usually mean desire in its more subdued form. However, as the authors of some discourses demonstrate (e.g., Discourse Thirteen), when properly regulated, *kāma* is the motive force behind our love for our families. Perhaps in this case we could speak of "desire," but for consistency's sake, I have used "lust."

13. Even though the translation is awkward, in this and the following several sentences I have tried to highlight the repeated use of the word "creation" (*sṛṣṭi*). For

this and other authors in this volume, much turns on correctly understanding the way the Lord has created the world.

14. Kena Upaniṣad 4.8. The original text identifies this quotation merely as *śruti,* or a "revealed text."

15. The mention of Vaśiṣṭha and Rāmacandra suggests this is a quotation from the Yoga-vāśiṣṭha Rāmāyaṇa, but this verse is not attested in contemporary print editions I have been able to consult. The same verse is cited by Rammohan Roy in several places: (1) in his preface to Īśā Upanishad (Roy 1973: 78), which was reprinted in *Tattvabodhinī Patrikā,* part 1, no. 4 (1765 Śaka), p. 32; (2) in his *Bhaṭṭācārya sahita vicāra* (Roy 1973: 110); and (3) in his *Cāri praśner uttara* (Roy 1973: 252). Rāmacandra Vidyāvāgīśa cites this same passage in his thirteenth published Brāhmo Samāj sermon (Vidyāvāgīśa 1977: 87).

16. This discourse is reprinted in *Tattvabodhinī Patrikā,* part 2, no. 16 (1766 Śaka), pp. 129–32. The Indian Institute Library in the Bodleian Library, Oxford, contains a bound set of the *Tattvabodhinī Patrikā,* presented to the library by Debendranath Tagore. In this set, someone has penciled beside this discourse the English initials "DT," lending support to the supposition that it was written by Debendranath (see the discussion regarding Debendranath's authorship in chapter 7).

17. Kaṭha Upanishad, 1.6c.

18. I have tried to convey how the author of this discourse translated the Sanskrit into Bengali (*sasyer nyāya manuṣya naṣṭa hay*), rather than how it might be translated more literally. In *Early Upanishads,* Patrick Olivelle renders the Sanskrit, "A mortal man ripens like grain" (1998: 374).

19. There is a play on the words *viśvāsa* ("trust") and *niśvāsa* ("breath") here. In the next sentence, this "breath" is equated with the Upanishadic "life breath," or *prāṇa.*

20. This discourse is somewhat unique for its use of the first-person singular, both in this sentence and below (compare the short prayer that is Discourse Sixteen). The author here speaks of "my body" (*āmār śarīra*) and "my intention" (*āmār abhiprāya*). Would we be wrong to find in these hints of self-narration further evidence of the hand of Debendranath, who was among the first to write an autobiography in Bengali?

21. Readers may recognize this parable as a variant of the episode from the Matsya Purāṇa recited in chapter 2 of Zimmer 1992.

22. God is characterized in essential (*svarūpa*) terms as pure consciousness and as such is beyond our senses. However, his manifest (*taṭastha*) characteristic is creator of the world, and we can know him as such. On Rammohan's earlier conception of this distinction, see the opening to his *Vedāntasāra* (Roy 1974: 63), his commentary on Brahmasūtra 1.1.2 (1974: 14–15), and his comments in *Bhaṭṭācāryer sahita vicāra* (1974: 109 and 113). In English, Rammohan spoke of these as the "absolute" and "relative" characteristics of the Supreme Being, respectively (Roy 1906: 122).

23. In the Bengali "alphabet," the consonants are understood to include an implicit short-a vowel. They are arranged by groups, or *vargas,* running from the initial phoneme *ka* to the final phoneme *kṣa.*

24. The author of this discourse twice refers to the Supreme Lord as being *caitanya-svarūpa.* There are obvious resonances with Rammohan Roy's characterization

of the Supreme Self (*paramātmā*) as *sarvavyāpī anirvacanīya caitanya-svarūpa* in the Anuṣṭhāna to his translation of Īśā Upanishad (Roy 1973: 80). The phrase is also reminiscent of Debendranath Tagore's characterization of God as *nirākāra, caitanya-svarūpa* in his autobiography (Tagore 1980: 19). Finally, this is the very same phrasing Vidyāsāgara chose when defining the Lord (*īśvara*) in his popular schoolbook, *Bodhodaya* (Vidyāsāgara 1972, 11:177).

25. An abbreviated version of this passage, as far as the words "next life," was published verbatim as an unsigned piece in *Tattvabodhinī Patrikā*, part 1, no. 1 (1765), p. 6. For an earlier translation, see Hatcher 1996a: 215.

26. For this author, "knowing" means "attaining through the intellect" (*buddhi*).

27. Kaṭha Upanishad 3.15.

28. Kaṭha Upanishad 3.12.

29. Though reminiscent of language used in Discourse Five (see note 19), the phrasing in Bengali is slightly different. Here the Supreme Brahman (rather than Supreme Lord) is described as being *caitanya-maya*.

30. The first line of this quotation is Muṇḍaka Upanishad 2.2.11d. The second line is a slight rewording of Śaṅkara's commentary on this passage, which reads: *brahma eva idaṃ viśvaṃ samastaṃ idaṃ jagad variṣṭhaṃ varatamaṃ* (*Ten Principal Upaniṣads* 1987: 164).

31. While it would make rather cumbersome English were we to translate it literally ("this world was not created solely for the purpose of our suffering"), it is important theologically to note that the author is concerned to emphasize God's purpose (*nimitta*) in creating as he does. Thus the word *nimitta* appears as many as six times in this short paragraph.

32. I have trimmed the text here just a bit for readability, as a literal translation seemed rather overdetermined. What the author says, more literally, is "so that what I ate would be bitter and pungent, what I heard would be monstrous and rude, what I smelled would be foul and sickening, what I saw would be ugly and frightening."

33. The important Bengali word here is *deśa*, which I elsewhere render as "nation." However, as this author emphasizes the way the Lord has created natural blessings, the word "land" seems more appropriate.

34. Reprinted in *Tattvabodhinī Patrikā*, part 2, no. 20 (1766 Śaka), pp. 153–54. In the Bodleian Library copy, this piece is initialed in pencil, "DT."

35. Kaṭha Upanishad 1.27. In his autobiography, Debendranath recalls the effect these words had on him, especially in light of his father's disappointment at his lack of interest in worldly affairs (Tagore 1980: 26).

36. Recalling earlier discourses, but somewhat differently phrased, the author refers to the Self as being *cidānanda-svarūpa*.

37. This discourse was reprinted in *Tattvabodhinī Patrikā*, part 1, no. 7 (1765 Śaka), pp. 55–56. I first published a translation in appendix 3 of my dissertation, "Yatna-Dharma: The Religious Worldview of Paṇḍit Īśvaracandra Vidyāsāgar" (Hatcher 1992). I have revised the translation to be consistent with terminology used throughout the present work.

38. When this discourse was reprinted in *Tattvabodhinī Patrikā* (see previous note), this sentence was omitted.

39. Mahābhārata 1.693.6.

40. One thinks here of the aphorism from the Hitopadeśa (introductory verse 11):

āhāranidrābhayamaithunaṃ ca sāmānyam etat paśubhir-nārāṇām
dharmo hi teṣām adhiko viśeṣo dharmeṇa hīnāḥ paśubhiḥ samānāḥ.

Men are like beasts in needing to eat and sleep, in feeling fear and having sexual intercourse, while it is *dharma* that sets them apart. Without *dharma*, they are like beasts.

41. This discourse corresponds to one later published in *Tattvabodhinī Patrikā*, part 1, no. 6 (1765 Śaka), which is also signed "R," but which omits the translation of the Sanskrit passage.

42. Taittirīya Upanishad 2.4.1. The text differs from that found in Olivelle's *Early Upanishads* (1998: 302) in using *kutaścana* for *kadācana*.

43. The word used here for "worldly concerns" is *viṣaya* rather than *viṣayajñāna*, but the sense seems clear. In an essay in the *Tattvabodhinī Patrikā* (part 1, no. 7, [1765 Śaka], p. 50), Rāmacandra Vidyāvāgīśa glosses the word *vṛttihīna* ("without means of support") as "devoid of attachment to *viṣaya*" (*viṣayāsakti rahita*), where *viṣaya* carries the sense of "material objects."

44. When the author says we should consider "what the world is really like," he means we should consider its *svabhāva*, its "essential nature." However, to use "essential nature" here would lend too technical a sense to the passage.

45. Yoga-vāśiṣṭha Rāmāyaṇa 2.18.41.

46. Kulārṇava Tantra 1.16.

47. Kulārṇava Tantra 1.17. The text cited differs from *Kulārṇavatantram* 2002: 5 in using *prāptva* for *tataḥ*.

48. Contrary to the typical pattern in these discourses, the meaning of the passage is conveyed by the three preceding sentences. I have been unable to identify the source of this Sanskirt passage.

49. Kaṭha Upanishad 2.1.

50. In the Muṇḍaka Upanishad, it is Śaunaka who approaches the sage Aṅgiras to inquire after ultimate knowledge. Aṅgiras teaches him the difference between a lower ritual knowledge and ultimate, saving knowledge. It is worth noting that in the Muṇḍaka, Śaunaka is styled a *mahāśāla*, or "great householder." No doubt this was an important point, for both Rammohan and his followers. In the present discourse, Śaunaka must choose between the desired (*preyas*) and the good (*śreyas*), a theme that is treated in Kaṭha Upanishad, which is quoted at the opening of this discourse. If this discourse was composed by Debendranath (as I argue in chapter 7), we might suppose the young Debendranath saw in Śaunaka a sort of kindred spirit, who (like him) was just beginning to come to grips with life's big questions.

51. Śaunaka is pondering, in the Bengali, the following pairs of opposites: *uttamādhama*, *sadasad*, *dharmādharma*, *sukhadukha*, and *kartavyākartavya*.

52. It is important to note that the two words used in succession here—"charmed" (*mohita*) and "charming" (*mohajanaka*)—bear an important relation to the fundamental problem preventing humans from realizing ultimate truth, namely "delusion" (*moha*).

53. Literally, "know that you are a veritable mechanism" (*yantrasvarūpa*).

54. This discourse is reprinted in *Tattvabodhinī Patrikā*, part 2, no. 18 (1766 Śaka), pp. 145–47. In the Bodleian Library copy of the *Tattvabodhinī Patrikā*, someone has penciled in beside this discourse the English initials "DT."

55. Kaṭha Upanishad 2.24.

56. The word used for "affection" throughout this essay is *sneha*.

57. Readers will notice that this discourse falls out of chronological sequence. There is no way to determine why this might be.

58. A translation of this discourse was first published in appendix 3 of my dissertation, "Yatna-Dharma: The Religious Worldview of Paṇḍit Īśvaracandra Vidyāsāgar" (Hatcher 1992). I have revised the translation to be consistent with terminology used throughout the present work.

59. Manusmṛti 2.88.

60. Bhāgavata Purāṇa 5.1.17.

61. This verse is cited by the Christian convert Krishnamohan Banerjea in a Bengali tract from 1847 in support of the same point made here: Christianity does not counsel renunciation of the householder's life (which Krishnamohan refers to as *saṃsārāśrama*), but instructs each of us to remain in the world to perform our duties and to worship God. God has created all of us as he has, and to renounce the world would be tantamount to rendering his creative efforts pointless. It would also prevent us from helping one another. Therefore, "everyone will acknowledge that we are required to pursue our worldly duties in keeping with mercy, truth, and reason" (Banerjea 1847: 47).

62. Attributing this quotation to a specific Sanskrit work has proven difficult. Fred Smith has suggested that such verses belong to a "floating corpus" of Sanskrit popular philosophical versification (personal email communication, 4 November 2004). My thanks also to B. V. Sastry for suggestions on interpreting this verse (email communication, 4 November 2004).

63. I have translated the phrase *dvaita nāi* as "One only" in order to suggest harmony with the key Brāhmo theological assertion that God is *ekamevādvitīyam*, "One only without an equal" (see the benediction to this text). If I am correct in attributing this discourse to Īśvaracandra Vidyāsāgara, it will interest readers to see him here enunciating a clear Vedantic theme, since he would later go on to reject Vedānta as a false philosophical system (Mitra 2000: 659). Any apparent contradiction, however, may be accounted for both by the group's consistent suspicion of Śaṅkara's Advaita Vedānta and by the fact that while the Sabhā initially viewed its work in terms of propagating Vedānta, after 1850 it began to distance itself from any vestiges of Vedic authority.

64. Manusmṛti 3.78.

65. It helps to know that 1840 was a leap year. For a complete listing of the calendar, see http://www.hf.rim.or.jp/~kaji/cal/cal.cgi?1840.

66. An unsigned version of this passage, minus the quotation from Chāndogya Upaniṣad and the initial paragraph, is reprinted in *Tattvabodhinī Patrikā*, part 2, no. 17 (1766 Śaka), 137–38.

67. Chāndogya Upanishad 3.14.1. The author of this discourse appears to loosely translate this verse in the first sentence of his discourse. For another translation, see Olivelle's *Early Upanishads* (1998: 208).

68. Taittirīya Upanishad 3.1. In Olivelle's *Early Upanishads* (1998: 308) the text reads *prayanti* for *prayasti*.

69. The phrasing is admittedly awkward, turning as it does on the repeated use of the word *vastu*, "thing." The original reads: *ye vastute ye vastur racanā śakti nāi, tāhā haite se vastu racanā kadāpi haite pāre nā.*

70. I have not been able to identify a source for this quotation, which the author glosses in the subsequent paragraph by "the inexpressibly splendid power of the Supreme Lord." The same quotation appears at the head of an essay by Rāmacandra Vidyāvāgīśa on the greatness of God (Vidyāvāgīśa 1845: 1).

71. "The heart's sense of religion" is my rendering of *antaḥkāraṇer dharma*.

72. Though unsigned in *Sabhyadiger vaktṛtā*, this discourse corresponds to one reprinted in *Tattvabodhinī Patrikā*, part 2, no. 9 (1766 Śaka), pp. 70–71, which is signed "A," lending support to the supposition that it was written by Akṣayakumāra Datta.

73. There is no way to explain the long gap between this and the preceding discourse, but it is surprising that the text records no discourse for the Bengali months of Caitra and Vaiśākha.

74. This discourse corresponds to a discourse printed in *Tattvabodhinī Patrikā* (part 2, no. 14 [1 1766 Śaka], pp. 108–9), with the omission of the Sanskrit verse and its translation. In the Bodleian Library copy of the *Tattvabodhinī Patrikā*, this discourse has been labeled in pencil as being by "DT."

75. Īśā Upanishad 7.

76. In this and the following two paragraphs, I have used the single word "intention" to capture the sense of such idioms as *mānasa*, *svecchānusāre* and *kartār icchā*.

77. In this passage, the relevant concepts are *dhārmika* ("righteous"), *adhārmika* ("unrighteous"), and *dharma* (which I here translate as "law").

78. This passage offers a fine illustration of the modern Bengali idiom of *yatna*, as a kind of careful or caring effort. On this, see chapter 4. This is a theme I have explored in some depth in my earlier study of Vidyāsāgara (Hatcher 1996a).

79. The text ends with the standard Brāhmo mantra, *ekamevādvitīyam*, which I have translated here as it was translated by the earliest followers of Rāmmohan (Vidyāvāgīśa 1844). The *mantra* represents one of the so-called great sayings (*mahāvākya*) of the Upanishads and can be found at Chāndogya Upanishad 6.2.1 (Olivelle's *Early Upanishads* 1998: 246).

Bibliography

SANSKRIT TEXTS AND TRANSLATIONS

Early Upanishads: Annotated Text and Translation. 1998. Translated by Patrick Olivelle. New York: Oxford University Press.

Hitopadeśa. 1929. Compiled by Śri Narayana Pandita. Bombay: Nirnaya Sagar.

Kulārṇavatantram. 2002. Caukhambā Surabhāratī Granthamālā, 353. Vārānasī: Caukhambā Surabhāratī Prakāśana.

The Mahābhārata. 1933–72. Edited by V. S. Sukthankar, S. K. Belvalkar, et al. Poona: Bhandarkar Oriental Research Institute.

Manusmṛti. 1990 [1983]. Edited by J. L. Shastri. Delhi: Motilal Banarsidass.

Śrīmad Bhāgavata Cūrṇikā ṭīkā. 1992. Edited by Rām Teja Pāṇḍeya. Delhi: Caukhamba Saṃskṛta Pratiṣṭhāna.

Ten Principal Upaniṣads with Śaṅkarabhāṣya. 1987. Delhi: Motilal Banarsidass.

Viṣṇu Purāṇa with Sanskrit Commentary of Sridharacharya. 1986. Edited by Thanesh Chandra Upreti. Vol. I. Parimal Sanskrit Series, No. 21. Delhi: Parimal.

The Yogavāśiṣṭha of Vālmīki. 1998. Edited by Kanta Gupta. Three vols. Delhi: Nag.

SECONDARY WORKS, BENGALI AND ENGLISH

Ahmad, Imtiaz, and Helmut Reifeld (Eds.). N.d. *Middle Class Values in India and Western Europe*. New Delhi: Social Science Press.

Ahmed, A. F. Salahuddin. 1976. *Social Ideas and Social Change in Bengal, 1818–1835*. 2nd ed. Calcutta: Riddhi.

Al-Azad, Alauddin. 1979. *A Study of the Life and Short Poems of Iswarchandra Gupta.* Dacca: Asiatic Society of Bangladesh.

Ali, M. M. 1965. *The Bengali Reaction to Christian Missionary Activities 1833–1857.* Mehrub, Chittagong: Mehrub.

Althusser, Louis. 2005 [1969]. *For Marx.* Translated by Ben Brewster. New York: Verso.

Babb, Lawrence. 1986. *Redemptive Encounters: Three Modern Styles in the Hindu Tradition.* Berkeley: University of California Press.

Bāgāl, Yogeścandra. 1977. "Debendranātha Ṭhākura." In *Sāhitya-sādhaka-caritamālā,* No. 45. Calcutta: Baṅgīya Sāhitya Pariṣat.

Ballantyne, James R. 1859. *Christianity Contrasted with Hindu Philosophy: An Essay in Five Books, Sanskrit and English.* London: James Madden.

Bandyopadhyay, Brajendranātha. 1973. "Rāmacandra Vidyāvāgīśa, Hariharānanda Tīrthasvāmī." In *Sāhitya-sādhaka-caritamālā,* No. 9. Calcutta: Baṅgīya Sāhitya Pariṣat.

Banerjea, Krishnamohan. 1833. *A Review of the Moonduck Oopunishad, Translated into English by Ram Mohun Roy.* Calcutta, N. p.

———. 1840. *Upadeśa kathā: Sermons Addressed to Native Christians and Inquirers; in Bengalee.* Calcutta: Bishop's College Press.

———. 1845. "Transition States of the Hindu Mind," *Calcutta Review* 3 (January–June): 102–47.

———. 1847. *Īśvarokta śāstra dhārā.* Calcutta: Samācar Candrikā.

———. 1903 [1861]. *Dialogues on the Hindu Philosophy, Comprising the Nyaya, the Sankhya, the Vedant; To Which Is Added a Discussion of the Authority of the Vedas.* 2nd ed. London: Christian Literature Society for India.

Banerjee, Sumanta. 1989. *The Parlour and the Streets: Elite and Popular Culture in Nineteenth Century Calcutta.* Calcutta: Seagull.

Banerjee, Swapna M. 2004. *Men, Women, and Domestics: Articulating Middle-Class Identity in Colonial Bengal.* New Delhi: Oxford University Press.

Basu, Prem Sundar (Ed.). 1940. *Life and Works of Brahmananda Keshav.* 2nd ed. Calcutta: Navavidhan Publication Committee.

Baumer, Rachel van M. 1975. "The Reinterpretation of Dharma in Nineteenth-Century Bengal: Righteous Conduct for Man in the Modern World." In *Aspects of Bengali History and Society,* edited by R. Baumer. Asian Studies at Hawaii, No. 12. Honolulu: University Press of Hawaii, 82–98.

Bhattacharya, Tithi. 2005. *Sentinels of Culture: Class, Education, and the Colonial Intellectual in Bengal.* New Delhi: Oxford University Press.

Biśvās, Dilīpakumāra. 1956. "Tattvabodhinī Sabhā o Debendranātha Ṭhākura," *Itihāsa* 5/1–6/1: 31–261.

———. 1958. "Maharshi Debendranath Tagore and the Tattvabodhini Sabha." In *Studies in the Bengal Renaissance,* edited by A. C. Gupta. Jadavpur: National Council of Education, 33–46.

———. 1989. "Rāmamohaner dharmacintā." In *Rāmamohana Smaraṇa,* edited by Pulinbihārī Sen et. al. Calcutta: Rāmamohana Rāya smṛtirakṣaṇa samiti.

Bloomfield, J. H. 1968. *Elite Conflict in a Plural Society: Twentieth-Century Bengal*. Berkeley: University of California Press.

Bose, Rajnarain. 1844. "Dāpher prativāda" [A Reply to Duff]. *Tattvabodhinī Patrikā* 14 (1 Āśvina 1766 Śaka). Reprinted in Ghoṣa 1981: 89–103.

———. 1845. "Vaidantic Doctrines Vindicated." *Tattvabodhinī Patrikā* 19 (1 Phālguṇa 1766 Śaka). Reprinted in Ghoṣa 1981: 103–14.

———. 1855. *Brāhmo Samājer vaktṛtā*. Calcutta: Vālmīki Yantra.

———. 1871. *Rājanārāyaṇa Basur vaktṛtā. Part 1*. 3rd rev. ed. Calcutta: Vālmīki Press.

———. 1872. "Hindudharmer śreṣṭhatā." Calcutta, N. p.

———. 1961. *Rājanārāyaṇa Basur ātmacarita*. Edited by Harihar Śeṭh. Calcutta: Orient.

Brahmasaṅgīta. 1861. Śrīlaśrīyukta varddhamānādhīśvara mahārājādhirāja mahatābcand bāhādurer vyaye satyasandhāyinī sabhā haite vitaraṇārtha barddamāna satyaprakāśayantre viśuddharūpe dvitīyabār mudrita haila. Burdwan: Satyaprakasha Press.

Brāhmo Addresses. 1870. *1791 Śaker Daśopadeśa*. Edited by Ānandacandra Vedāntavāgīśa. Calcutta: Ādi Brāhma Samāj.

Burch, George Bosworth. 1976. *The Search for the Absolute in Neo-Vedanta: K. C. Bhattacharya*. Honolulu: University of Hawaii Press.

Caṭṭopādhyāya, Harimohan. 1867. *Jīvana-carita: Sara Rādhākānta Bāhādura Ke, Si, Es, Āi*. Calcutta: Baṅgavidyā Prakāśikā Press.

Chakravarty, Satis Chandra. 1935. *The Father of Modern India*. Calcutta: Rammohan Centenary Committee.

Chattopadhyay, Gautam. 1965. *Awakening in Bengal in Early Nineteenth Century (Selected Documents)*. Vol. 1. Calcutta: Progressive.

———. 1978. *Bengal: Early Nineteenth Century (Selected Documents)*. Calcutta: Research India.

Collet, Sophia Dobson. 1988. *The Life and Letters of Raja Rammohun Roy*. Reprint ed. Edited by D. K. Biswas and P. C. Ganguli. Calcutta: Sadharan Brahmo Samaj.

Damen, Frans. L. 1988. *Crisis and Renewal in the Brahmo Samaj (1860–1884)*. Leuven: Catholic University Press.

Dāśgupta, Śāntikumāra, and Haribandhu Mukhaṭi. 1974. *Īśvara Gupta Racanāvalī*. Calcutta: Dattacaudhurī and Sons.

Datta, Bhavatoṣa (Ed.). 1968. *Bankimcandra Caṭṭopādhyāya: Īśvaracandra Gupter jīvanacarita o kavitva*. Calcutta: Jijnasa.

De, Barun. 1977. "A Historiographical Critique of Renaissance Analogues for Nineteenth Century India." In *Perspectives in Social Sciences*, vol. 1, edited by Barun De. Calcutta: Oxford University Press, 178–218.

Defoe, Daniel. 1961. *Robinson Crusoe*. New York: New American Library.

Deb, Braja Mohan. 1843. *On the Supreme God or an Inquiry into Truth in the Matter of Spiritual and Idol-Worship*. Translated from the Bengali and Sanskrit Originals, with notes, by the Rev. W. Morton, LMS. Calcutta: Asiatic Press.

de Vries, Jan. 1994. "The Industrial Revolution and the Industrious Revolution," *Journal of Economic History* 54/2: 249–70.

Duff, Alexander. 1839. *India and India Missions*. Edinburgh: John Johnstone.

———. 1845. "Vedantism, What Is It?" *Calcutta Review* 4/7: 50–61.

Dutt, Romesh Chunder. 1877. *The Literature of Bengal*. Calcutta: I. C. Bose.

Farquhar, J. N. 1967 [1914]. *Modern Religious Movements in India*. Reprint ed. Delhi: Munshiram Manoharlal.

Ghoṣa, Benoy. (Ed.). 1963. *Sāmāyika-patre bāṅglār samāja-citra. Part 2: 1840–1905: "Tattvabodhinī patrikā"-r racanā-saṃkalana*. Calcutta: Vīkṣaṇ.

———. 1978. *Janasabhār sāhitya*. Enlarged ed. Calcutta: Papyrus.

———. 1981. *Sāmāyika-patre bāṅglār samāja-citra. Part 5: Tattvabodhinī Patrikā, 2.* Calcutta: Papyrus.

———. 1984. *Vidyāsāgara o bāṅgālī samāj*. Calcutta: Orient Longman.

Ghosh, Parimal. 2004. "Where Have All the 'Bhadraloks' Gone?" *Economic and Political Weekly* 39/3 (January 17): 247–51.

Gītāvalī. 1846. Calcutta, N. p.

Gupta, Īśvaracandra. 1857. *Prabodhaprabhākara. Part 1*. Calcutta: Prabhākara Yantra.

Halbfass, Wilhelm. 1988. *India and Europe: An Essay in Understanding*. Albany: State University of New York Press.

Hatcher, Brian A. 1992. "Yatna-Dharma: The Religious Worldview of Paṇḍit Īśvaracandra Vidyāsāgara." Ph.D. dissertation, Harvard University.

———. 1996a. *Idioms of Improvement: Vidyāsāgar and Cultural Encounter in Bengal*. Calcutta: Oxford University Press.

———. 1996b. "Indigent Brahmans, Industrious Pandits: Bourgeois Ideology and Sanskrit Pandits in Colonial Calcutta." In *Comparative Studies of South Asia, Africa and the Middle East* 16/1: 15–26.

———. 1999. *Eclecticism and Modern Hindu Discourse*. New York: Oxford University Press.

———. 2001. "Great Men Waking: Paradigms in the Historiography of the Bengal Renaissance." In *Bengal: Rethinking History: Essays in Historiography*, edited by Sekhar Bandyopadhyay. New Delhi: Manohar, 135–63.

———. 2004. "Contemporary Hindu Thought." In *Contemporary Hinduism: Ritual, Culture, and Practice*, edited by Robin Rinehart. New York: ABC-Clio, 179–211.

———. 2005. "What's Become of the Pandit? Rethinking the History of Sanskrit Scholars in Colonial Bengal," *Modern Asian Studies* 39/3: 683–723.

———. 2006. "Remembering Rammohan: An Essay on the (Re-)emergence of Modern Hinduism," *History of Religions* 46/1: 50–80.

Hawley, John Stratton. 2001. "Modern India and the Question of Middle-Class Religion," *International Journal of Hindu Studies* 5/3: 217–25.

Hay, Stephen (Ed.). 1963. *Dialogue between a Theist and an Idolater: Brāhma Pauttalik Samvād.—An 1820 Tract Probably by Rammohun Roy*. Calcutta: Firma KLM.

Hervieu-Léger, Danièle. 2000. *Religion as a Chain of Memory*. Cambridge: Polity Press, 2000.

Hesse, Hermann. 1969. *Steppenwolf*. Translated by Basil Creighton. New York: Bantam.

Johnston, G. A. (Ed.). 1915. *Selections from the Scottish Philosophy of Common Sense.* Chicago: Open Court.

Joshi, Sanjay. 2001. *Fractured Modernity: Making of a Middle Class in Colonial North India.* New Delhi: Oxford University Press.

Killingley, Dermot. 1976. "Vedanta and Modernity." In *Indian Society and the Beginnings of Modernization, c. 1830–1850*, edited by Philips and Wainwright. London: School of Oriental and African Studies, 127–40.

———. 1981. "Rammohan Roy on the Vedanta Sutras." *Religion* 11: 151–169.

———. (Trans.). 1982. *The Only True God: Works on Religion by Rammohun Roy.* Newcastle upon Tyne: Grevatt and Grevatt.

———. 1993. *Rammohun Roy in Hindu and Christian Tradition: The Teape Lectures 1990.* Newcastle upon Tyne: Grevatt and Grevatt.

King, Richard. 1999. *Orientalism and Religion: Postcolonial Theory, India, and "The Mystic East."* New York: Routledge.

Kling, Blair. 1976. *Partner in Empire: Dwarkanath Tagore and the Age of Enterprise in Eastern India.* Berkeley: University of California Press.

Kopf, David. 1969. *British Orientalism and the Bengal Renaissance.* Berkeley: University of California Press.

———. 1979. *The Brahmo Samaj and the Shaping of the Modern Indian Mind.* Princeton, N.J.: Princeton University Press.

Leonard, G. S. 1879. *A History of the Brahmo Samaj from Its Rise to the Present Day.* Calcutta, N.p.

Long, James. 1846. "Excerpt from a Communication to the Church Missionary Society," *Church Missionary Record* (London) 17: 84.

———. 1848. *Handbook of Bengali Missions.* Calcutta, N.p.

Lutgendorf, Philip. 1997. "Monkey in the Middle: The Status of Hanuman in Popular Hinduism," *Religion* 27/4: 311–32.

Maharṣi Debendranāth. 1907. *Bhārata-gaurava-granthāvalī.* Calcutta: J. M. Basu.

Majumdar, B. B. 1934. *History of Political Thought: From Rammohan to Dayananda (1821–84).* Calcutta: University of Calcutta Press.

Majumdar, J. K. 1983 [1941]. *Raja Rammohun Roy and Progressive Movements in India.* Calcutta: Sadharan Brahmo Samaj.

Mitra, Indra. 2000 [1992]. *Karuṇāsāgara Vidyāsāgara.* 2nd. ed. Calcutta: Ananda.

Moitra, Suresh Chandra (Comp.). 1979. *Selections from Jnanannesan.* Calcutta: Prajna.

Muir, Ramsay. 1969. *The Making of British India, 1756–1858.* Karachi: Oxford University Press.

Mukerji, Bitika. 1983. *Neo-Vedanta and Modernity.* Varanasi: Ashutosh Prakashan Sansthan.

Mukherjee, S. N. 1977. *Calcutta: Myths and History.* Calcutta: Subarnarekha.

Mukhopādhyāya, Śyāmacaraṇa. 1877. *Cuḍālā Upākhyāna.* Calcutta: Purāṇaprakāśa Yantra.

———. 1879. *Key to Rijupatha, Part III.* 8th ed. Calcutta: A. T. Ghoshal.

Mullens, Joseph. 1852. *Vedantism, Brahmism, and Christianity Examined and Compared: A Prize Essay*. Calcutta: Calcutta Christian Tract and Book Society.

O'Malley, L. S. S., with Monmohan Chakravarti. 1985 [1912]. *Bengal District Gazeteers: Hooghly*. New Delhi: Logos.

Palit, Cittabrata. 1980. *New Viewpoints on Nineteenth Century Bengal*. Calcutta: Progressive.

Pennington, Brian. 2001. "Constructing Colonial Dharma: A Chronicle of Emergent Hinduism, 1830–1831," *Journal of the American Academy of Religion* 69/3: 577–603.

———. 2005. *Was Hinduism Invented? Britons, Indians, and the Colonial Construction of Religion*. New York: Oxford University Press.

Prabhavananda, Swami. 1964. *The Sermon on the Mount according to Vedanta*. London: George Allen and Unwin.

Rāy, Mahendranāth. 1885. *Śrīyukta Bābu Akṣayakumāra Datter Jīvanavṛttānta*. Calcutta, N.p.

Raychaudhuri, Tapan. 1988. *Europe Reconsidered: Perceptions of the West in Nineteenth Century Bengal*. New Delhi: Oxford University Press.

Robertson, Bruce Carlisle. 1995. *Raja Rammohan Roy: The Father of Modern India*. New Delhi: Oxford University Press.

Roy, Rammohun. 1906. *The English Works of Raja Rammohun Roy with an English Translation of "Tuhfatul muwahhiddin."* Allahabad: Panini Office.

———. 1933. *Rammohun Roy: The Man and His Work*. Centenary Publicity Booklet. Calcutta: Amal Home.

———. 1973. *Rāmamohana Racanāvalī*. Edited by Ajitkumāra Ghoṣa. Calcutta: Haraph Prakāśanī.

———. 1974. *Vedāntagrantha*. Edited by Īśānacandra Rāy. Calcutta: Sādhāraṇa Brāhmo Samāj.

Sabhyadiger Vaktṛtā. *See* Tattvabodhinī Sabhā 1841.

Sanyal, Rajat. 1980. *Voluntary Associations and the Urban Public Life in Bengal (1815–1876)*. Calcutta: Riddhi-India.

Sarkar, Hem Chandra. 1931. *The Religion of the Brahmo Samaj*. 3rd ed. Calcutta: Classic Press.

Sarkar, Sumit. 1997. *Writing Social History*. New Delhi: Oxford University Press.

Sarkar, Susobhan. 1958. "Derozio and Young Bengal." In *Studies in the Bengal Renaissance*, edited by A. C. Gupta. Jadavpur: National Council of Education, 16–32.

Śāstrī, Śivanātha. 1911. *History of the Brahmo Samaj*. 2 vols. Calcutta: R. Chatterjee.

———. 1983. *Rāmtānu Lāhiḍī o tatkālīna Baṅgasamāja*. Reprint ed. Calcutta: New Age.

Sen, Amiya Kumar. 1979. *Tattwabodhini Sabha and the Bengal Renaissance*. Calcutta: Sadharan Brahmo Samaj.

Sen, Asok. 1977. *Iswar Chandra Vidyasagar and His Elusive Milestones*. Calcutta: Riddhi-India.

Sinha, Samita. 1993. *Pandits in a Changing Environment: Sanskrit Centres of Learning in Nineteenth Century Bengal*. Calcutta: Sarat Book House.

Tagore, Debendranath. 1861. *Upaniṣadaḥ: Śrīyukta Bābu Devendranātha Ṭhākura mahāśayānumatyanusāreṇa tatkṛta vṛttisahakṛta bāṅgalānuvāda sahitāḥ*. Edited by Ānandacandravedāntavāgīśa. Calcutta: Prākṛta yantra.

———. 1909. *The Autobiography of Maharshi Devendranath Tagore*. Translated from the original Bengali by Satyendranath Tagore and Indira Devi. Calcutta: S. K. Lahiri.

———. 1957 [1854]. *Brāhmasamājer pañcaviṃśati vatsarer parīkṣita vṛttānta*. Reprint ed. Calcutta: Sādhāraṇa Brāhma Samāj.

———. 1965 [1861]. *Brāhma Samājer vyākhyāna*. Calcutta: Sādhāraṇa Brāhmo Samāj.

———. 1975 [1850]. *Brāhma Dharmaḥ*. Calcutta: Sādhāraṇa Brāhmo Samāj.

———. 1980 [1898]. *Maharṣi Debendranātha Ṭhākurer ātmajīvanī*. Reprint edition by Arabinda Mitra and Aśīm Āmed. Calcutta: Chariot International.

Takeuchi, Keiji. 1997. *The Philosophy of Brahmo Samaj: Rammohun Roy and Devendranath Tagore*. Calcutta: Bookfront Publication Forum.

Tattvabodinī Sabhā. 1841. *Sabhyadiger Vaktṛtā. Tattvabodhinī Sabhā. Part 1.* 17 Agrahāyaṇa 1761 avadhi 5 Jyaiṣṭha 1762 paryanta. Calcutta: Tattvabodhinī Sabhā.

———. 1844. *Varṇamālā. Part 2*. Calcutta: Tattvabodhinī Sabhā.

———. 1846. *1768 Śaker Sāmvatsarika āya vyaya sthitir nirūpaṇa pustaka*. Calcutta: Tattvabodhinī Sabhā.

———. 1848. *1770 Śaker Sāmvatsarika āya vyaya sthitir nirūpaṇa pustaka*. Calcutta: Tattvabodhinī Sabhā.

———. 1850. *1772 Śaker Sāmvatsarika āya vyaya sthitir nirūpaṇa pustaka*. Calcutta: Tattvabodhinī Sabhā.

———. 1854. *1776 Śaker sāmvatsarika āya vyaya sthitir nirupaṇa pustaka*. Calcutta: Tattvabodhinī Sabhā.

Terdiman, R. 1993. *Present Past: Modernity and the Memory Crisis*. Ithaca, N.Y.: Cornell University Press.

Vidyāsāgara, Īśvaracandra. 1972. *Vidyāsāgara-racanāsaṃgraha*. 3 vols. Edited by Gopāl Hāldār. Calcutta: Sākṣaratā Prakāśana.

Vidyāvāgīśa. Rāmacandra. 1836. *Parameśvarer upāsanāviṣaye prathama vyākhyāna avadhi dvādaśa vyākhyāna paryanta*. Calcutta: Prajñā.

———. 1844. *Second Discourse on the Spiritual Worship of God, Delivered by Ramchundru Shurma, at the Brahma Sumaj, on Wednesday, the 13th of Bhadru, 1750 Shukabda.* Translated from Bengallee by Chundrushekur Dev. Calcutta: Tuttubodhiney.

———. 1845. *Parameśvarer mahimā*. Calcutta: Tattvabodhinī Sabhā.

———. 1849. *Parameśvarer upāsanā viṣaye prathamāvadhi saptadaśa vyākhyāna*. Calcutta: Tattvabodhinī Sabhā.

———. 1977. *Brāhmasamājer vyākhyāna*. Calcutta: Sādhāraṇa Brāhmo Samāj.

Viśvāsa, Nakuḍacandra. 1887. *Akṣayacarita*. Calcutta, N.p.

Viswanathan, Gauri. 1990. *Masks of Conquest: Literary Study and British Rule in India*. London: Faber and Faber.

Waghorne, Joanne. 1999. "The Diaspora of the Gods: Hindu Temples in the New World System," *Journal of Asian Studies* 58/3: 648–86.

———. 2005. *The Diaspora of the Gods: Modern Hindu Temples in an Urban Middle-Class World*. New York: Oxford University Press.

Weber, Max. 1958. *Protestant Ethic and the Spirit of Capitalism*. New York: Scribners'.
Wilson, Bryan. 1983. *Religion in Sociological Perspective*. New York: Oxford University Press.
Zimmer, Heinrich. 1992. *Myths and Symbols in Indian Art and Civilization*. Princeton, N.J.: Princeton University Press.

Index

CPSIA information can be obtained at www.ICGtesting.com
Printed in the USA
BVOW03s0458040314

346597BV00002B/2/P

9 780199 374991